Church New Jerusalem

Book of Worship

Prepared for the use of the New Church

Church New Jerusalem

Book of Worship
Prepared for the use of the New Church

ISBN/EAN: 9783337038595

Printed in Europe, USA, Canada, Australia, Japan

Cover: Foto ©Lupo / pixelio.de

More available books at **www.hansebooks.com**

THE

BOOK OF WORSHIP:

PREPARED FOR THE USE OF

THE NEW CHURCH,

BY ORDER OF THE GENERAL CONVENTION.

―――― NEW YORK EDITION. ――――

PUBLISHED BY
THE NEW CHURCH BOARD OF PUBLICATIONS,
No. 20 COOPER UNION, NEW YORK.
1876.

PREFACE.

THE Book of Worship now offered to the New Church, has been prepared, under the direction of the Executive Committee of the General Convention, by a commitee of nine, representing the views and practices of the several parts of the Church.

As the Committee believed the commonly accepted version of the Word to be, on the whole, better adapted to the uses of worship in the New Church than any other translation at present attainable, it has been adopted as the basis of the present work, such corrections only having been made as were obviously necessary.

The Morning and Evening Services have been arranged with a view to their use in a variety of ways conforming with the various usages in the Church. The rubrics are therefore mostly optional, leaving the choice of matter and the order of the several parts to be determined by the wants of the different congregations.

These services are followed by the variable portions referred to in the rubrics, of which a liberal provision is made in order to meet as far as practicable the various requirements of different congregations. They consist of music for the Sanctus and Doxologies; seventeen Responsive Services; passages from the Word to be read when desired in the place of those inserted in the services; Prayers; Selections from the Psalms, arranged for responsive reading; Selections with Chants; Anthems, and Hymns. Nothing has been omitted which is known to be wanted; and nothing inserted which is not desired by some.

Three editions of the book are published. The first, designated, for convenience, the "Boston Edition," preserves the name JEHOVAH in its original forms, wherever it occurs in passages from The Word; in the second, to be known as the "New York Edition," the name LORD is used for JEHOVAH, as in the English Bible; the third, called the "Psalter Edition," is like the New York Edition, but contains a fuller collection of Prayers, including the Litany, also the entire book of Psalms, divided into portions for daily morning and evening readings, and arranged to be read in alternate verses. The other editions contain twenty-one selections from the Psalms, arranged to be read by alternate lines. The first thirteen of these selections may be used for the Morning Service on the thirteen Sundays of each quarter; leaving the next three for occasional Evening Services. The seventeenth lesson is suitable for Thanksgiving Day, the eighteenth for Christmas, the nineteenth for Good Friday, the twentieth for Easter. The use of the lessons is not limited, however, to this arrangement.

Those who prefer to have the reading of the Commandments preceded by a short introductory lesson, will find the following selections useful for that purpose. Thirteen lessons are recommended, to correspond to the number of Sundays in each quarter. These may be abbreviated, if shorter lessons are preferred, by omitting some of the verses. They are all from the Book of Deuteronomy, (*1*) iv. 1–14, 40; (*2*) iv. 23–40; (*3*) v. 22–33; (*4*) vi. 1–13, 17; (*5*) vi. 17–25; (*6*) vii. 1–11; (*7*) vii. 11—viii. 1; (*8*)

PREFACE.

viii ; (*9*) x. 12—xi. 1 ; (*10*) xi. 8–21 ; (*11*) xi. 22–32 ; (*12*) xxx. 1–10 ; (*13*) xxx. 11–20.

The Selections include all that were in general use in the Liturgy, with a few additions. The Chants also are in great part from the Liturgy ; but they have been thoroughly revised, and many excellent chants, new and old, have been added, by Prof. GEORGE J. WEBB, to whom the Church has been indebted almost from the beginning for guidance in the appropriate singing of sacred words

The Selections and Chants are followed by a number of Chant Anthems by Mr. Webb, which offer a new and promising musical form for the words of Scripture songs ; also by a small collection of good Anthems, selected with special reference to congregational use.

A carefully chosen collection of Hymns, the most suitable for the New Church that could be found, is printed with appropriate music, which also has been revised and approved by Mr. Webb.

JOHN WORCESTER,	J. C. AGER,	FRANK SEWALL,
JAMES REED,	C. H. MANN,	WILLARD G. DAY,
S. F. DIKE,	CHAUNCEY GILES,	EDWIN GOULD.

CONTENTS.

	PAGE
ORDER FOR MORNING SERVICE	1
ORDER FOR EVENING SERVICE	5
THE SANCTUS AND DOXOLOGIES	7

RESPONSIVE SERVICES:

i. The Commandments from Exodus and Mark.	11
ii. The Commandments from Deuteronomy and Matthew	13
iii. The Ten Commandments from Exodus	15
iv. The Ten Commandments from Deuteronomy	17
v. Response to the Commandments	20
vi. The Blessings	22
vii. The Blessings, with Responses	23
viii. The Two Great Commandments	25
ix. The New Jerusalem	27
x. The Law of Love	30
xi. Psalm of Thanksgiving	31
xii. The Holy Supper	34
xiii. The Incarnation of the LORD	36
xiv. Penitence	37
xv. The Resurrection of the LORD	39
xvi. The Ascension and Glorification of the LORD	40
xvii. The Holy Spirit or the Divine Proceeding of the LORD	41

INTRODUCTORY SENTENCES AND PRAYERS:

Introductory Sentences	43
Introductory Prayers	44
Sentences introductory to Prayer	45
Prayers from the Word	47
The Lord's Prayer	48
Confessions	48
Prayers and Thanksgivings	49

LESSONS FROM THE PSALMS—For Responsive Reading	57

SELECTIONS AND CHANTS:

Introductory	1
Penitential	19
Praise and Thanksgiving	52
Prophecy and Promise	85
Descriptive	113

CONTENTS.

ANTHEMS: PAGE

    Chant Anthems 129
    Anthems 154
    The Faith of the New Church 192
    Te Dominum 197

HYMNS:

    Praise and Adoration 199
    Supplication 224
    Penitential 238
    Faith and Trust 243
    Divine Providence 258
    The Word 273
    The Church 278
    Heaven 282
    The Lord's Day 289
    Morning 292
    Evening 295
    Close of Worship 304
    Baptism 312
    Holy Supper 314
    Ordination 319
    Dedication 320
    Anniversaries 321
    Thanksgiving 324
    National Hymn 328
    Christmas—Incarnation and Redemption 329
    Easter—The Resurrection 346
    Ascension 349
    The Holy Spirit 350
    The Holy City 352
    The Second Coming 354
    Doxologies 355

INDEXES:

    First Lines of the Selections 357
    Authors of the Chants 360
    Anthems with Names of Authors 361
    First Lines of the Hymns, and Authors 362
    Tunes with Names of Composers 365
    Numerical Index of Tunes 366
    Lessons for Festival Services 368

LORD, I have loved the habitation of thy house, and the place where thine honor dwelleth.

How lovely are thy tabernacles, O LORD of Hosts.

BLESSED are they that dwell in thy house, they are continually praising Thee.

I WILL come into thy house in the multitude of thy mercy: in thy fear will I worship toward thy holy temple.

LET the words of my mouth, and the meditation of my heart, be acceptable in thy sight, O LORD, my Strength and my Redeemer.

LET thy mercies come also unto me, O LORD, even thy salvation according to thy Word.

O SEND out thy light and thy truth: let them lead me; let them bring me into thy holy hill, and to thy tabernacles.

PEACE be within thy walls; prosperity within thy palaces. For my brethren and companions' sakes, I will now say, Peace be within thee.

ORDER

OF

WORSHIP USED IN THIS SOCIETY.

I.

¶ *Voluntary upon the Organ, and when convenient, an Anthem may be sung by the Choir.*

II.

¶ *The Minister alone rising, and opening the Word, repeats one or more of the following sentences:*

THE LORD is in his holy temple; let all the earth keep silence before Him.

ENTER into his gates with thanksgiving, into his courts with praise: be thankful unto Him, and bless his name. For the LORD is good; his mercy is everlasting; and his truth endureth to all generations.

SEEK ye the LORD while He may be found. Call ye upon Him while He is near. Let the wicked forsake his way, and the unrighteous man his thoughts; and let him return unto the LORD, and He will have mercy upon him; and to our God, for He will abundantly pardon.

EXALT ye the LORD our GOD, and worship at his footstool, for He is holy.

For Thou art not a God that hath pleasure in wickedness:
Neither shall evil dwell with Thee.

The vainglorious shall not stand in thy sight:
Thou hatest all workers of iniquity.

Thou wilt destroy them that speak falsehood:
The Lord will abhor the man of blood and deceit.

But as for me, I will come into thy house in the multitude of thy mercy:
In thy fear will I worship toward thy holy temple.

Lead me, O Lord, in thy righteousness, because of my
 enemies:
Make thy way straight before my face.

¶ *All will sing a Selection or Hymn, to be announced by the Minister.*

V.

¶ *The Minister will then say:*

O COME, let us worship and bow down, let us kneel before the Lord our Maker.

¶ *All kneeling, such Prayers as may be desired from the Collection or other sources may be said, always closing with the Lord's Prayer.*

OUR Father, who art in the heavens: Hallowed be Thy name. Thy kingdom come. Thy will be done, as in heaven, so also upon the earth. Give us this day our daily bread. And forgive us our debts as we also forgive our debtors. And lead us not into temptation: but deliver us from evil. For Thine is the Kingdom, and the Power, and the Glory, forever. *Amen.*

VI.

¶ *The People sitting, the Minister will read the first Lesson from the Word.*

VII.

¶ *All rising, the Minister will say:*

TO JESUS CHRIST the LORD be glory and dominion forever and ever. Amen.

¶ *And the People will sing a Doxology from pp. 9, 10.*

¶ *The Minister and People may then read responsively a Lesson from the Psalms, pp. 57-90.*

VIII.

¶ *At the close of the Responsive Service the Minister will announce and all will sing a Selection or Hymn. Or the whole of Part VII. being omitted, a Selection, Hymn, or Anthem may be sung.*

IX.

¶ *The Second Lesson from the Word.*

X.

¶ *All rising, here will follow the Commandments, or some other Responsive Service from the Collection, or an Anthem or Hymn may be sung.*

XI.

¶ *The Sermon.*

XII.

¶ *Prayer.*

XIII.

¶ *All will sing a Selection, Anthem, or Hymn.*

¶ *The Benediction.*

THE grace of our LORD JESUS CHRIST be with you all. Amen.

¶ *When the Service is read by a Layman, he will say:*

THE LORD keep our going out and our coming in, from this time forth and forever more. Amen.

ORDER

FOR

MORNING SERVICE.

———•❈•———

¶ *All standing, the Minister may read one or more of the following sentences, or from those in the Collection:*

THE LORD is in his holy temple : let all the earth keep silence before Him.

ENTER into his gates with thanksgiving, and into his courts with praise : be thankful unto Him, and bless his name. For the LORD is good ; his mercy is everlasting ; and his truth endureth to all generations.

SEEK ye the LORD while He may be found, call ye upon Him while He is near. Let the wicked forsake his way, and the unrighteous man his thoughts ; and let him return unto the LORD, and He will have mercy upon him ; and to our GOD, for He will abundantly pardon.

EXALT ye the LORD our GOD, and worship at his footstool, for He is holy.

¶ *Or, the Minister only may rise, and after the opening sentence or sentences all may kneel, and the Minister say one or more of the following introductory Prayers, or from those in the Collection:*

SEARCH me, O God, and know my heart; try me, and know my thoughts; and see if there be any wicked way in me; and lead me in the way everlasting.

CAUSE me to hear thy loving kindness in the morning; for in Thee do I trust; cause me to know the way wherein I should walk; for I lift up my soul unto Thee.

LET the words of my mouth, and the meditation of my heart, be acceptable in thy sight, O Lord, my Strength and my Redeemer.

¶ *All standing, the Minister and People may read the following; or, in place of this or following it, one of the responsive lessons from the Psalms:*

GIVE ear to my words, O Lord:
    Consider my meditation.

Hearken to the voice of my cry, my King and my God:
    For unto Thee will I pray.

My voice shalt Thou hear in the morning, O Lord:
    In the morning will I direct my prayer unto Thee, and will look up.

For Thou art not a God that hath pleasure in wickedness:
    Neither shall evil dwell with Thee.

The vainglorious shall not stand in thy sight:
    Thou hatest all workers of iniquity.

Thou wilt destroy them that speak falsehood:
    The Lord will abhor the man of blood and deceit.

But as for me, I will come into thy house in the multitude of thy mercy:
    In thy fear will I worship toward thy holy temple.

Lead me, O LORD, in thy righteousness, because of mine enemies.

Make thy way straight before my face.

¶ *Here may follow the Sanctus [pp. 7–9], or one of the supplicatory Selections [pp. 20—53.]*

¶ *Then may be read the lesson introductory to the Commandments, or the Lesson from the Old Testament, followed by the Commandments or other Responsive Service from the Collection.*

¶ *The Minister will then say:*

O COME, let us worship and bow down; let us kneel before the LORD our Maker.

¶ *All kneeling, such Prayers as may be desired from the Collection may be said, always closing with the Lord's Prayer; or, preceding the Prayers, the following may be said:*

HAVE mercy upon me, O GOD, according to thy loving-kindness: according to the multitude of thy tender mercies, blot out my transgressions. Wash me thoroughly from mine iniquity, and cleanse me from my sin. For I acknowledge my transgressions, and my sin is ever before me.

OUR FATHER, who art in the heavens: Hallowed be Thy name. Thy kingdom come. Thy will be done, as in heaven, so also upon the earth. Give us this day our daily bread. And forgive us our debts as we also forgive our debtors. And lead us not into temptation; but deliver us from evil. For Thine is the Kingdom, and the Power, and the Glory, forever. *Amen.*

¶ *Here, all standing, the following may be sung: [Music, pp. 7 and 8.]*

HOLY, holy, holy, JEHOVAH of Hosts: All the earth is full of his glory. *Amen.*

¶ *The responsive lesson from the Psalms may here follow; and at the end may be sung one of the Doxologies on pp. 9 and 10, or a Selection.*

¶ *The Minister may read, the People sitting, a lesson introductory to the Commandments, or the Lesson from the Old Testament; after which may be sung, all standing:* [*For music, see pp. 8 and 9.*]

HOLY, holy, holy, LORD GOD Almighty: Who was, and who is, and who is to come.

¶ *Here may follow the Commandments or other Responsive Service from the Collection, or the Te Dominum or a Selection.*

¶ *At the close of the Responsive Service a Selection may be sung.*

¶ *Here may follow the Lessons from the Word, or the Lesson from the New Testament, when the Lesson from the Old Testament has been read as above.*

¶ *Then, all standing, the Benedictus on page 58 (of the Selections) may be sung, or some other Selection, or an Anthem or a Hymn.*

¶ *The Sermon.*

¶ *The Sermon may be followed by an Ascription or Prayer, after which may be read or chanted, by the Minister and People, the Declaration of Faith on pages 192 or 196.*

¶ *Here may be sung a Selection, Anthem or Hymn, which may be followed by the closing Prayers.*

¶ *The Benediction.*

THE grace of our Lord Jesus Christ be with you all. Amen.

¶ *When the service is read by a layman, in place of the Benediction, he will say:*

THE LORD keep our going out and our coming in, from this time forth and forevermore. *Amen.*

ORDER

FOR

EVENING SERVICE.

¶ *All standing, the Minister may read one or more of the following sentences, or from those in the Collection.*

THE LORD is in his holy temple; let all the earth keep silence before Him.

HOLINESS becometh thine house, O LORD, forever.

BLESS ye the LORD, all ye servants of the LORD, who by night stand in the house of the LORD : lift up your hands in the sanctuary and bless the LORD. The LORD that made heaven and earth, bless thee out of Zion.

THUS saith the LORD, that created the heavens; GOD Himself, that formed the earth and made it. I am the LORD; and there is none else; a just GOD and a Saviour, there is none besides Me.

LOOK unto Me, and be ye saved, all the ends of the earth; for I am GOD, and there is none else.

COME unto Me, all ye that labor and are heavy laden, and I will give you rest. Take my yoke upon you, and learn of Me; for I am meek, and lowly in heart; and ye shall find rest to your souls.

¶ *Here one of supplicatory Selections on pages 20–53 may be sung, or read responsively.*

¶ *Then may follow one or more of the introductions to prayer from the Collection, or the following:*

O COME, let us worship and bow down ; let us kneel before the LORD our Maker.

¶ *All kneeling, the* LORD'S PRAYER *will be said, preceded by such of the Confessions and Prayers, from the Collection, as may be desired.*

OUR FATHER, who art in the heavens: Hallowed be Thy name. Thy kingdom come. Thy will be done, as in heaven, so also upon the earth. Give us this day our daily bread. And forgive us our debts as we also forgive our debtors. And lead us not into temptation ; but deliver us from evil. For Thine is the Kingdom, and the Power, and the Glory, forever. *Amen.*

¶ *All standing, the Sanctus may be sung:* [*See pages 7–9.*]

¶ *Then may be read by the Minister and People one of the responsive lessons from the Psalms, followed by one of the Doxologies on pages 9 and 10, or by a Selection. Or, in place of the responsive reading, a Selection may be sung, followed by a Doxology.*

¶ *Here shall follow, the People sitting, the reading from the Word. If there be two lessons, at the end of the first, the following, or a Selection, or both, may be sung:* [*For music, see pp. 8 and 9.*]

HOLY, holy, holy LORD GOD Almighty,
Who was, and who is, and who is to come.

¶ *At the end of the reading from the Word, the Magnificat on page 57, or some other suitable Selection, may be sung.*

¶ *Then may follow the Sermon or other instruction.*

¶ *Then may be sung a Selection, Anthem, or Hymn, which may be followed by the Declaration of Faith, the closing Prayers, and the Benediction.*

THE grace of our LORD JESUS CHRIST be with you all. *Amen.*

[NOTE.—When the service is read by a layman, the sentence at the end of the Morning Service will be used.]

THE SANCTUS AND DOXOLOGIES.

WITH MUSIC.

I.

DOXOLOGIES.

IV.

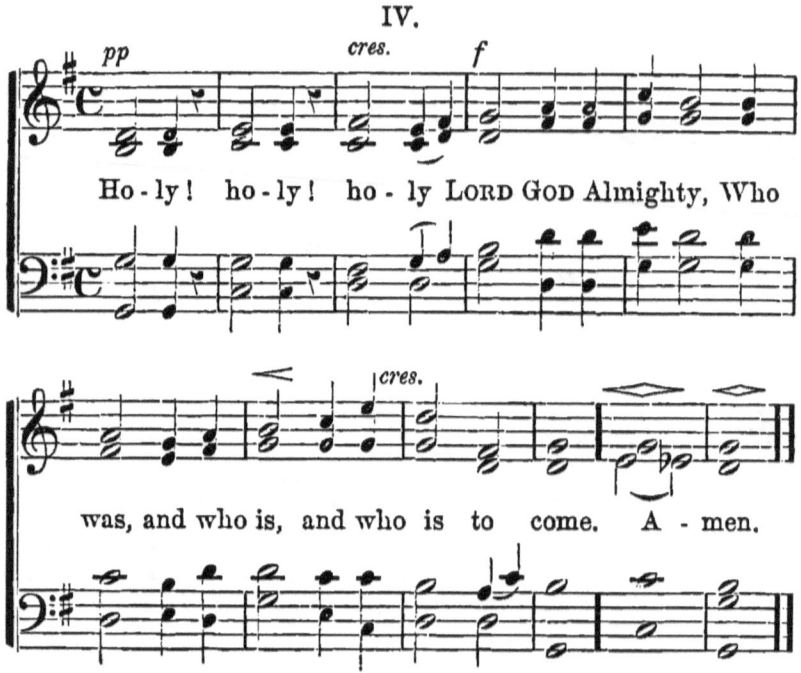

Ho-ly! ho-ly! ho-ly Lord God Almighty, Who was, and who is, and who is to come. A-men.

DOXOLOGIES.

I.

¶ *Minister:*

TO Jesus Christ the Lord be glory and dominion forever and ever. *Amen.*

¶ *People:*

HE is the Alpha | and the O|mega,
 The Beginning and the | End, the | First and the | Last :

Who is, and who was, and who | is to | come :
The | Al|migh|ty.

DOXOLOGIES.

II.

TO Jesus Christ the Lord be glory | and do|minion,
For|ever and | ever : A|men.

He is the Alpha and the Omega, the Beginning and the End,
the | First and the | Last :
Who is, and who was, and who is to come, the | Al|migh|ty.

III.

GLORY be to the Lord, the | heavenly | King :
Father and | Saviour | Jesus | Christ.

Whom alone the heavens and | all the | earth :
Shall worship and adore, world | without | end.   A|men.

IV.

GLORY and dominion be unto the Lord | Jesus | Christ :
For|ever and | ever : A|men.

Who is, and who was, and who | is to | come :
The | Al|migh|ty.

RESPONSIVE SERVICES.

I.

THE COMMANDMENTS.

EXODUS XX. MARK XII.

AND God spake all these words, saying:

I am the LORD thy GOD, who have brought thee out of the land of Egypt, out of the house of bondage. Thou shalt have no other gods before Me. Thou shalt not make unto thee any graven image, or any likeness of any thing that is in heaven above, or that is in the earth beneath, or that is in the water under the earth: thou shalt not bow down thyself to them, nor serve them: for I, the LORD thy GOD, am a jealous GOD, visiting the iniquities of the fathers upon the children unto the third and fourth generation of them that hate Me; and showing mercy unto the thousandth generation of them that love Me and keep my commandments.

Thou shalt not take the name of the LORD thy GOD in vain: for the LORD will not hold him guiltless that taketh his name in vain.

Remember the Sabbath day to keep it holy. Six days shalt thou labor, and do all thy work; but the seventh day is the Sabbath of the LORD thy GOD; in it thou shalt not do any work, thou, nor thy son, nor thy daughter, thy man-servant, nor thy maid-servant, nor thy cattle, nor thy stranger that is within thy gates: for in six days the LORD made heaven and earth, the sea, and all that in them is, and rested the seventh day : wherefore the LORD blessed the Sabbath day, and hallowed it.

Honor thy father and thy mother; that thy days may be long upon the land which the LORD thy GOD giveth thee.

Thou shalt not kill.

Thou shalt not commit adultery.

Thou shalt not steal.

Thou shalt not bear false witness against thy neighbor.

Thou shalt not covet thy neighbor's house.

Thou shalt not covet thy neighbor's wife, nor his man-servant, nor his maid-servant, nor his ox, nor his ass, nor any thing that is thy neighbor's.

¶ *Then may follow the Two Great Commandments, the Minister first saying, " Remember also the Two Great Commandments of our* LORD JESUS CHRIST."

HEAR, O Israel, the LORD our GOD is one LORD. And thou shalt love the LORD thy GOD with all thy heart, and with all thy soul, and with all thy mind, and with all thy strength : this is the first commandment. And the second is like, namely this, Thou shalt love thy neighbor as thyself. There is none other commandment greater than these.

¶ *The People will answer:*

ALL that the LORD hath spoken,
We will do and hear.

¶ *Then the Minister may say:*

BLESSED are they that do his commandments, that they may have right to the tree of life, and may enter in through the gates into the city.

¶ *Then may follow Selection* 49, *on page* 36, *or some other suitable Selection.*

II.
THE COMMANDMENTS.
Deut. v. Matt. xxii.

THE Lord talked with you face to face in the mount, out of the midst of the fire, saying:

I am the Lord thy God, who brought thee out of the land of Egypt, out of the house of bondage. Thou shalt have none other gods before Me. Thou shalt not make thee any graven image, or any likeness of any thing that is in heaven above, or that is in the earth beneath, or that is in the waters beneath the earth: thou shalt not bow down thyself to them, nor serve them: for I, the Lord thy God, am a jealous God, visiting the iniquity of the fathers upon the children, unto the third and fourth generation of them that hate Me; and showing mercy unto the thousandth generation of them that love Me and keep my commandments.

Thou shalt not take the name of the Lord thy God in vain: for the Lord will not hold him guiltless that taketh his name in vain.

Keep the Sabbath day to sanctify it, as the Lord thy God hath commanded thee. Six days shalt thou labor, and do all thy work; but the seventh day is the Sabbath of the Lord thy God: in it thou shalt not do any work, thou, nor thy son, nor thy daughter, nor thy manservant, nor thy maid-servant, nor thine ox, nor thine ass, nor any of thy cattle, nor thy stranger that is within thy gates; that thy man-servant and thy maid-servant may rest as well as thou. And remember that thou wast a servant in the land of Egypt, and that the Lord thy God brought thee out thence through a mighty hand and by an outstretched arm: therefore the LORD thy GOD commanded thee to keep the Sabbath day.

Honor thy father and thy mother, as the LORD thy GOD hath commanded thee; that thy days may be prolonged, and that it may go well with thee, in the land which the LORD thy GOD giveth thee.

Thou shalt not kill.

Neither shalt thou commit adultery.

Neither shalt thou steal.

Neither shalt thou bear false witness against thy neighbor.

Neither shalt thou desire thy neighbor's wife.

Neither shalt thou covet thy neighbor's house, his field, or his man-servant, or his maid-servant, his ox, or his ass, or anything that is thy neighbor's.

¶ *Then may follow the Two Great Commandments, the Minister first saying, "Remember also the Two Great Commandments of our* LORD JESUS CHRIST."

THOU shalt love the LORD thy GOD with all thy heart, and with all thy soul, and with all thy mind. This is the first and great Commandment. And the second is like unto it. Thou shalt love thy neighbor as thyself. On these two commandments hang all the law and the prophets.

¶ *The People may answer:*

ALL that the LORD hath spoken, We will do and hear.

¶ *Then the Minister may say:*

BLESSED are they that do His commandments, that they may have right to the tree of life, and may enter in through the gates into the city.

¶ *Then may follow Selection 53, on page 39, or some other suitable Selection.*

III.
THE TEN COMMANDMENTS.
Exodus xx.

AND God spake all these words, saying:

I am the Lord thy God, who have brought thee out of the land of Egypt, out of the house of bondage. Thou shalt have no other gods before Me. Thou shalt not make unto thee any graven image, or any likeness of any thing that is in heaven above, or that is in the earth beneath, or that is in the water under the earth: thou shalt not bow down thyself to them, nor serve them: for I, the Lord thy God, am a jealous God, visiting the iniquities of the fathers upon the children unto the third and fourth generation of them that hate Me; and showing mercy unto the thousandth generation of them that love Me and keep my commandments.

Holy, holy, holy, is the | Lord of | Hosts:
The whole | earth is | full · of his | glory.

Thou shalt not take the name of the Lord thy God in vain: for the Lord will not hold him guiltless that taketh his name in vain.

He hath commanded his | cove·nant for | ever:
Holy and | reve·rend | is his | Name.

Remember the Sabbath day to keep it holy. Six days shalt thou labor, and do all thy work; but the seventh day is the Sabbath of the LORD thy GOD; in it thou shalt not do any work, thou, nor thy son, nor thy daughter, thy man-servant, nor thy maid-servant, nor thy cattle, nor thy stranger that is within thy gates: for in six days the LORD made heaven and earth, the sea, and all that in them is, and rested the seventh day: wherefore the LORD blessed the Sabbath day, and hallowed it.

    The LORD is in his | holy | temple:
    Let all the | earth keep | si·lence be|fore Him.

Honor thy father and thy mother; that thy days may be long upon the land which the LORD thy GOD giveth thee.

    Thy hands have made me, and | fashioned | me:
    Make me to understand, that I may | learn | thy com|mandments.

Thou shalt not kill.

    With the merciful Thou wilt | show thy·self | merciful:
    With an upright man Thou wilt | show thy|self | upright.

Thou shalt not commit adultery.

    With the pure Thou wilt | show thy·self | pure:
    And with the froward Thou wilt | show thy|self | froward.

Thou shalt not steal.

    Order my | steps in thy | Word:
    And let not any iniquity have do|minion | over | me.

Thou shalt not bear false witness against thy neighbor.

<blockquote>
I have chosen the | way of | truth :
Thy judgments | have I | laid be|fore me.
</blockquote>

Thou shalt not covet thy neighbor's house.

<blockquote>
Incline my heart to thy | testi|monies :
And | not to | cove·tous|ness.
</blockquote>

Thou shalt not covet thy neighbor's wife, nor his man-servant, nor his maid-servant, nor his ox, nor his ass, nor any thing that is thy neighbor's.

<blockquote>
All that the | Lord hath | spoken :
We will | do | and | hear.
</blockquote>

IV.
THE TEN COMMANDMENTS.

Deut. v.

THE Lord talked with you face to face in the mount, out of the midst of the fire, saying :

I am the Lord thy God, who brought thee out of the land of Egypt, out of the house of bondage. Thou shalt have none other gods before Me. Thou shalt not make thee any graven image, or any likeness of any thing that is in heaven above, or that is in the earth beneath, or that is in the waters beneath the earth : thou shalt not bow down thyself to them, nor serve them : for I, the Lord thy God, am a jealous God, visiting the iniquity of the fathers upon the children, unto the third and fourth generation of them that hate Me ; and showing mercy unto the thousandth generation of them that love Me, and keep my commandments.

Holy, holy, holy, Lord | God Al|mighty;
Who was, and who | is, and who | is to | come.

Thou shalt not take the name of the Lord thy God in vain: for the Lord will not hold him guiltless that taketh his name in vain.

Who shall not fear | Thee, O | Lord,
And glorify thy name? for | Thou a|lone art | holy.

Keep the Sabbath day to sanctify it, as the Lord thy God hath commanded thee. Six days shalt thou labor, and do all thy work; but the seventh day is the Sabbath of the Lord thy God: in it thou shalt not do any work, thou, nor thy son, nor thy daughter, nor thy man-servant, nor thy maid-servant, nor thine ox, nor thine ass, nor any of thy cattle, nor thy stranger that is within thy gates; that thy man-servant and thy maid-servant may rest as well as thou. And remember that thou wast a servant in the land of Egypt, and that the Lord thy God brought thee out thence through a mighty hand and by an outstretched arm: therefore the Lord thy God commanded thee to keep the Sabbath day.

This is the day which the | Lord hath | made:
We will re|joice · and be | glad in | it.

Honor thy father and thy mother, as the Lord thy God hath commanded thee; that thy days may be prolonged, and that it may go well with thee, in the land which the Lord thy God giveth thee.

The righteous shall in|herit the | land,
And | dwell there|in for|ever.

Thou shalt not kill.

Let thy mercies come unto me, that | I may | live ;
For thy | law is | my de|light.

Neither shalt thou commit adultery.

Thy word is | very | pure :
Therefore thy | servant | loveth | it.

Neither shalt thou steal.

Righteous art | Thou, O | LORD ;
And | upright | are thy | judgments.

Neither shalt thou bear false witness against thy neighbor.

Through thy precepts I get | under|standing :
Therefore every | false way | do I | hate.

Neither shalt thou desire thy neighbor's wife.

I have in|clined my | heart
To perform thy statutes | always, | to the | end.

Neither shalt thou covet thy neighbor's house, his field, or his man-servant, or his maid-servant, his ox, or his ass, or any thing that is thy neighbor's.

Thou art | near, O | LORD ;
And | all · thy com|mandments are | truth.

V.
RESPONSE TO THE COMMANDMENTS.

¶ *When the Commandments are read by the Minister as in the Services on pp. 11-14, the following Response may be repeated by the people silently, or be read, or chanted, at the end of each Commandment; or, the others being omitted, that which follows the 10th Commandment, may alone be used.*

¶ *Response after Commandments I-IX:*

LORD, have mercy upon me : and incline my heart to keep this law.

¶ *Response after Commandment X:*

LORD, have mercy upon me : and write all these thy laws in my heart, I beseech Thee.

¶ *When sung, one of the following Chants may be used:*

I.

After Commandments I-IX.

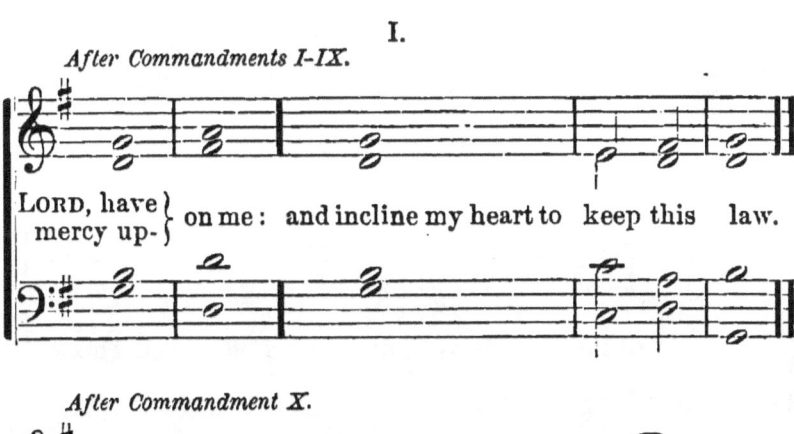

After Commandment X.

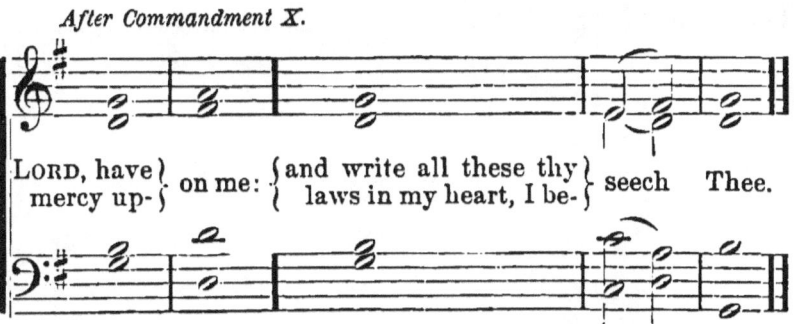

II.

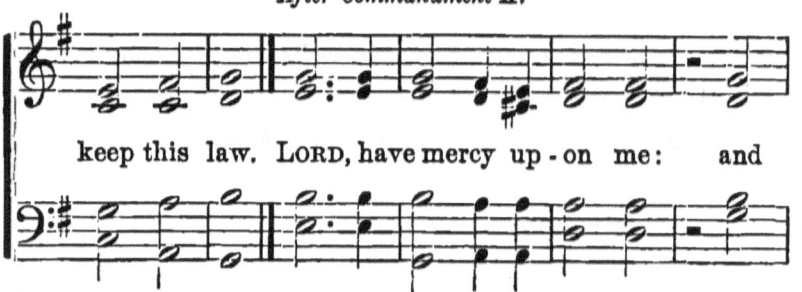

VI.
THE BLESSINGS.
Matthew V.

AND seeing the multitudes, He went up into a mountain : and when He had sat down, his disciples came unto Him. And He opened his mouth, and taught them, saying,

Blessed are the poor in spirit : for theirs is the kingdom of heaven.

Blessed are they that mourn : for they shall be comforted.

Blessed are the meek : for they shall inherit the earth.

Blessed are they that do hunger and thirst after righteousness : for they shall be filled.

Blessed are the merciful : for they shall obtain mercy.

Blessed are the pure in heart : for they shall see God.

Blessed are the peacemakers : for they shall be called the children of God.

Blessed are they that are persecuted for righteousness' sake : for theirs is the kingdom of heaven.

Blessed are ye, when they shall revile you, and persecute you, and shall say all manner of evil against you falsely, for my sake.

Rejoice and be exceeding glad ; for great is your reward in heaven : for so persecuted they the prophets who were before you.

¶ *The People may answer:*

THE law was given by Moses ; but grace and truth came by Jesus Christ.

¶ *Then may follow a Selection.*

VII.
THE BLESSINGS.

AND seeing the multitudes, He went up into a mountain : and when He had sat down, his disciples came unto Him. And He opened his mouth, and taught them, saying :

Blessed are the poor in spirit : for theirs is the kingdom of heaven.

* *This note is sung only when two syllables fall to this measure.*

The LORD is nigh unto the broken in | heart :
And saveth such as be of a | contrite | spirit.

Blessed are they that mourn : for they shall be comforted.

This is my comfort in my af|fliction :
For thy | Word hath | quickened me.

Blessed are the meek : for they shall inherit the earth.

The meek will He guide in | judgment :
And the meek will He | teach his | way.

Blessed are they that do hunger and thirst after righteousness : for they shall be filled.

He shall receive blessing from the | LORD :
And righteousness from the GOD of | his sal|vation.

Blessed are the merciful : for they shall obtain mercy.

* *This note is sung only when two syllables fall to this measure.*

He that trusteth in the | Lord :
Mercy shall compass | him a|bout.

Blessed are the pure in heart : for they shall see God.

Create in me a clean heart, O | God :
And renew a right | spir·it with|in me.

Blessed are the peacemakers : for they shall be called the children of God.

Behold, how good and how pleasant it | is :
For brethren to dwell to|geth·er in | unity.

Blessed are they that are persecuted for righteousness' sake : for theirs is the kingdom of heaven.

The salvation of the righteous is of the | Lord ;
He is their Strength in the | time of | trouble.

Blessed are ye, when they shall revile you, and persecute you, and shall say all manner of evil against you falsely, for my sake.

The angel of the Lord en|campeth
Around them that fear Him : and de|liver·eth | them.

Rejoice and be exceeding glad : for great is your reward in heaven : for so persecuted they the prophets who were before you.

Blessed be the Lord the God of | Israel :
From everlasting and to everlasting : A|men, and A|men.

¶ *Here a Selection may be sung.*

VIII.
THE TWO GREAT COMMANDMENTS.

NOW these are the commandments, the statutes, and the judgments, which the LORD your GOD commanded to teach you, that ye might do them in the land whither ye pass over to possess it; that thou mightest fear the LORD thy GOD, to keep all his statutes and his commandments, which I command thee, thou, and thy son, and thy son's son, all the days of thy life; and that thy days may be prolonged. Hear, therefore, O Israel, and observe to do; that it may be well with thee, and that ye may increase mightily, as the LORD GOD of thy fathers hath promised thee, in the land that floweth with milk and honey.

THE first of all the commandments is, Hear, O Israel; the LORD our GOD is one LORD. And thou shalt love the LORD thy GOD with all thy heart, and with all thy soul, and with all thy mind, and with all thy strength: this is the first commandment.

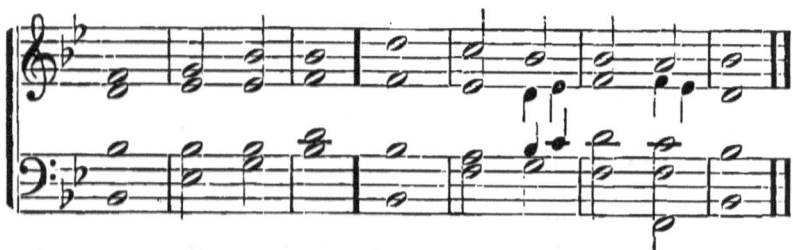

1 Thou art | worthy, O | LORD,
   To receive | glory, and | honor, and | power:

2 For Thou hast cre|ated all | things;
   And for thy pleasure they | are, and | were cre|ated.

AND the second is like, namely this, Thou shalt love thy neighbor as thyself. There is none other commandment greater than these.

All the paths of the Lord are | mercy and | truth,
To those that keep his covenant | and his | testi|monies.

And these words which I command thee this day shall be in thy heart; and thou shalt teach them diligently unto thy children, and shalt talk of them when thou sittest in thy house, and when thou walkest by the way, and when thou liest down, and when thou risest up. And thou shalt bind them for a sign upon thy hand, and they shall be as frontlets between thine eyes. And thou shalt write them upon the posts of thy house, and on thy gates.

1 Behold, the | Lord our | God
   Hath showed us his | glory | and his | greatness:

2 And we have | heard his | voice
   Out of the | midst | of the | fire:

3 We have | seen this | day,
   That God doth | talk with | man, and he | liveth.

4 And the Lord commanded us to do | all these | statutes.
   To fear the Lord our | God, for our | good | always:

5 That He might pre|serve · us a|live,
   As | it | is this | day.

6 And it shall be our | righteous|ness,
   That we observe to | do all | these com|mandments,

7 Before the | Lord our | God,
   As | He · hath com|manded | us.

IX.
THE NEW JERUSALEM.

AND I saw a new heaven and a new earth: for the first heaven and the first earth were passed away; and there was no more sea. And I, John, saw the holy city, New Jerusalem, coming down from GOD out of heaven, prepared as a bride adorned for her husband. And I heard a great voice out of heaven saying, Behold, the tabernacle of GOD is with men, and He will dwell with them, and they shall be his people, and GOD himself shall be with them, their GOD.

And GOD shall wipe away all | tears · from their | eyes;
And death shall | be no | more;
Neither shall there be mourning, nor crying, nor | pain any |
For the former things are | passed a|way. [more;

AND he that sat upon the throne said, Behold, I make all things new. I am Alpha and Omega, the Beginning and the End. I will give unto him that is athirst of the fountain of the water of life freely.

    And the Spirit and the | Bride say, | Come.
    And let him that | heareth say, | Come.
    And let him that | thirsteth | come.
    And let him that willeth take water of | life | freely.

And there came unto me one of the seven angels, and talked with me, saying, Come hither, I will show thee the Bride, the Lamb's wife. And he carried me away in the spirit to a great and high mountain, and showed me that great city, the holy Jerusalem, descending out of heaven from God, having the glory of God : and her light was like unto a stone most precious, even like a jasper stone, clear as crystal ; and had a wall great and high, and had twelve gates, and at the gates twelve angels, and names written thereon, which are the names of the twelve tribes of the children of Israel.

And the city had no | need of the | sun,
Neither of the moon, to | shine in | it :
For the glory of God did | lighten | it,
And the Lamb is the | light there|of.

And the wall of the city had twelve foundations, and in them the names of the twelve apostles of the Lamb. And he that talked with me had a golden reed to measure the city, and the gates thereof, and the wall thereof. And the city lieth four-square ; and the length is as large as the breadth : and he measured the city with the reed, twelve thousand furlongs : the length and the breadth and the height of it are equal. And he measured the wall thereof, an hundred forty and four cubits, the measure of a man, that is, of an angel. And I saw no temple therein: for the LORD GOD Almighty and the LAMB are the temple of it.

> And there shall in no wise enter | into | it
> Any thing | that de|fileth,
> Or worketh abomination, or | mak·eth a | lie:
> But they that are written in the LAMB's | book of | life.

AND he shewed me a pure river of water of life, clear as crystal, proceeding out of the throne of GOD and of the LAMB. In the midst of the street of it, and on either side of the river, was the tree of life, which bare twelve manner of fruits, and yielded her fruit every month: and the leaves of the tree were for the healing of the nations.

> And the throne of GOD and of the LAMB shall | be in | it;
> And his servants shall | serve | Him:
> And they shall | see his | face;
> And his name shall | be · in their | foreheads.

AND he saith unto me, Seal not the words of the prophecy of this book: for the time is at hand. He that is unjust, let him be unjust still: and he that is filthy, let him be filthy still: and he that is righteous, let him be righteous still: and he that is holy, let him be holy still. And, behold, I come quickly; and my reward is with me, to render to every one according as his work shall be. I am the Alpha and the Omega, the Beginning and the End, the First and the Last.

> Blessed are they that | do · his com|mandments,
> That they may have right to the | tree of | life,
> And may | enter | in
> Through the gates | into the | city.

X.
THE LAW OF LOVE.

THINK not that I am come to destroy the Law or the Prophets : I am not come to destroy, but to fulfill. For verily I say unto you : Till heaven and earth pass, one jot or one tittle shall in no wise pass from the Law, till all be fulfilled. Whosoever, therefore, shall break one of the least of these commandments, and shall teach men so, shall be called the least in the kingdom of the heavens : but whosoever shall do and teach them, the same shall be called great in the kingdom of the heavens.

For|ever, O | Lord,
Thy word is es|tablished | in the | heavens :
Thy faithfulness is unto all | gener|ations.
Thou hast established the | earth, and it | standeth | firm.

AND Jesus said : The first of all the commandments is, Hear, O Israel, the Lord our God is one Lord : And thou shalt love the Lord thy God with all thy heart, and with all thy soul, and with all thy mind, and with all thy strength.

With my whole heart have I | sought | Thee :
O let me not | wander from | thy com|mandments.
Thy word have I | hid in mine | heart :
That I might not | sin a|gainst | Thee.

AND the second is like unto it, Thou shalt love thy neighbor as thyself. On these two commandments hang all the Law and the Prophets.

Blessed are the perfect | in the | way,
Who walk in the | law | of the | LORD.
Blessed are they that keep his | testi|monies :
That seek | Him with | all the | heart.

A NEW commandment I give unto you, That ye love one another. As I have loved you, that ye also love one another. By this will all men know that ye are my disciples, if ye have love one to another.

Search me, O GOD, and | know my | heart :
Try me, and | know | my | thoughts :
And see if there be any wicked | way in | me :
And lead me in the | way | ever|lasting.

THEREFORE all things whatsoever ye would that men should do to you, do ye even so to them : for this is the Law and the Prophets.

The law was | given by | Moses :
Grace and truth | came by | JESUS | CHRIST.
And of his fullness have we | all re|ceived :
And | grace for | grace : A|men.

XI.

PSALM OF THANKSGIVING.

PSALM CVII.

O GIVE thanks unto the LORD, for He is good ; for his mercy endureth forever. Let the redeemed of the LORD say so, whom He hath redeemed from the hand of the enemy; and gathered them out of the lands, from the east and from the west, from the north and from the south. They wandered in the wilderness in a solitary way; they found no city to dwell in. Hungry and thirsty their soul fainted in them. Then they cried unto the Lord in their trouble, and He delivered them out of their distresses. And He led them forth by the right way, that they might go to a city of habitation.

O that men would praise the | Lord for his | goodness,
And for his wonderful | works to the | children of | men:
For He satisfieth the | longing | soul,
And filleth the | hungry | soul with | goodness.

Such as sit in darkness and the shadow of death, being bound in affliction and iron: because they rebelled against the words of God, and contemned the counsel of the Most High: therefore He brought down their heart with labor; they fell down, and there was none to help. Then they cried unto the Lord in their trouble, and He saved them out of their distresses. He brought them out of darkness and the shadow of death, and brake their bands in sunder.

> O that men would praise the | Lord for his | goodness,
> And for his wonderful | works to the | children of | men :
> For He hath broken the | gates of | brass,
> And cut the | bars of | iron in | sunder.

Fools because of their transgression and because of their iniquities are afflicted. Their soul abhorreth all manner of meat; and they draw near unto the gates of death. Then they cry unto the Lord in their trouble, and He saveth them out of their distresses. He sent his word and healed them, and delivered them from their destructions.

> O that men would praise the | Lord for his | goodness,
> And for his wonderful | works to the | children of | men :
> And let them sacrifice the sacrifices | of thanks giving,
> And de|clare his | works with re|joicing.

They that go down to the sea in ships, that do business in great waters; these see the works of the Lord, and his wonders in the deep. For He commandeth and raiseth the stormy wind, which lifteth up the waves thereof. They mount up to heaven, they go down again to the depths: their soul is melted because of trouble. They reel and stagger like a drunken man, and all their wisdom is brought to naught. Then they cry unto the Lord in their trouble, and He bringeth them out of their distresses. He maketh the storm a calm, and the waves thereof are still. Then are they glad because they are quiet; and He bringeth them unto the haven of their desire.

> O that men would praise the | Lord for his | goodness,
> And for his wonderful | works to the | children of | men :
> Let them exalt Him also in the congregation | of the | people,
> And praise Him in the as|sembly | of the | elders.

XII.
THE HOLY SUPPER.

IN this mountain shall the LORD of Hosts make unto all people a feast of fat things, a feast of wines on the lees, of fat things full of marrow, of wines on the lees well refined. And He will destroy in this mountain the face of the covering cast over all people, and the vail that is spread over all nations. He will swallow up death in victory; and the LORD GOD will wipe away tears from off all faces; and the rebuke of his people shall He take away from off all the earth: for the LORD hath spoken it.

And it shall be said in that day, Lo, | this · is our | GOD;
We have waited for | Him, and | He will | save us:

This is the LORD; we have | waited | for Him;
We will be glad and re|joice in | his sal|vation.

BEHOLD, I stand at the door, and knock; if any man hear my voice, and open the door, I will come in to him, and will sup with him, and he with Me.

I will go unto the | altar of | GOD:
Unto GOD the | gladness | of my | joy.

IF thou bring thy gift to the altar, and there rememberest that thy brother hath aught against thee, leave there thy gift before the altar, and go thy way; first be reconciled to thy brother, and then come and offer thy gift.

Search me, O God, and | know my | heart :
Try | me, and | know my | thoughts :
And see if there be any wicked | way in | me :
And lead me in the | way | ever|lasting.

A NEW commandment I give unto you, That ye love one another. As I have loved you, that ye also love one another.

I will wash my | hands in | innocence :
So will I | compass thine | altar, O | Lord :
That I may publish with the voice of | thanks|giving :
And tell of | all thy | wondrous | works.

I AM the Good Shepherd, and know my sheep, and am known of mine ; and I lay down my life for the sheep.

Thou preparest a | table be|fore me,
In the | presence | of mine | enemies ;
Thou anointest my | head with | oil ;
My | cup | runneth | over.

I AM the bread of life : he that cometh unto Me shall never hunger, and he that believeth on Me shall never thirst.

What shall I | render to the | Lord,
For all his | bene·fits | toward | me ?
I will take the | cup · of sal|vation,
And call upon the | name | of the | Lord.

I AM the living bread which came down from heaven ; if any one eat of this bread, he shall live forever : and the bread that I will give is my flesh, which I will give for the life of the world.

Unto Him that | loved | us,
And washed us from our | sins in | his own | blood,
And hath made us kings and priests unto | God · and his | Father,
To Him be glory and dominion for | ever and | ever : A|men.

XIII.
THE INCARNATION OF THE LORD.

IN the beginning was the Word, and the Word was with God, and the Word was God: and the Word was made flesh and dwelt among us.

>Thou, O Lord, art our Father, | our Re|deemer;
>Thy | name is from | ever|lasting.

And there were in the same country shepherds abiding in the field, keeping watch over their flock by night: and, lo, the angel of the Lord came upon them, and the glory of the Lord shone round about them; and they were sore afraid.

>Arise, shine, for thy | light is | come,
>And the glory of the | Lord is | risen up|on thee.

And the angel said unto them, Fear not: for, behold, I bring you good tidings of great joy, which shall be to all people.

>How beautiful up|on the | mountains
>Are the feet of | him that | bringeth good | tidings:
>
>That pro'claimeth | peace:
>That | bringeth good | tidings of | good.

For unto you is born this day in the city of David a Saviour, which is Christ the Lord: and this shall be a sign unto you; ye shall find the babe wrapped in swaddling clothes, lying in a manger.

Unto us a | Child is | born ;
Unto | us a | Son·is | given :

And the government shall be up|on his | shoulder,
And his name shall be called Wonderful, Counsellor, the Mighty God, Father of e|terni·ty, the | Prince of | Peace.

And suddenly there was with the angel a multitude of the heavenly host, praising God, and saying :

Glory to | God in the | highest,
On earth | peace, among | men good | will.

I will declare the decree the Lord hath said unto me: Thou art my son ; this day have I begotten thee.

¶ *Here may be sung Selection* 10, *page* 6, *or some other suitable Selcction.*

XIV.

PENITENCE.

O MY people, what have I done unto thee, and wherein have I wearied thee? Answer me. For I brought thee up out of the land of Egypt, and redeemed thee out of the house of bondage.

All we, like sheep, have | gone a|stray :
We have turned, every | one to his | own | way.

Thou calledst in trouble, and I delivered thee ; I answered thee in the secret place of thunder : I proved thee at the waters of Meribah.

Whither shall I | go · from thy | Spirit?
Or whither shall I | flee | from thy | presence?
If I ascend up into heaven, | Thou art | there:
If I make my bed in | hell, be,hold, Thou art | there.

O THAT thou hadst hearkened to my commandments: then had thy peace been as a river, and thy righteousness as the waves of the sea.

If Thou, O LORD, shouldst | mark in|iquities,
O | LORD, | who shall | stand?
But with | Thee is for|giveness,
That | Thou | mayst be | feared.

WHAT more could have been done to my vineyard that I have not done in it? Wherefore when I looked that it should bring forth grapes, brought it forth wild grapes?

Return, we beseech Thee, O | GOD of | hosts:
Look down from heaven, and be,hold, and | visit this | vine,
And the vineyard which thy right | hand hath | planted,
And the branch that Thou | madest | strong for thy|self.

O ISRAEL, thou hast destroyed thyself; thou hast fallen by thine iniquity: but in Me is thine help.

Have mercy upon | me, O | GOD,
According to thy | loving-|kind'ness;
According to the multitude of thy | tender | mercies,
Blot | out | my trans|gressions.

O ISRAEL, I have blotted out as a thick cloud thy transgressions, and as a cloud thy sins: return unto Me, for I have redeemed thee.

So will we not go | back from | Thee;
Quicken us, and we will | call up|on thy | name.
Turn us again, O LORD | GOD of | hosts:
And cause thy face to | shine, and we | shall be | saved.

O ISRAEL: return unto the LORD thy GOD.

¶ *Then may be sung Selection* 11, *on page* 7, *or some other suitable Selection.*

XV.

THE RESURRECTION OF THE LORD.

I AM the Resurrection and the Life : he that believeth in Me, though he were dead, yet shall he live ; and whosoever liveth and believeth in Me shall never die.

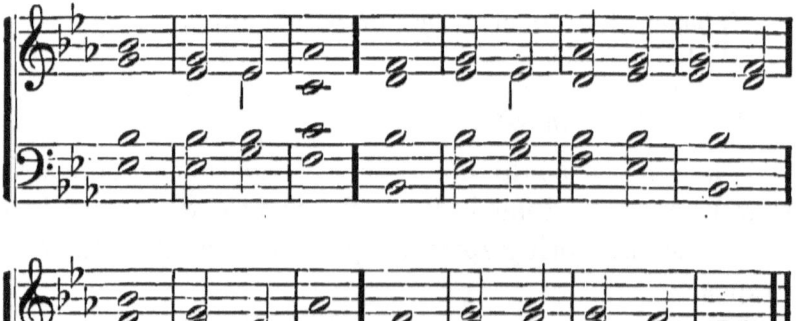

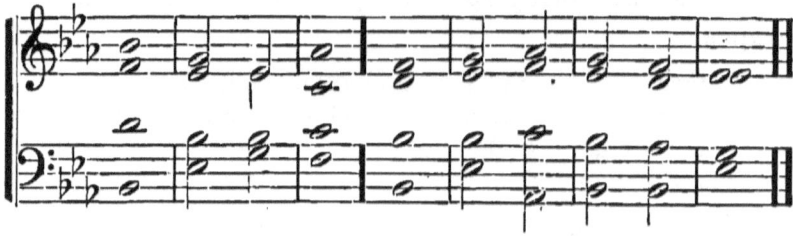

> The Lord | is my | light
> And my sal|vation ; | whom shall I | fear?
> The Lord is the | strength of my | life ;
> Of | whom shall I | be a|fraid ?

The angel of the Lord descended from heaven, and came and rolled back the stone from the door, and sat upon it ; his countenance was like lightning, and his raiment white as snow.

> They cried unto the | Lord in their | trouble,
> And He saved them | out of | their dis|tresses ;
> He brought them out of darkness and the | shadow of | death,
> And | brake their | bands in | sunder.

And the angel said unto the woman, Fear not, for I know that ye seek Jesus, who was crucified : He is not here ; He is risen, as He said :

For Thou wilt not leave my | soul in | hell ;
Neither wilt Thou suffer thine Holy | One to | see cor|ruption;
Thou wilt show me the | path of | life ;
In thy | presence is | fullness of | joy.

FEAR not: I am He that liveth and was dead ; and, lo! I am alive forevermore, Amen : and have the keys of death and of hell.

Worthy is the Lamb | that was | slain
To receive power and riches and wisdom and strength and | honor and | glory and | blessing :
Blessing and honor and | glory and | power,
Be unto Him that sitteth upon the throne, and unto the Lamb, for | ever and | ever. A|men.

I AM the LORD thy GOD, who have brought thee up out of the land of Egypt, out of the house of bondage : Thou shalt have no other gods before me.

¶ *Here may be sung Selection* 151, *page* 116, *or some other suitable Selection.*

XVI.

THE ASCENSION AND GLORIFICATION OF THE LORD.

I ASCEND unto my Father and to your Father, unto my GOD and your GOD.

Be Thou exalted, O GOD, a|bove the | heavens :
And thy glory a|bove | all the | earth.

No man hath ascended up to heaven but He that hath come down from heaven; even the Son of man, who is in heaven.

> The kingdoms of this world are become the kingdoms of our Lord and | of his | Christ,
> And He shall | reign for | ever and | ever.

And I, if I be lifted up from the earth, will draw all men unto Me.

> Whom have I in | heaven but | Thee;
> And there is none upon earth that I de|sire be|sides | Thee.

Behold, I send the promise of my Father upon you; but tarry ye in the city of Jerusalem until ye be endued with power from on high.

> Out of Zion shall go | forth the | Law;
> And the Word of the | Lord from Je|rusa|lem.

And He lifted up his hands and blessed them; and while He blessed them He was parted from them and carried up into heaven.

> The Lord hath prepared his | throne in the | heavens,
> And his kingdom | ruleth | over | all.

I am the Alpha and the Omega, the Beginning and the End, saith the Lord: Who is, and who was, and who is to come, the Almighty.

¶ *Here may be sung Selection 73, page 55, or some other suitable Selection.*

XVII.

THE HOLY SPIRIT, OR THE DIVINE PROCEEDING OF THE LORD.

If a man love Me he will keep my words, and my Father will love him; and We will come to him, and make our abode with him.

Thou art gone up on high, Thou hast led cap|tivity | captive.
Thou hast received gifts for men, yea, for the re|bellious | also,
That the Lord | God might | dwell a|mong them.

The wind bloweth where it listeth, and thou hearest the sound thereof, but canst not tell whence it cometh, nor whither it goeth : so is every one that is born of the Spirit.

Thou sendest | forth thy | Spirit ;
They | are cre|ated ;
And Thou re|newest the | face of the | earth.

The Comforter, which is the Holy Ghost, whom the Father will send in my name, he shall teach you all things, and bring all things to your remembrance, whatsoever I have said unto you.

He that | hath an | ear,
Let | — him | hear,
What the Spirit | saith | unto the | Churches.

I will not leave you comfortless. I will come to you : because I live ye shall live also: at that day ye shall know that I am in my Father, and ye in Me, and I in you.

¶ *Here may be sung Selection* 115, *page* 87, *or some other suitable Selection.*

INTRODUCTORY
SENTENCES AND PRAYERS.

INTRODUCTORY SENTENCES.

THE LORD is in his holy temple; let all the earth keep silence before Him.

ENTER into his gates with thanksgiving, and into his courts with praise: be thankful unto Him, and bless his name. For the LORD is good; his mercy is everlasting; and his truth endureth to all generations.

GIVE unto the LORD, O ye kindreds of the people: give unto the LORD glory and strength: give unto the LORD the glory due unto his name: bring an offering, and come into his courts: O worship the LORD in the beauty of holiness: tremble before Him all the earth.

SEEK ye the LORD while He may be found, call ye upon Him while He is near. Let the wicked forsake his way, and the unrighteous man his thoughts; and let him return unto the LORD, and He will have mercy upon him; and to our GOD, for He will abundantly pardon.

EXALT ye the LORD our GOD, and worship at his footstool, for He is holy.

ONE thing have I desired of the LORD, that will I seek after; that I may dwell in the house of the LORD all the days of my life, to behold the beauty of the LORD, and to inquire in his temple.

For from the rising of the sun even unto the going down of the same, my name shall be great among the Gentiles; and in every place incense shall be offered unto my name, and a pure offering: for my name shall be great among the heathen, saith the Lord of Hosts.

Wherewith shall I come before the Lord, and bow myself before the High God? Shall I come before Him with burnt offerings, with calves of a year old? Will the Lord be pleased with thousands of rams, or with ten thousands of rivers of oil? Shall I give my first-born for my transgression, the fruit of my body for the sins of my soul? He hath showed thee, O man, what is good; and what doth the Lord require of thee, but to do justly, and to love mercy, and to walk humbly with thy God?

What shall I render to the Lord for all his benefits toward me? I will take the cup of salvation, and call upon the name of the Lord. I will pay my vows to the Lord now in the presence of all his people, in the courts of the house of the Lord, in the midst of thee, O Jerusalem.

Holiness becometh thine house, O Lord, forever.

The sun shall be no more thy light by day, neither for brightness shall the moon give light unto thee: but the Lord shall be unto thee an everlasting light, and thy God thy glory.

Bless ye the Lord, all ye servants of the Lord, who by night stand in the house of the Lord: lift up your hands in the sanctuary and bless the Lord. The Lord that made heaven and earth, bless thee out of Zion.

INTRODUCTORY PRAYERS.

Search me, O God, and know my heart; try me, and know my thoughts; and see if there be any wicked way in me; and lead me in the way everlasting.

Cause me to hear thy loving kindness in the morning; for in Thee do I trust; cause me to know the way wherein I should walk; for I lift up my soul unto Thee.

O Lord, open Thou my lips ; and my mouth shall shew forth thy praise. For Thou desirest not sacrifice ; else would I give ; Thou delightest not in burnt offering. The sacrifices of God are a broken spirit : a broken and a contrite heart, O God, Thou wilt not despise.

Let the words of my mouth, and the meditation of my heart, be acceptable in thy sight, O Lord, my Strength and my Redeemer

Unto Thee lift I up mine eyes, O Thou that dwellest in the heavens.

Quicken me, O Lord, according to thy Word. Accept, I beseech Thee, the free-will offerings of my mouth, O Lord, and teach me thy judgments.

Help us, O God of our salvation : for the glory of thy name ; and deliver us, and purge away our sins ; for thy name's sake.

SENTENCES INTRODUCTORY TO PRAYER.

Thus saith the Lord, the King of Israel, and his Redeemer, the Lord of Hosts ; I am the first, and I am the last, and beside Me there is no God

Thus saith the Lord, that created the heavens : God Himself, that formed the earth and made it. I am the Lord ; and there is none else ; a just God and a Saviour, there is none besides Me.

Look unto Me, and be ye saved, all the ends of the earth ; for I am God, and there is none else.

Come unto Me, all ye that labor and are heavy laden, and I will give you rest. Take my yoke upon you, and learn of Me ; for I am meek, and lowly in heart ; and ye shall find rest to your souls.

And I say unto you, Ask, and it shall be given you ; seek, and ye shall find ; knock, and it shall be opened unto you. For every one that asketh, receiveth ; and he that seeketh, findeth ; and to him that knocketh, it shall be opened.

THE hour cometh, nud now is, when the true worshippers shall worship the FATHER in spirit and in truth; for the FATHER seeketh such to worship Him. GOD is a Spirit; and they that worship Him, must worship in spirit and in truth.

BLESSED is he whose transgression is forgiven, whose sin is covered. Blessed is the man unto whom the LORD imputeth not iniquity, and in whose spirit there is no guile.

I SAID, I will confess my transgressions unto the LORD, and Thou forgavest the iniquity of my sin. For this shall every one that is godly pray unto Thee in a time when Thou mayest be found: surely in the floods of great waters they shall not come nigh unto him.

I AM the Way, and the Truth, and the Life. No one cometh unto the FATHER but by Me. If ye had known Me ye would have known my FATHER also: and from henceforth ye know Him and have seen Him. He that hath seen Me hath seen the FATHER.

I AM the vine, ye are the branches; he that abideth in Me, and I in him, the same bringeth forth much fruit: for without Me ye can do nothing. . . . . . . If ye abide in Me, and my words abide in you, ye shall ask what ye will, and it shall be done unto you.

IF ye then, being evil, know how to give good gifts unto your children; how much more shall the Heavenly FATHER give the Holy Spirit to them that ask Him.

AGAIN I say unto you, that if two of you shall agree on earth, as touching any thing that they shall ask, it shall be done for them of my FATHER who is in Heaven: for where two or three are gathered together in my name, there am I in the midst of them.

WHAT things soever ye desire when ye pray, believe that ye receive them, and ye shall have them. And when ye stand praying, forgive, if ye have aught against any: that your FATHER also who is in heaven may forgive you your trespasses. But if ye do not forgive, neither will your FATHER who is in heaven forgive your trespasses.

SENTENCES INTRODUCTORY TO PRAYER.

O COME let us worship and bow down: let us kneel before the LORD our Maker.

BRETHREN: The Word of God assures us that he that asketh, receiveth, he that seeketh, findeth, and to him that knocketh, it shall be opened; and that to the humble and contrite heart, the LORD is ever near: let us therefore, with humility and faith, draw near to the LORD, to confess before Him our sins, to implore his mercies and forgiveness, to seek light and strength from Him for all our needs, and to thank Him for his unspeakable goodness to us; humbly kneeling and saying:

PRAYERS FROM THE WORD.

UNTO Thee, O LORD, do I lift up my soul. O my GOD, I trust in Thee: let me not be ashamed, let not mine enemies triumph over me. Show me thy ways, O LORD; teach me thy paths. Lead me in thy truth, and teach me; for Thou art the GOD of my salvation: on Thee do I wait all the day

REMEMBER, O LORD, thy tender mercies and thy loving kindnesses; for they have been ever of old. Remember not the sins of my youth, nor my transgressions: according to thy mercy remember Thou me for thy goodness' sake, O LORD.

UNTO Thee, O LORD, do I lift up my soul. For Thou, O LORD, art good, and ready to forgive; and plenteous in mercy to all that call upon Thee. Give ear, O LORD, to my prayer; and attend to the voice of my supplications. In the day of my trouble I will call upon Thee: for Thou wilt answer me. Among the gods there is none like unto Thee, O LORD; neither are there any works like unto thy works. All nations whom Thou hast made shall come and worship before Thee, O LORD; and shall glorify thy name. For Thou art great, and doest wondrous things: Thou art GOD alone.

TEACH me thy way, O LORD; I will walk in thy truth: unite my heart to fear thy name. I will praise Thee, O LORD my GOD, with all my heart: and I will glorify thy name for evermore.

THE LORD'S PRAYER.

OUR FATHER, who art in the heavens: Hallowed be Thy name. Thy kingdom come. Thy will be done, as in heaven, so also upon the earth. Give us this day our daily bread. And forgive us our debts as we also forgive our debtors. And lead us not into temptation; but deliver us from evil. For Thine is the Kingdom, and the Power, and the Glory, forever. *Amen.*

CONFESSIONS.

HAVE mercy upon me, O GOD, according to thy loving kindness: according to the multitude of thy tender mercies, blot out my transgressions. Wash me thoroughly from mine iniquity, and cleanse me from my sin. For I acknowledge my transgressions, and my sin is ever before me.

O LORD our GOD, we confess that we have sinned against Thee in thought, word, and deed; we have erred from thy ways; we have followed the devices of our own hearts, and there is no health in us. But Thou, O LORD, art good and ready to forgive, and plenteous in mercy unto all them that call upon Thee. Help us, O GOD of our salvation, for the glory of thy name, and deliver us, and purge away our sins, for thy name's sake. *Amen.*

O LORD, our heavenly Father, who, of thy great mercy, hast promised forgiveness of sins to all them that repent and turn unto Thee, have mercy upon us: deliver us from all our evils, strengthen us in all goodness, and bring us unto everlasting life. *Amen.*

WE confess, O Heavenly Father, that in thought, word, and work, we have sinned against heaven and in thy sight, and are not worthy to be called thy children. But Thou, O LORD, art good, and ready to forgive, and plenteous in mercy to all them that call upon Thee. Lead us, O LORD, to true repentance. Search our hearts by the light of thy truth, and renew a right spirit within us, that we may be enabled to see and acknowledge our evils, and to shun them as sins against Thee, and in the faithful and diligent performance of our duties, may learn to do justly, and love mercy, and walk humbly with Thee our GOD. *Amen.*

PRAYERS AND THANKSGIVINGS.

¶ *For the Divine Blessing on the Worship and Instruction.*

O LORD, our heavenly FATHER, by whose mercy we are enabled to meet together to offer unto Thee our united prayer and praise, and to meditate upon thy Word : We thank Thee for the privileges of Divine worship, for the ministry of thy Holy Gospel, and for all the means which Thou hast appointed for our spiritual instruction and the attainment of everlasting life. Bless now, we beseech Thee, O LORD, our assembling in thy Name. Enable us so to dispose our thoughts and affections that our worship may be acceptable in thy sight. Grant that thy Holy Word may be taught in its purity and received in humble and willing hearts. Give us a spiritual discernment of its heavenly wisdom, and guide us in a faithful application of it to our own lives. May thy words so abide in us, that we may abide in Thee. Awaken and strengthen in us a more abiding interest in what is spiritual and eternal, and a more abiding love to Thee and to the neighbor. Lead us to acknowledge thy providence in all the experiences of life, and in all things to follow Thee in the regeneration. *Amen.*

¶ *For Divine Direction.*

ORDER our steps in thy Word, O LORD, and let not any iniquity have dominion over us. Give us strength against our inward foes. Deliver us from all idolatry of self and of the world, from all error, pride, and self-will. Save us from all rejection of thy truth, from prejudice, blindness, and hardness of heart. Lead us, O LORD, and teach us, that we may avoid all secret sin and open transgression ; that we may be free from malice and unkindness, from selfish and covetous desires, from ingratitude to Thee and to our neighbor, from worldly-mindedness and discontent. Help us to forgive our enemies, to love our neighbor as ourselves, and to do unto others as we would that they should do unto us. Hold up our goings in thy paths, that our footsteps slip not. Keep our tongues from evil and our lips from speaking guile ; that we may depart from evil and do good ; may seek peace and pursue it. *Amen.*

¶ *For the Profitable Reading of the Word.*

O LORD JESUS CHRIST our Saviour, who hast given us thy Word to be a lamp to our feet and a light unto our path : Grant that we may reverently and attentively read and hear its holy lessons, and, thinking upon thy commandments to do them, may find in them the words of eternal life. *Amen.*

¶ *For all men.*

O LORD JESUS CHRIST, the Creator and Preserver of all mankind : We humbly beseech Thee for all sorts and conditions of men, that Thou wouldest make thy ways known unto them, thy salvation unto all nations. And for thy Church throughout all the world we pray, that it may be so guided and governed by thy good spirit that all who call themselves after thy name, may be led into the way of truth, and hold the faith in unity of spirit, in the bond of peace, and in righteousness of life. Be merciful to all who are in any way afflicted in mind, body, or estate ; comfort and relieve them according to their several necessities, giving them patience under their sufferings, and a happy issue out of all their afflictions. *Amen.*

¶ *A General Thanksgiving.*

O LORD JESUS CHRIST, Father of all mercies, we, thine unworthy servants, do give Thee most humble and hearty thanks for all thy goodness and loving-kindness to us and to all men. We thank Thee for our creation and preservation, and for all the blessings of this life ; but, above all, for thine inestimable love in the redemption of the world through thy glorified Humanity, for the means of grace, and for the hope of everlasting life. And we beseech Thee, O Lord, give us that due sense of all thy mercies, that our hearts may be unfeignedly thankful, and that we may show forth thy praise, not only with our lips, but in our lives ; by giving up ourselves to thy service, and walking before Thee in holiness and righteousness all our days. *Amen.*

¶ *For the Word.*

WE give Thee thanks, O LORD, the Father of Lights, from whom cometh down every good and perfect gift, for thy written Word, whereby Thou dost maintain the communion of angels and men, and dost point out to man the way to heaven. Grant us diligently to read and hear the same, that in thy light we may see light ; endue us with purity and singleness of heart, that we may receive thy truth in sincerity and keep it pure and undefiled ; and enable us, by faithful obedience to thy commandments, to become not only hearers but doers of thy Word. *Amen.* B

¶ *For the New Jerusalem.*

MOST merciful LORD and Saviour JESUS CHRIST, who, by thy Second Coming in the power and great glory of thy Word, hast enabled us to acknowledge Thee the only God of heaven and earth, our Creator, Redeemer, and Regenerator : We pray Thee for the prosperity of thy holy Church, the New Jerusalem, descending from Thee out of heaven. Dispel, we beseech Thee, the darkness that prevents thine appearing ; open the eyes of the blind and the ears of the deaf, and reveal thyself, most blessed Redeemer, to thine erring creatures, as the Husband of thy Church, the true and only object of her love and worship. And grant that wheresoever thy Church doth appear on the face of the earth, it may be so led by thy Holy Spirit, that all who accept its heavenly doctrines, may, with one accord, maintain the same in purity of heart and holiness of life. *Amen.*

¶ *For the Ministry and People.*

MOST merciful and blessed LORD and Saviour, thou true Shepherd of Israel, from whom cometh every good and perfect gift : Send down upon the ministers of thy Church, and all the congregations committed to their charge, the healthful spirit of thy grace, and so refresh them with the continual dew of thy blessing, that they may truly serve Thee and magnify thy Holy Name. *Amen.*

¶ *For Country and Rulers.*

O LORD, our Heavenly Father, Almighty Ruler of the world, King of kings and Lord of lords : Defend and bless thy servant the President of these United States, and all others in authority. Give them faithfulness and strength, integrity and judgment, in administering the affairs of our common country. And endue all classes of the people with a spirit of obedience, charity, and good will, that justice and equity may everywhere prevail, and peace and harmony be established throughout the earth. *Amen.*

¶ *For Sincerity.*

O LORD, our heavenly Father, to whom all hearts are open, all desires known, and from whom no secrets are hid : Cleanse the thoughts of our hearts, by the inspiration of thy Holy Spirit, that we may perfectly love Thee, and worthily magnify thy Holy Name. *Amen.*

¶ For the Divine Presence.

ALMIGHTY and everlasting LORD JESUS CHRIST, whose tabernacle is with men, and who art ever nigh unto the humble and contrite heart: Shed down thy Holy Spirit, we beseech Thee, on all that are here assembled, that, every unholy thought and affection being put away, we may worthily utter thy praise, meekly learn thy Word, and render thanks for all thy mercies. And this we ask for thy Name's sake, O LORD, who art Emmanuel, GOD with us. *Amen.*

¶ For the Divine Guidance.

O LORD JESUS CHRIST, who art the true Light that lighteneth every one that cometh into the world: Shine, we pray Thee, into our hearts; that, the darkness of evil and of error being driven away, we may see clearly the way of thy commandments, and humbly and gladly walk therein, to the avoidance of all evil and to the performance of such good and useful works as Thou wilt have us do. Grant this for thy mercy's sake. *Amen.*

¶ For Divine Assistance.

O LORD our Father in the Heavens, we lift up our eyes unto Thee, from whom alone cometh our help. Hear us, O LORD; show us thy mercy, and forgive us our sins. Enlighten us by thy Word. Enable us to receive it with simplicity and sincerity of heart, and to keep it whole and undefiled. Purify our affections, that we may refuse the evil and choose the good, and give us strength and knowledge, that through obedience to thy commandments we may attain unto everlasting life. *Amen.*

¶ For Direction and Strength.

O LORD, who alone canst enlighten the mind and point out the way to everlasting life, give us understanding that we may learn thy commandments, and strengthen us that we may walk steadfastly therein. Enable us to deny ourselves, to take up our cross and to follow Thee. Grant unto us the spirit of true religion. Dispose us to be kind and gentle, tender and compassionate, patient and forgiving, just and upright, loving one another as Thou hast loved us. In times of trouble, be Thou our support; in weakness and temptation, be Thou our strength. Guide us continually by thy Holy Spirit, and grant that, by a life of obedience, faith, and love, we may diligently serve Thee and glorify thy holy name. *Amen.*

¶ *For Unity.*

O LORD our heavenly Father, who hast constituted thy Church in heaven and on earth one fold under one Shepherd, grant that all who know and love Thee may be united in one holy bond of faith and charity. Inspire us with meekness, patience, long-suffering, and forbearance one toward another, and enable us, with one heart and one soul, to labor together in promoting the interests of religion and the welfare of all around us: that Thou, who art the GOD of love and peace, mayest be our GOD and dwell among us, and that we may be thy people, zealous of good works, and ever devoted to thy service. *Amen.*

¶ *For Submission.*

O LORD our Saviour and Redeemer, who hast bidden us to leave all and follow Thee: Deliver us, we pray Thee, from the love of self and of the world. Increase within us the love of thy holy name. Help us to deny ourselves, to take up our cross, and to follow Thee. And in all our trials and adversities, grant us patience and resignation to thy holy will. *Amen.*

¶ *For a Forgiving Spirit.*

O HOLY and ever blessed LORD, teach us, we beseech Thee, to love one another, to exercise forbearance and forgiveness toward our enemies; to recompense no man evil for evil, but to be merciful even as Thou, our Father in Heaven, art merciful; that so we may continually follow after Thee in all our doings, and be more and more conformed to thine image and likeness. *Amen.*

¶ *For Trust in God.*

O LORD, our heavenly Father, our mighty Redeemer and Saviour, who orderest all things for our eternal good: Mercifully enlighten our minds, and give us a firm and abiding trust in thy love and care. Silence our murmurings, quiet our fears, and dispel our doubts, that, rising above our afflictions and our anxieties, we may rest on Thee, the Rock of everlasting strength. *Amen.*

¶ *For Resignation.*

O LORD, Thou Fountain of goodness, whose tender mercies are over all thy works, and who hast compassion on them that fear Thee, even as a father pitieth his children: amid the many changes and sorrows of this earthly life, grant us a patient resignation to thy will, and contentment under all the rulings of thy Providence. *Amen.*

¶ *For Peace.*

O LORD, from whom alone all holy desires, all just counsels, and all good works do proceed : Give unto thy servants that peace which the world can not give ; that our hearts may be inclined to obey thy commandments, and that we, being defended from the fear of our enemies, may pass our time in rest and quietness, through thy merciful deliverance and protection. *Amen.*

¶ *For Thanksgiving Day.*

O LORD, Giver of all good and Fountain of mercies, in whom are all the springs of our life : All glory, thanks, and praise be unto Thee for thine eternal and overflowing goodness ; for thy faithfulness, which is from one generation to another ; for thy mercies, which are new every morning and more than we can number ; for seed-time and harvest ; for summer and winter ; for childhood and age ; for health and reason ; for food, clothing, and shelter ; for thy fatherly care over us in sickness and in health, in joy and in sorrow, in life and in death ; for friends, and kindred, and kind benefactors ; for home and country ; for thy Church and for thy Holy Word ; yea, Lord, for that there is nothing for which we may not bless and give thanks unto Thee : and therefore do we lift up our hands in the sanctuary, and call upon thy Name, and pay our vows in the presence of all thy people, confessing that Thou art good to all and that thy tender mercies are over all thy works. *Amen.*

¶ *For Christmas.*

O LORD JESUS CHRIST, our Redeemer and Saviour, who in thine infinite mercy wast pleased to take upon Thee our fallen nature, and to be born into the world : Grant, we beseech Thee, so to be born spiritually in each one of us, that heavenly peace and good will may descend into our hearts, and reign therein forever. *Amen.*

¶ *For Easter.*

O LORD our Redeemer, who didst bow the heavens and come down for our salvation, and who hast overcome death and opened unto us the gates of everlasting life ; mercifully grant that a resurrection from all spiritual death may be wrought in us, whereby we may be raised up into communion with Thee, and dwell evermore in thy presence, who livest and reignest, the only GOD of heaven and earth, forever. *Amen.*

¶ *For Ascension.*

GRANT, we beseech Thee, O LORD, that as we believe Thee in thy glorified Humanity to have ascended into the heavens, so may we in heart and mind thither ascend, and with Thee continually dwell, who livest and reignest, the only GOD of heaven and earth, forever. *Amen.*

¶ *For the Holy Spirit.*

O LORD JESUS CHRIST, who, through the glorification of thy Humanity, didst send down thy Holy Spirit to be the light of our life and the inspiration of our hearts; grant that we may so receive this precious gift, that we may bring forth fruit and that our fruit may remain. In our trials and temptations, leave us not comfortless, but make thy presence so known and felt, that thy joy may be in us and that our joy may be full. *Amen.*

¶ *In Preparation for the Holy Supper.*

HAVE mercy upon us, O GOD, according to thy loving-kindness; according to the multitude of thy tender mercies, blot out our transgressions. For we acknowledge our transgressions, and our sins are ever before us. We confess that we have sinned against Thee, in thought, word, and deed, and are not worthy to be called thy children. But Thou, O LORD, art good, and ready to forgive, and plenteous in mercy to all them that call upon Thee. To the broken in heart Thou hast promised to be near, and to save such as be of a contrite spirit. Grant us a spirit of sincere contrition, that, searching our hearts by the light of thy truth, we may be enabled to see and acknowledge our evils, and to shun them as sins against Thee. And may we be thus delivered, O LORD, from all idolatry of self and the world, from all pride and self-will, from all prejudice, blindness, and hardness of heart, from covetousness and ambition, from all feelings of animosity and resentment, and contempt for those whom we dislike. And give us that sense of our own weakness, which compels us to seek help from Thee, that we may be thus led to look for strength and support to those means which Thou hast provided. And by such sincere repentance and humility, may we be prepared, O LORD, for thy Holy Supper, that our hearts may be opened to receive of thy Divine Body and Blood, and that we may be brought thereby not only into thy presence, but into that conjunction with Thee which is eternal life. *Amen.*

¶ *Prayers for the Close of Worship.*

GRANT, we beseech Thee, O LORD our GOD, that the words which we have heard this day may, through thy grace, be so engrafted in our hearts, that they may bring forth in us the fruits of righteousness, to the salvation of our souls, the edification of thy church, and the honor and glory of thy holy name. *Amen.*

O LORD, our Heavenly Father, impress upon our minds the truths of thy Word: open our eyes to behold the wonders of thy law: shed abroad thy love in our hearts, and enable us to do thy will. Continue unto us thy favor, which is life, and thy lovingkindness, which is better than life. Guide us by thy counsel, and receive us at last into thy presence. *Amen.*

DIRECT us, O LORD, in all our doings with thy most gracious favor, and further us with thy continual help; that in all our works begun, continued, and ended in Thee, we may glorify thy holy name, and finally, by thy mercy, obtain everlasting life. *Amen.*

ALMIGHTY FATHER, the Fountain of all wisdom, who knowest our necessities before we ask, and our ignorance in asking: We beseech Thee to have compassion upon our infirmities; and those things which, for our unworthiness, we dare not, and for our blindness, we can not ask, vouchsafe, O LORD, to give us, for thine own mercy's sake. *Amen.*

O LORD our GOD, who hast given us grace with one accord to make our common supplications unto Thee, and hast promised that where two or three are gathered together in thy Name, Thou wilt be in the midst of them to grant their requests: Fulfill now, O LORD, the petitions of thy servants, as may be most profitable for them, granting us in this world knowledge of thy truth, and in the world to come life everlasting. *Amen.*

LESSONS FROM THE PSALMS.

FOR RESPONSIVE READING.

LESSON I.

PSALM XXV.

UNTO Thee, O Lord, do I lift up my soul.
O my God, I trust in Thee:
Let me not be ashamed;
Let not mine enemies triumph over me.
Yea, let none that wait on Thee be ashamed:
Let them be ashamed who transgress without cause.
Show me thy ways, O Lord;
Teach Thou me thy paths.
Lead me in thy truth, and teach me:
For Thou art the God of my salvation; on Thee do I wait all the day.
Remember, O Lord, thy tender mercies and thy loving-kindnesses;
For they are from everlasting.
Remember not the sins of my youth, nor my transgressions:
According to thy mercy remember Thou me, for thy goodness' sake, O Lord.
Good and upright is the Lord:
Therefore will He teach sinners in the way.
The meek will He guide in judgment:
And the meek will He teach his way.
All the paths of the Lord are mercy and truth to those that keep his covenant and his testimonies.
For thy name's sake, O Lord, pardon mine iniquity; for it is great.
What man is he that feareth the Lord?
Him shall He teach in the way that he shall choose.

His soul shall dwell in good ;
And his seed shall inherit the earth.
The secret of the LORD is with them that fear Him ;
And his covenant, to give them knowledge.
Mine eyes are ever toward the LORD ;
For He shall pluck my feet out of the net.
Turn Thee unto me, and have mercy upon me ;
For I am desolate and afflicted.
The troubles of my heart are enlarged :
O bring Thou me out of my distresses.
Look upon mine affliction and my pain ;
And forgive all my sins.
Consider mine enemies ; for they are many ;
And they hate me with cruel hatred.
O keep my soul, and deliver me :
Let me not be ashamed, for I put my trust in Thee.
Let integrity and uprightness preserve me, for I wait on Thee.
Redeem Israel, O God, out of all his troubles.

PSALM XXIII.

THE LORD is my Shepherd ;
I shall not want.
He maketh me to lie down in green pastures :
He leadeth me beside the still waters.
He restoreth my soul :
He leadeth me in the paths of righteousness for his name's sake.
Yea, though I walk through the valley of the shadow of death, I will fear no evil :
For Thou art with me ; thy rod and thy staff they comfort me.
Thou preparest a table before me in the presence of mine enemies :
Thou anointest my head with oil ; my cup runneth over.
Surely goodness and mercy shall follow me all the days of my life ;
And I shall dwell in the house of the Lord for ever.

LESSON II.

PSALM XXXI.

IN Thee, O LORD, do I put my trust ; let me never be ashamed :
Deliver me in thy righteousness.
Bow down thine ear to me ; deliver me speedily :
Be Thou to me a rock of strength, for an house of defence to save me.

For Thou art my rock and my fortress :
Therefore for thy name's sake lead me, and guide me.
Pull me out of the net that they have privily laid for me :
For Thou art my strength.
Into thine hand I commit my spirit :
Thou hast redeemed me, O Lord God of truth.
I have hated them that regard lying vanities :
But I have trusted in the Lord.
I will be glad and rejoice in thy mercy :
For Thou hast considered my trouble; Thou hast known my soul in adversities:
And hast not shut me up into the hand of the enemy :
Thou hast set my feet in a large place.
Have mercy upon me, O LORD, for I am in trouble :
Mine eye is consumed with grief, yea, my soul and my belly.
For my life is spent with grief, and my years with sighing :
My strength faileth because of mine iniquity, and my bones are consumed.
I was a reproach among all mine enemies, but especially among my neighbors, and a fear to mine acquaintance :
They that did see me without fled from me.
I am forgotten as a dead man out of mind :
I am like a broken vessel.
For I have heard the slander of many : fear was on every side :
While they took counsel together against me, they devised to take away my life.
But I trusted in Thee, O LORD :
I said, Thou art my God.
My times are in thy hand :
Deliver me from the hand of mine enemies, and from them that persecute me.
Make thy face to shine upon thy servant :
Save me for thy mercies' sake.

PSALM XXVIII.

UNTO Thee will I cry, O LORD, my rock ; be not silent unto me :
Lest, if Thou be silent to me, I become like them that go down into the pit.
Hear the voice of my supplications, when I cry unto Thee ;
When I lift up my hands toward thy holy oracle.
Draw me not away with the wicked, and with the workers of iniquity,
Which speak peace to their neighbors, but mischief is in their hearts.

Give them according to their deeds, and according to the wickedness of their endeavors :
Give them according to the work of their hands; render to them their desert.
Blessed be the LORD, because He hath heard the voice of my supplications.
The Lord is my strength and my shield;
My heart trusted in Him, and I am helped :
Therefore my heart greatly rejoiceth, and with my song I will praise Him.
The LORD is their strength :
And He is the saving strength of his anointed.
Save thy people, and bless thine inheritance :
Feed them also, and lift them up for ever.

LESSON III.

PSALM XXI.

THE king shall joy in thy strength, O LORD,
And in thy salvation how greatly shall he rejoice!
Thou hast given him his heart's desire ;
And hast not withholden the request of his lips.
For Thou meetest him with the blessings of goodness ;
Thou settest a crown of pure gold on his head.
He asked life of Thee, and Thou gavest it him ;
Length of days for ever and ever.
His glory is great in thy salvation ;
Honor and majesty hast Thou laid upon him.
For Thou hast made him most blessed for ever :
Thou hast made him glad with the joy of thy countenance.
For the king trusted in the LORD ;
And through the mercy of the most High he shall not be moved.
Be Thou exalted, O LORD, in thine own strength :
So will we sing and praise thy power.

PSALM XXXIV.

I WILL bless the LORD at all times :
His praise shall continually be in my mouth.
My soul shall make her boast in the LORD :
The humble shall hear, and be glad.
O magnify the LORD with me ;
And let us exalt his name together.

I sought the LORD and He heard me ;
And delivered me from all my fears.
They looked unto Him, and were lightened :
And their faces were not ashamed.
O. taste and see that the LORD is good ;
Blessed is the man that trusteth in Him.
O fear the LORD, ye his saints :
For there is no want to them that fear Him.
Keep thy tongue from evil, and thy lips from speaking guile.
Depart from evil, and do good ; seek peace, and pursue it.
The eyes of the LORD are upon the righteous ;
And his ears are open unto their cry.
The face of the LORD is against them that do evil :
To cut off the remembrance of them from the earth.
The righteous cry, and the LORD heareth ;
And delivereth them out of all their troubles.
The LORD is nigh unto the broken in heart ;
And saveth such as be of a contrite spirit.
Many are the afflictions of the righteous :
But the Lord doth deliver him from them all.
He keepeth all his bones :
Not one of them is broken.
Evil shall slay the wicked :
And they that hate the righteous shall be condemned.
The LORD redeemeth the soul of his servants :
And none of them that trust in Him shall be condemned.

LESSON IV.

PSALM XXXVII.

FRET not thyself because of evildoers ;
Neither be thou envious against the workers of iniquity.
For they shall soon be cut down like the grass ;
And shall wither as the green herb.
Trust in the LORD, and do good ;
So shalt thou dwell in the land, and verily thou shalt be fed.
Delight thyself also in the LORD ;
And He shall give thee the desires of thine heart.
Commit thy way unto the LORD :
Trust also in Him ; and He shall bring it to pass.
And He shall bring forth thy righteousness as the light ;
And thy judgment as the noonday.

Rest in the Lord, and wait patiently for Him :
Fret not thyself because of him who prospereth in his way, because of the man who bringeth wicked devices to pass.
Cease from anger, and forsake wrath :
Fret not thyself in any wise to do evil.
For evildoers shall be cut off :
But those that wait upon the Lord, they shall inherit the earth.
For yet a little while, and the wicked shall not be :
Yea, thou shalt diligently consider his place, and it shall not be.
But the meek shall inherit the earth :
And shall delight themselves in the abundance of peace.
The LORD knoweth the days of the upright ;
And their inheritance shall be for ever.
They shall not be ashamed in the evil time :
And in the days of famine they shall be satisfied.
But the wicked shall perish, and the enemies of the LORD shall be as the fat of lambs :
They shall consume ; into smoke shall they consume away
The wicked borroweth, and payeth not again :
But the righteous showeth mercy, and giveth.
For such as be blessed of Him shall inherit the earth ;
And they that be cursed of Him shall be cut off.
The steps of a good man are ordered by the LORD :
And He delighteth in his way.
Though he fall, he shall not be utterly cast down :
For the Lord upholdeth him with his hand.
I have been young, and now am old ;
Yet have I not seen the righteous forsaken, nor his seed begging bread.
He is gracious all the day, and lendeth ;
And his seed is blessed.
Depart from evil, and do good ;
And dwell for evermore.
For the LORD loveth judgment, and forsaketh not his saints ;
They are preserved for ever ;
But the seed of the wicked shall be cut off :
The righteous shall inherit the land and dwell therein for ever.
The mouth of the righteous speaketh wisdom ;
And his tongue doth talk of judgment.
The law of his GOD is in his heart ;
None of his steps shall slide.
The wicked watcheth the righteous ;
And seeketh to slay him.

The LORD will not leave him in his hand;
Nor condemn him when he is judged.
Wait on the LORD, and keep his way, and He shall exalt thee to inherit the land:
When the wicked are cut off, thou shalt see it.
I have seen the wicked in great power;
And spreading himself like a green bay tree.
Yet he passed away, and, lo, he was not:
Yea, I sought him, but he could not be found.
Mark the perfect man, and behold the upright:
For the end of that man is peace.
But the transgressors shall be destroyed together:
The end of the wicked shall be cut off.
But the salvation of the righteous is of the LORD:
He is their strength in the time of trouble.
And the LORD shall help them, and deliver them:
He shall deliver them from the wicked, and save them, because they trust in Him.

LESSON V.

PSALM XLII.

AS the hart panteth for the brooks of water;
So panteth my soul for Thee, O God.
My soul thirsteth for GOD, for the living GOD:
When shall I come and appear before God?
My tears have been my meat day and night;
While they continually say unto me, Where is thy God?
Why art thou cast down, O my soul? and why art thou disquieted in me?
Hope thou in God; for I shall yet praise Him for the help of his countenance.
O my GOD, my soul is cast down within me:
Therefore will I remember Thee from the land of Jordan, and of Hermon, from the hill Mizar.
Deep calleth unto deep at the noise of thy waterspouts:
All thy waves and thy billows are gone over me.
Yet the LORD will command his loving kindness in the daytime;
And in the night his song shall be with me, and my prayer unto the God of my life.
I will say unto GOD my Rock, Why hast Thou forgotten me?
Why go I mourning because of the oppression of the enemy?

As with a sword in my bones, mine enemies reproach me ;
While they say daily unto me, Where is thy God?
Why art thou cast down, O my soul? and why art thou disquieted within me?
Hope thou in God; for I shall yet praise Him, who is the health of my countenance, and my God.

PSALM LXII.

TRULY my soul waiteth upon God :
From Him cometh my salvation.
He only is my rock and my salvation ;
He is my defence, I shall not be greatly moved.
How long will ye assault a man?
How long will ye all shatter him like a bowing wall or a tottering fence?
They only consult to cast him down from his eminence ; they delight in lies :
They bless with their mouth, but they curse inwardly.
My soul, wait thou only upon God :
For my expectation is from Him.
He only is my rock and my salvation :
He is my defence; I shall not be moved.
In GOD is my salvation and my glory :
The rock of my strength, and my refuge, is in God.
Trust in Him at all times, ye people ; pour out your heart before Him :
God is a refuge for us.
Surely men of low degree are vanity, and men of high degree are a lie :
To be laid in the balance, they are altogether lighter than vanity.
Trust not in oppression, and become not vain in robbery :
If riches increase, set not your heart upon them.
God hath spoken once, twice have I heard it ;
That power belongeth unto God.
Also unto Thee, O LORD, belongeth mercy :
For Thou renderest to every man according to his work.
Help us, O GOD of our salvation, for the glory of thy name :
And deliver us, and purge away our sins, for thy name's sake.

LESSON VI.

PSALM XLIII.

JUDGE me, O GOD, and plead my cause against an ungodly nation:
O deliver me from the man of deceit and iniquity.
For Thou art the GOD of my strength: why dost Thou cast me off?
Why go I mourning because of the oppression of the enemy?
O send out thy light and thy truth; let them lead me:
Let them bring me unto thy holy hill, and to thy tabernacles.
Then will I go unto the altar of GOD, unto GOD the gladness of my joy:
And I will praise Thee upon the harp, O God my God.
Why art thou bowed down, O my soul? and why art thou disquieted within me?
Hope in God; for I shall yet praise Him, who is the health of my countenance, and my God.

PSALM LI.

HAVE mercy upon me, O GOD, according to thy loving-kindness:
According to the multitude of thy mercies blot out my transgressions.
Wash me thoroughly from mine iniquity;
And cleanse me from my sin.
For I acknowledge my transgressions:
And my sin is ever before me.
Against Thee, Thee only, have I sinned, and done evil in thy sight:
That Thou mightest be justified when Thou speakest, and be clear when Thou judgest.
Purge me with hyssop, and I shall be clean:
Wash me, and I shall be whiter than snow.
Make me to hear joy and gladness:
That the bones which Thou hast broken may rejoice.
Hide thy face from my sins;
And blot out all mine iniquities.
Create in me a clean heart, O GOD;
And renew a right spirit within me.
Cast me not away from thy presence;
And take not thy Holy Spirit from me.
Restore unto me the joy of thy salvation;
And uphold me with thy free Spirit.

I will teach transgressors thy way ;
And sinners shall be converted unto Thee.
Deliver me from blood, O GOD, Thou GOD of my salvation :
And my tongue shall sing aloud of thy righteousness.
O LORD, open Thou my lips ;
And my mouth shall show forth thy praise.
For Thou desirest not sacrifice ; else would I give :
Thou delightest not in burnt offering.
The sacrifices of GOD are a broken spirit :
A broken and a contrite heart, O God, Thou wilt not despise.
Do good in thy good pleasure unto Zion :
Build Thou the walls of Jerusalem.

PSALM XLVI.

GOD is our refuge and strength ;
A very present help in trouble.
Therefore will not we fear, though the earth be removed ;
And though the mountains be cast into the midst of the seas.
Though the waters thereof roar and be troubled ;
Though the mountains shake with the swelling thereof.
There is a river, whose streams shall make glad the city of GOD ;
The holy place of the tabernacles of the Most High.
GOD is the midst of her, she shall not be moved :
God will help her at the dawn of the morning.
The heathen raged: the kingdoms were moved :
He uttered his voice, the earth did melt.
The LORD of Hosts is with us ;
The God of Jacob is our refuge.
Come, behold the works of the LORD, what desolations He hath made in the earth.
He maketh wars to cease unto the end of the earth.
He breaketh the bow, and cutteth the spear in sunder ;
He burneth the chariots in the fire.
Be still, and know that I am GOD :
I will be exalted among the heathen, I will be exalted in the earth.
The LORD of Hosts is with us ;
The God of Jacob is our refuge.

LESSON VII.

PSALM LIV.

SAVE me, O GOD, by thy name ;
And judge me by thy strength.

Hear my prayer, O GOD;
Give ear to the words of my mouth.

For strangers are risen up against me, and oppressors seek after my soul:
They have not set God before them.

Behold, GOD is mine helper:
The Lord is with them that uphold my soul.

He shall reward evil unto mine enemies:
Cut them off in thy truth.

I will freely sacrifice unto Thee:
I will praise thy name, O Lord; for it is good.

For He hath delivered me out of all trouble:
And mine eye hath looked upon mine enemies.

PSALM LXI.

HEAR my cry, O GOD;
Attend unto my prayer.

From the end of the earth will I cry unto Thee:
When mine heart is overwhelmed, lead me to the Rock that is higher than I.

For Thou hast been a shelter for me;
A strong tower from the enemy.

I will abide in thy tabernacle for ever:
I will trust in the covert of thy wings.

For Thou, O GOD, hast heard my vows:
Thou hast given me the heritage of those that fear thy name.

Thou wilt add days to the days of the king:
His years as generation and generation.

He shall abide before GOD for ever:
O prepare mercy and truth, let them preserve him.

So will I sing praise unto thy name for ever;
That I may daily perform my vows.

PSALM LV.

GIVE ear to my prayer, O GOD;
And hide not Thyself from my supplication.

Attend unto me, and hear me:
I mourn in my complaint, and make a noise:

Because of the voice of the enemy, because of the oppression of the wicked:
For they cast iniquity upon me, and in anger do they hate me.

My heart is sore pained within me:
And the terrors of death are fallen upon me.

Fearfulness and trembling are come upon me;
And horror hath overwhelmed me.
And I said, Oh that I had wings like a dove!
For then would I fly away, and be at rest.
Lo, then would I wander far off, and remain in the wilderness.
I would hasten my escape from the windy storm and tempest.
As for me, I will call upon God;
And the Lord shall save me.
Evening, and morning, and at noon, will I pray, and cry aloud:
And He will hear my voice.
He will deliver my soul in peace from the battle that was against me:
For there are many with me.
God shall hear, and afflict them, even He that abideth of old.
Because they have no changes, therefore they fear not God.
He hath put forth his hands against such as be at peace with him;
He hath broken his covenant.
The words of his mouth were smoother than butter, but war was in his heart:
His words were softer than oil, yet were they drawn swords.
Cast thy burden upon the Lord, and He will sustain thee:
He will never suffer the righteous to be moved.

LESSON VIII.

PSALM LXX.

MAKE haste, O God, to deliver me:
Make haste to help me, O Lord.
Let them be ashamed and confounded that seek after my soul:
Let them be turned backward, and put to confusion, that desire my hurt.
Let all those that seek Thee rejoice and be glad in Thee:
And let such as love thy salvation say continually, Let God be magnified.
But I am poor and needy: make haste unto me, O God:
Thou art my help and my deliverer, O Lord, make no delay.

PSALM LXXI.

IN Thee, O Lord, do I put my trust:
Let me never be put to confusion.
Deliver me in thy righteousness, and cause me to escape:
Incline thine ear unto me, and save me.

Be Thou my strong habitation, whereunto I may continually resort:
Thou hast given commandment to save me, for Thou art my rock and my fortress.
Deliver me, O my God, out of the hand of the wicked;
Out of the hand of the unrighteous and cruel man.
For Thou art my hope, O Lord God:
Thou hast been my trust from my youth.
I am as a wonder unto many;
But Thou art my strong refuge.
Let my mouth be filled with thy praise;
And with thy honor all the day.
Cast me not off in the time of old age:
Forsake me not when my strength faileth.
For mine enemies speak against me:
And they that lay wait for my soul take counsel together:
They say, God hath forsaken him:
Persecute and take him, for there is none to deliver.
O God, be not far from me:
O my God, make haste for my help.
Let them be confounded and consumed that are adversaries to my soul:
Let them be covered with reproach and dishonor that seek my hurt.
But I will hope continually;
And will yet praise Thee more and more.
My mouth shall show forth thy righteousness and thy salvation all the day;
For I know not the numbers thereof.
I will go in the strength of the Lord God:
I will make mention of thy righteousness, of thine only.
O God, Thou hast taught me from my youth:
And hitherto have I declared thy wondrous works.
Now also when I am old and greyheaded, O God, forsake me not;
Until I have showed thy strength unto a generation, and thy power to every one that is to come.
Thy righteousness, also, O God, is very high, who hast done great things:
O God, who is like unto Thee!
Thou, who hast showed me great and sore troubles, shalt quicken me again;
And shalt bring me up again from the depths of the earth.
Thou shalt increase my greatness;
And comfort me on every side.

I will also praise Thee with the psaltery, even thy truth, O my
    God:
Unto Thee will I sing with the harp, O Thou Holy One of Israel.
My lips shall greatly rejoice when I sing unto Thee;
And my soul, which Thou hast redeemed.
My tongue also shall talk of thy righteousness all the day long:
*For they are confounded, for they are brought unto shame, that
    seek my hurt.*

LESSON IX.

PSALM LXXII.

GIVE the king thy judgments, O God;
And thy righteousness unto the king's son.
He shall judge thy people with righteousness;
And thy poor with judgment.
The mountains shall bring peace to the people;
And the little hills, by righteousness.
He shall judge the poor of the people;
He shall save the children of the needy, and shall crush the oppressor.
They shall fear Thee as long as the sun and moon endure;
Throughout all generations.
He shall come down like rain upon the mown grass:
As showers that water the earth.
In his days shall the righteous flourish;
And abundance of peace till the moon be no more.
He shall have dominion also from sea to sea;
And from the river unto the ends of the earth.
They that dwell in the wilderness shall bow before Him:
And his enemies shall lick the dust.
The kings of Tarshish and of the isles shall bring presents:
The kings of Sheba and Seba shall offer gifts.
Yea, all kings shall bow down to him:
All nations shall serve him.
For he shall deliver the needy when he crieth;
The poor also, and him that hath no helper.
He shall spare the poor and needy;
And shall save the souls of the needy.
He shall redeem their soul from deceit and violence:
And precious shall their blood be in his sight.
And he shall live, and to him shall be given of the gold of Sheba:
*Prayer also shall be made for him continually; and daily shall
    he be praised.*

PSALM LXXXVIII.

O LORD God of my salvation, I have cried day and night before Thee :
Let my prayer come before Thee, incline thine ear unto my cry :
For my soul is full of troubles :
And my life draweth nigh unto the grave.
I am counted with them that go down into the pit :
I am as a man that hath no strength :
I am neglected among the dead, like the slain that lie in the grave, whom Thou rememberest no more :
And they are cut off from thy hand.
Thou hast laid me in the lowest pit :
In darkness, in the deeps.
Thy wrath lieth hard upon me ;
And Thou hast afflicted me with all thy waves.
Thou hast put away mine acquaintance far from me ; Thou hast made me an abomination unto them :
I am shut up, and I cannot come forth.
Mine eye mourneth by reason of affliction :
I have called daily upon Thee, O Lord, I have stretched out my hands unto Thee.
Wilt Thou show wonders to the dead ?
Shall the dead arise and praise Thee ?
Shall thy loving-kindness be declared in the grave ?
Or thy faithfulness in destruction ?
Shall thy wonders be known in the dark ?
And thy righteousness in the land of forgetfulness ?
But unto Thee have I cried, O LORD ;
And in the morning shall my prayer come before Thee.

LESSON X.

PSALM LXXXV.

THOU hast been favorable, O LORD, to thy land :
Thou hast brought back the captivity of Jacob.
Thou hast forgiven the iniquity of thy people :
Thou hast covered all their sin.
Thou hast taken away all thy wrath :
Thou hast turned away from the burning of thine anger.
Restore us, O GOD of our salvation ;
And turn away thine anger from us.

Wilt Thou be angry with us for ever?
Wilt Thou prolong thine anger to all generations?
Wilt Thou not revive us again :
That thy people may rejoice in Thee?
Make us to see thy mercy, O LORD ;
And grant us thy salvation.
I will hear what GOD the LORD will speak ; for He will speak peace unto his people, and to his saints :
But let them not turn again to folly.
Surely his salvation is near them that fear Him ;
That glory may dwell in our land.
Mercy and truth are met together ;
Righteousness and peace have kissed each other.
Truth shall spring out of the earth ;
And righteousness shall look down from the heavens.
Yea, the LORD shall give good ;
And our land shall yield her increase.
Righteousness shall go before Him ;
And shall set us in the way of his steps.

PSALM LXXX.

GIVE ear, O Shepherd of Israel, Thou that leadest Joseph like a flock :
Thou that dwellest between the cherubim, shine forth.
Before Ephraim and Benjamin and Manasseh stir up thy strength;
And come and save us.
Turn us again, O GOD, and cause thy face to shine ; and we shall be saved.
O Lord God of hosts, how long wilt Thou be angry against the prayer of thy people.
Thou feedest them with the bread of tears ;
And givest them tears to drink in great measure.
Thou makest us a strife unto our neighbors :
And our enemies laugh among themselves.
Turn us again, O GOD of hosts ;
And cause thy face to shine, and we shall be saved.
Thou hast brought a vine out of Egypt :
Thou hast cast out the nations and planted it.
Thou preparedst room before it ;
And didst cause it to take deep root, and it filled the land.
The hills were covered with the shadow of it ;
And the boughs thereof were like the cedars of God.
She sent out her boughs unto the sea ;
And her branches unto the river.

Why hast Thou then broken down her hedges ;
So that all they which pass by the way do pluck her?
The boar out of the wood doth waste it ;
And the wild beast of the field doth devour it.
Return, we beseech Thee, O GOD of hosts :
Look down from heaven, and behold, and visit this vine :
And the vineyard which thy right hand hath planted ;
And the branch that Thou madest strong for thyself.
It is burned with fire, it is cut down :
They perish at the rebuke of thy countenance.
Let thy hand be upon the man of thy right hand ;
Upon the son of man whom Thou madest strong for thyself.
So will not we go back from Thee :
Quicken us, and we will call upon thy name.
Turn us again, O LORD GOD of hosts ;
Cause thy face to shine, and we shall be saved.

LESSON XI.

PSALM CVII.

O GIVE thanks unto the LORD, for He is good :
For his mercy is for ever.
Thus shall the redeemed of the LORD say ;
Whom He hath redeemed from the hand of the enemy :
And hath gathered them out of the lands, from the east, and from the west ;
From the north, and from the south.
They wandered in the wilderness in a desolate way ;
They found no city of habitation.
They were hungry and thirsty ;
Their soul did faint within them.
Then they cried unto the LORD in their trouble ;
He delivered them out of their distresses.
And He led them forth by a straight way ;
To go to a city of habitation.
Let them confess to the LORD his mercy.
And his wonderful works to the children of men!
For He satisfieth the longing soul ;
And filleth the hungry soul with good.
Such as sit in darkness and in the shadow of death ;
Being bound in affliction and iron :
Because they rebelled against the words of GOD ;
And contemned the counsel of the Most High :

Therefore He brought down their heart with labor:
They fell down, and there was none to help.
Then they cried unto the LORD in their trouble;
He saved them out of their distresses.
He brought them out of darkness and the shadow of death;
And brake their bands in sunder.
Let them confess to the LORD his mercy:
And his wonderful works to the children of men!
For He hath broken the gates of brass
And cut the bars of iron in sunder.
Fools because of their transgression, and because of their iniquities, are afflicted.
Their soul abhorreth all manner of meat, and they draw near unto the gates of death.
Then they cry unto the LORD in their trouble;
He saveth them out of their distresses.
He sent his word, and healed them;
And delivered them from their destructions.
Let them confess to the LORD his mercy;
And his wonderful works to the children of men!
And let them sacrifice the sacrifices of thanksgiving;
And declare his works with rejoicing.
They that go down to the sea in ships;
That do business in great waters.
These see the works of the LORD;
And his wonders in the deep.
For He commandeth, and raiseth the stormy wind;
Which lifteth up the waves thereof.
They mount up to heaven, they go down again to the depths:
Their soul is melted because of trouble.
They reel and stagger like a drunken man;
And all their wisdom is brought to naught.
Then they cry unto the LORD in their trouble;
And He bringeth them out of their distresses.
He maketh the storm a calm;
And the waves thereof are still.
Then are they glad because they are quiet;
And He bringeth them unto the haven of their desire.
Let them confess to the LORD his mercy;
And his wonderful works to the children of men!
Let them exalt Him in the congregation of the people;
And praise Him in the assembly of the elders.
He turneth rivers into a wilderness;
Springs of water into dry ground:

A fruitful land into barrenness ;
For the wickedness of them that dwell therein.
He turneth the wilderness into a pool of waters ;
And dry land into water-springs.
And there He maketh the hungry to dwell ;
That they may prepare a city for habitation :
And sow the fields, and plant vineyards ;
Which may yield fruits of increase.
He blesseth them also, and they are multiplied greatly ;
And He suffereth not their cattle to decrease.
Again, they are minished and brought low ;
Through oppression, affliction, and sorrow.
He poureth contempt upon princes ;
And causeth them to wander in a pathless waste.
Yet setteth He the poor on high from affliction ;
And maketh him families like a flock.
The righteous shall see, and rejoice :
And all iniquity shall stop her mouth.
Whoso is wise, and will observe these things ;
Even they shall understand the loving-kindness of the Lord.

LESSON XII.

PSALM CXIX.

THOU art my portion, O Lord :
I have said that I would keep thy words.
I entreated thy favor with all the heart :
Be merciful unto me according to thy word.
I thought upon my ways, and turned my feet to thy testimonies.
I made haste, and delayed not to keep thy commandments.
The bands of the wicked have robbed me :
But I have not forgotten thy law.
At midnight I will rise to give thanks unto Thee ;
Because of the judgments of thy justice.
I am a companion of all them that fear Thee ;
And of them that keep thy precepts.
The earth, O Lord, is full of thy mercy :
Teach Thou me thy statutes.
Thy hands have made me and fashioned me :
Make me to understand, that I may learn thy commandments.

They that fear Thee will be glad when they see me;
Because I have hoped in thy word.
I know, O LORD, that thy judgments are justice;
And that Thou in faithfulness hast afflicted me.
Let, I pray Thee, thy merciful kindness be for my comfort;
According to thy word to thy servant.
Let thy tender mercies come unto me, that I may live;
For thy law is my delight.
Let the proud be ashamed; for they dealt perversely with me without a cause:
I will meditate in thy precepts.
Let those that fear Thee turn unto me;
And those that know thy testimonies.
Let my heart be sound in thy statutes;
That I may not be ashamed.
My soul fainteth for thy salvation:
But I hope in thy word.
Mine eyes fail for thy word;
Saying, When wilt Thou comfort me?
For I am become like a bottle in the smoke;
Yet do I not forget thy statutes.
How many are the days of thy servant?
When wilt Thou execute judgment on them that persecute me?
The proud have digged pits for me;
Which are not according to thy law.
All thy commandments are faithfulness:
They persecute me with falsehood; help Thou me.
They had almost consumed me upon earth;
But I did not forsake thy precepts.
Quicken me according to thy loving-kindness;
And I will keep the testimony of thy mouth.
O how I love thy law!
It is my meditation all the day.
Thou hast made me wiser than mine enemies, through thy commandments:
For they are ever with me.
I have more understanding than all my teachers:
For thy testimonies are my meditation.
I understand more than the ancients;
Because I keep thy precepts.
I have refrained my feet from every evil way;
That I might keep thy word.
I have not departed from thy judgments:
For Thou hast taught me.

How sweet are thy words to my taste !
Sweeter than honey unto my mouth!
Through thy precepts I get understanding :
Therefore I hate every path of falsehood.

LESSON XIII.

PSALM CXIX.

I CRIED with all the heart ; hear me, O LORD :
I will keep thy statutes.
I cried unto Thee : O save me ;
And I shall keep thy testimonies.
I prevented the dawn and cried :
I hoped in thy word.
Mine eyes prevent the night watches ;
That I might meditate in thy word.
Hear my voice according unto thy loving-kindness :
O Lord, quicken me according to thy judgment.
They draw near that follow mischief :
They are far from thy law.
Thou art near, O LORD, and all thy commandments are truth.
Concerning thy testimonies, I have known of old that Thou hast founded them for ever.
Consider mine affliction, and deliver me :
For I do not forget thy law.
Plead my cause, and deliver me :
Quicken me according to thy word.
Salvation is far from the wicked :
For they seek not thy statutes.
Great are thy tender mercies, O LORD :
Quicken me according to thy judgments.
Many are my persecutors and mine enemies :
Yet do I not decline from thy testimonies.
I beheld the transgressors, and was grieved :
Because they did not keep thy word.
Consider how I love thy precepts :
Quicken me, O Lord, according to thy loving-kindness.
Thy word is true from the beginning :
And every one of thy righteous judgments endureth for ever.
Princes have persecuted me without a cause :
But my heart doth tremble at thy word.
I rejoice at thy word, as one that findeth great spoil.
Falsehood do I hate and abhor ; but thy law do I love.

Seven times a day do I praise Thee ;
Because of the judgments of thy justice.
Great peace have they who love thy law :
And no stumbling block have they.
O Lord, I have hoped for thy salvation ;
And thy commandments have I done.
My soul hath kept thy testimonies ;
And I do love them exceedingly.
I have kept thy precepts and thy testimonies :
For all my ways are before Thee.
Let my cry come near before Thee, O Lord :
Make me to understand according to thy word.
Let my supplication come before Thee :
Deliver me according to thy word.
I have longed for thy salvation, O Lord ;
And thy law is my delight.
I have gone astray, like a lost sheep :
Seek thy servant, for I do not forget thy commandments.

LESSON XIV.

PSALM LXXXIX.

I WILL sing of the mercies of the Lord for ever :
With my mouth will I make known thy faithfulness to all generations.
For I have said, Mercy shall be built up for ever :
Thy faithfulness shalt thou establish in the very heavens.
I have made a covenant with my chosen ;
I have sworn unto David my servant :
Thy seed will I establish for ever ;
And build up thy throne to all generations.
And the heavens shall praise thy wonders, O Lord :
Thy faithfulness also in the congregation of the saints.
For who in heaven can be compared to the Lord?
Who among the sons of the Gods can be likened to the Lord?
God is greatly to be feared in the assembly of the saints ;
And to be reverenced by all them that are about Him.
O Lord God of Hosts, who is like unto Thee, mighty Lord?
Or to thy faithfulness round about Thee?
Thou rulest the raging of the sea :
When the waves thereof arise, Thou stillest them.

Thou hast broken Rahab in pieces, as one that is slain :
Thou hast scattered thine enemies with the arm of thy strength.
The heavens are thine, the earth is also thine :
The world and the fulness thereof, Thou hast founded them.
The north and the south, Thou hast created them :
Tabor and Hermon shall rejoice in thy name.
Thou hast a mighty arm :
Strong is thy hand, high is thy right hand.
Justice and judgment are the foundation of thy throne :
Mercy and truth shall go before thy face.
Blessed is the people that know the joyful sound :
They shall walk, O Lord, in the light of thy countenance.
In thy name shall they rejoice all the day :
And in thy righteousness shall they be exalted.
For Thou art the glory of their strength :
And in thy favor our horn shall be exalted.
For the LORD is our defence ;
And the Holy One of Israel our King.
Then Thou spakest in vision to thy holy one, and saidst, I have laid help upon one that is mighty ;
I have exalted one chosen out of the people.
I have found David my servant ;
With my holy oil have I anointed him:
With whom my hand shall be established ;
Mine arm also shall strengthen him.
The enemy shall not beset him ;
Nor the son of wickedness afflict him.
And I will beat down his foes before his face ;
And I will smite them that hate him.
But my faithfulness and my mercy shall be with him :
And in my name shall his horn be exalted.
I will set his hand also in the sea ;
And his right hand in the rivers.
He shall cry unto me, Thou art my Father ;
My God, and the rock of my salvation.
I will also make him my first-born ;
Higher than the kings of the earth.
My mercy will I keep for him for evermore ;
And my covenant shall stand fast with him.
His seed also will I make to endure for ever ;
And his throne as the days of heaven.
If his children forsake my law, and walk not in my judgments ;
If they break my statutes, and keep not my commandments :

Then will I visit their transgression with the rod ;
And their iniquity with stripes.
Nevertheless my loving-kindness will I not utterly take from him :
Nor suffer my faithfulness to fail.
My covenant will I not break ;
Nor alter the thing that is gone out of my lips.
Once have I sworn by my holiness that I will not lie unto David.
His seed shall endure for ever, and his throne as the sun before me.
It shall be established for ever as the moon ;
And as a faithful witness in heaven.
Blessed be the LORD for evermore :
Amen and Amen.

LESSON XV.

PSALM CXIX.

THY word is a lamp unto my feet ;
And a light unto my path.
I have sworn, and I will perform ;
That I will keep the judgments of thy justice.
I am afflicted very much :
Quicken me, O Lord, according to thy word.
Accept, I beseech Thee, the free-will offerings of my mouth, O LORD ;
And teach Thou me thy judgments.
My soul is continually in my hand :
Yet do I not forget thy law.
The wicked have laid a snare for me :
Yet I have not wandered from thy precepts.
Thy testimonies have I taken as an heritage for ever :
For they are the rejoicing of my heart.
I hate divided thoughts :
But thy law do I love.
Thou art my hiding place and my shield :
I hope in thy word.
Depart from me, ye evildoers :
For I will keep the commandments of my God.
Uphold me according unto thy word, that I may live :
And let me not be ashamed of my hope.
Hold Thou me up, and I shall be safe :
And I will have respect unto thy statutes continually.

Thou hast trodden down all them that err from thy statutes:
For their deceit is falsehood.
Thou puttest away all the wicked of the earth like dross:
Therefore I love thy testimonies.
My flesh trembleth for fear of Thee;
And I am afraid of thy judgments.
I have done judgment and justice:
Leave me not to mine oppressors.
Be surety for thy servant for good:
Let not the proud oppress me.
Mine eyes fail for thy salvation;
And for the word of thy righteousness.
Deal with thy servant according to thy mercy;
And teach Thou me thy statutes.
I am thy servant; give me understanding;
That I may know thy testimonies.
It is time for Thee, O LORD, to work:
For they have made void thy law.
Therefore I love thy commandments more than gold;
And more than fine gold.
Therefore all thy precepts concerning all things do I esteem right;
And every false way do I hate.
Thy testimonies are wonderful:
Therefore doth my soul keep them.
The entrance of thy words giveth light:
It giveth understanding to the simple.
I opened my mouth, and panted:
For I longed for thy commandments.
Look Thou upon me, and be merciful unto me;
As Thou usest to do unto those that love thy name.
Order my steps in thy word:
And let not any iniquity have dominion over me.
Deliver me from the oppression of man:
So will I keep thy precepts.
Make thy face to shine upon thy servant;
And teach Thou me thy statutes.

LESSON XVI.

PSALM CXLIV.

BLESSED be the LORD my strength;
Who teacheth my hands to war, and my fingers to fight:
My goodness, and my fortress; my high tower, and my deliverer:
My shield and He in whom I trust; who subdueth my people under me.
LORD, what is man, that Thou takest knowledge of him!
The son of man, that Thou makest account of him!
Man is like to vanity:
His days are as a shadow that passeth away.
Bow thy heavens, O LORD, and come down:
Touch the mountains, and they shall smoke.
Cast forth lightning, and scatter them:
Shoot out thine arrows, and destroy them.
Send thine hand from above; rid me, and deliver me out of great waters;
From the hand of strange children; whose mouth speaketh vanity, and their right hand is a right hand of falsehood.
I will sing a new song unto Thee, O GOD:
Upon a psaltery and an instrument of ten strings will I sing praises unto Thee.
It is He that giveth salvation unto kings:
Who delivereth David his servant from the hurtful sword.
Rid me, and deliver me from the hand of strange children;
Whose mouth speaketh vanity, and their right hand is a right hand of falsehood:
That our sons may be as plants grown up in their youth;
That our daughters may be as corner stones, polished after the similitude of a palace:
That our garners may be full, affording all manner of store:
That our sheep may bring forth thousands and ten thousands in our streets:
That our oxen may be strong to labor;
That there be no breaking in, nor going out; nor any complaining in our streets.
Happy are the people, who are in such a state:
Happy are the people whose God is the Lord.

PSALM CXLV.

I WILL extol Thee, my GOD, O King;
And I will bless thy name for ever and ever.

Every day will I bless Thee ;
And I will praise thy name for ever and ever.
Great is the LORD, and greatly to be praised ;
And unsearchable is his greatness.
Generation to generation shall praise thy works ;
And shall declare thy mighty acts.
I will speak of the glorious honor of thy majesty ;
And of thy wondrous works.
And men shall speak of the might of thy terrible acts :
And I will declare thy greatness.
The memory of thy great goodness shall they proclaim ;
And shall sing aloud of thy righteousness.
The LORD is gracious, and full of compassion :
Slow to anger, and great in mercy.
The LORD is good to all :
And his mercies are over all his works.
All thy works shall praise Thee, O LORD ;
And thy saints shall bless Thee.
They shall speak of the glory of thy kingdom ;
And talk of thy might ;
To make known to the sons of men his mighty acts ;
And the glorious majesty of his kingdom.
Thy kingdom is an everlasting kingdom ;
And thy dominion throughout all generations.
The LORD upholdeth all that fall ;
And raiseth up all the bowed down.
The eyes of all wait upon Thee ;
And Thou givest them their meat in its season.
Thou dost open thine hand ;
And satisfy the desire of every living thing.
The LORD is righteous in all his ways ;
And kind in all his works.
The LORD is nigh unto all that call upon Him ;
To all that call upon Him in truth.
He will fulfil the desire of them that fear Him :
He also will hear their cry, and will save them.
The LORD preserveth all that love Him :
But all the wicked will He destroy.
My mouth shall speak the praise of the LORD :
And let all flesh bless his holy name for ever and ever.

LESSON XVII.

PSALM XXXIII.

REJOICE in the LORD, O ye righteous:
Praise is comely for the upright.
Praise the LORD with harp:
Sing unto Him with the psaltery of ten strings.
Sing unto Him a new song.
Play skilfully with a loud noise.
For the Word of the LORD is right:
And all his works are done in truth.
He loveth righteousness and judgment:
The earth is full of the goodness of the Lord.
By the Word of the LORD were the heavens made:
And all the host of them by the breath of his mouth.
He gathered the waters of the sea together as an heap:
He layeth up the deep in storehouses.
Let all the earth fear the LORD:
Let all the inhabitants of the world stand in awe of Him.
For He spake, and it was:
He commanded, and it stood fast.
The LORD bringeth the counsel of the heathen to nought:
He maketh the devices of the people of none effect.
The counsel of the LORD standeth for ever;
The thoughts of his heart to all generations.
Blessed is the nation whose God is the LORD:
The people He hath chosen for his own inheritance.
The LORD looketh from the heavens, He beholdeth all the sons of men.
From the place of his habitation He looketh upon all the inhabitants of the earth.
He fashioneth their hearts alike:
He considereth all their works.
There is no king saved by the multitude of an host:
A mighty man is not delivered by much strength.
An horse is a vain thing for safety:
Neither shall he deliver any by his great strength.
Behold, the eye of the LORD is upon them that fear Him;
Upon them that hope in his mercy:
To deliver their soul from death;
And to keep them alive in famine.

Our soul waiteth for the LORD :
He is our help and our shield.
For our heart shall rejoice in Him ;
Because we have trusted in his holy name.

PSALM LXVII.

GOD be merciful unto us, and bless us ;
And cause his face to shine upon us.
That thy way may be known upon earth ;
Thy saving health among all nations.
Let the people praise Thee, O GOD :
Let all the people praise Thee.
O let the nations be glad and sing for joy :
For Thou shalt judge the people righteously, and govern the nations upon earth.
Let the people praise Thee, O GOD ;
Let all the people praise Thee.
The earth shall yield her increase :
God, our own God, shall bless us.
GOD shall bless us :
And all the ends of the earth shall fear Him.

LESSON XVIII.

PSALM XVIII.

I WILL love Thee, O LORD, my strength.
The Lord is my rock, and my fortress, and my deliverer :
My GOD, my strength, in whom I will trust :
My buckler, and the horn of my salvation, and my high tower.
I will call upon the LORD, who is to be praised :
So shall I be saved from mine enemies.
The sorrows of death compassed me ;
And the floods of ungodly men made me afraid.
The sorrows of hell compassed me about :
The snares of death prevented me.
In my distress I called upon the LORD, and cried unto my GOD :
He heard my voice out of his temple, and my cry came before Him, into his ears.
Then the earth shook and trembled :
The foundations also of the hills moved and were shaken, because He was wroth.

There went up a smoke out of his nostrils ;
And fire out of his mouth devoured; coals were kindled by it.
He bowed the heavens also, and came down :
And darkness was under his feet.
And He rode upon a cherub, and did fly :
Yea, He did fly upon the wings of the wind.
He made darkness his secret place ;
His pavilion round about Him was dark waters and thick clouds of the skies.
At the brightness that was before Him his thick clouds passed ;
There were hail stones and coals of fire.
The LORD also thundered in the heavens, and the Most High uttered his voice ;
There were hail stones and coals of fire.
Yea, He sent out his arrows, and scattered them ;
And He shot out lightnings, and discomfited them.
Then the channels of waters were seen, and the foundations of the world were discovered ;
At thy rebuke, O Lord, at the blast of the breath of thy nostrils.
He sent from above, He took me ;
He drew me out of many waters.
He delivered me from my strong enemy ;
And from them which hated me ; for they were stronger than I.
They fell upon me in the day of my calamity :
But the Lord was my stay.
He brought me forth also into a large place;
He delivered me because He delighted in me.
The LORD rewarded me according to my righteousness :
According to the cleanness of my hands hath He recompensed me.
For I have kept the ways of the LORD ;
And have not wickedly departed from my God.
For all his judgments were before me ;
And I did not put away his statutes from me.
I was also upright before Him ;
And I kept myself from mine iniquity.
Therefore hath the LORD recompensed me according to my righteousness ;
According to the cleanness of my hands before his eyes.
With the merciful Thou wilt show thyself merciful :
With an upright man Thou wilt show thyself upright.
With the pure Thou wilt show thyself pure ;
And with the froward Thou wilt show thyself froward.
For Thou wilt save the afflicted people ;
But wilt bring down lofty looks.

Therefore will I give thanks unto Thee, O LORD, among the nations ;
And I will sing praises unto thy name.

LESSON XIX.

PSALM LXIX.

O GOD, Thou knowest my foolishness ;
And my sins are not hid from Thee.
Let not them that wait on Thee, O LORD GOD of Hosts, be ashamed for my sake :
Let not those that seek Thee be confounded for my sake, O God of Israel.
Because for thy sake I have borne reproach :
Shame hath covered my face.
I am become a stranger unto my brethren ;
And an alien unto my mother's children.
For the zeal of thine house hath eaten me up :
And the reproaches of them that reproached Thee are fallen upon me.
I made sackcloth also my garment ;
And I became a by-word to them.
They that sit in the gate speak against me ;
And I am the song of the drunkards.
But as for me, my prayer is unto Thee, O LORD, in an acceptable time :
O God, in the multitude of thy mercy hear me, in the truth of thy salvation.
Deliver me out of the mire, and let me not sink :
Let me be delivered from them that hate me, and out of the deep waters.
Let not the waterflood overflow me, neither let the deep swallow me up ;
And let not the pit shut her mouth upon me.
Hear me, O LORD ; for thy loving-kindness is good :
Turn unto me according to the multitude of thy tender mercies.
And hide not thy face from thy servant :
For I am in trouble ; hear me speedily.
Draw nigh unto my soul, and redeem it :
Deliver me because of mine enemies.
Thou hast known my reproach, and my shame, and my dishonor :
Mine adversaries are all before Thee.

Reproach hath broken my heart, and I am full of heaviness :
And I looked for pity, but there was none, and for comforters,
  but I found none.
They gave me also gall for my meat ;
And in my thirst they gave me vinegar to drink.
Let their table become a snare before them :
And let their good fortune become a trap.
Let their eyes be darkened, that they see not ;
And cause their loins continually to shake.
Pour out thine indignation upon them ;
And let thy wrathful anger take hold of them.
Let their habitation be desolate ;
And let none dwell in their tents.
For they persecute him whom thou hast smitten ;
And they talk of the pain of those whom thou hast wounded.
Add iniquity unto their iniquity :
And let them not come into thy righteousness.
Let them be blotted out of the book of the living ;
And let them not be written with the righteous.
But I am poor and sorrowful :
Let thy salvation, O God, set me up on high.
I will praise the name of GOD with a song ;
And will magnify Him with thanksgiving.
The afflicted shall see this, and be glad :
And your heart shall live that seek God.

LESSON XX.

PSALM XVI.

THE LORD is the portion of mine inheritance and of my cup :
  Thou dost maintain my lot.
The lines are fallen to me in pleasant places :
Yea, I have a goodly heritage.
I will bless the LORD, who hath given me counsel :
My reins also instruct me in the nights.
I have set the LORD always before me :
Because He is at my right hand, I shall not be moved.
Therefore my heart is glad, and my glory rejoiceth :
My flesh shall also rest in hope.
For Thou wilt not leave my soul in hell ;
Neither wilt Thou suffer thine Holy One to see corruption.

Thou wilt show me the path of life :
In thy presence is fulness of joy ; at thy right hand are pleasures for evermore.

PSALM XXX.

I WILL extol Thee, O LORD, for Thou hast lifted me up ;
And hast not made mine enemies to rejoice over me.
O LORD my GOD, I cried unto Thee ;
And Thou hast healed me.
O LORD, Thou hast brought up my soul from the grave :
Thou hast kept me alive, that I should not go down to the pit.
Sing unto the LORD, O ye saints of his ;
And give thanks at the remembrance of his holiness.
For his anger is but for a moment ; in his favor is life :
Weeping may endure for a night, but joy cometh in the morning.
LORD, by thy favor Thou hast made my mountain to stand strong :
Thou didst hide thy face, and I was troubled.
I cried unto Thee, O LORD ;
And unto the Lord I made supplication.
What profit is there in my blood, when I go down to the pit ?
Shall the dust praise Thee ? shall it declare thy truth.
Hear, O LORD, and have mercy upon me :
O Lord, be Thou my helper.
Thou hast turned for me my mourning into dancing :
Thou hast put off my sackcloth, and girded me with gladness :
Therefore shall my glory sing praise to Thee, and not be silent.
O Lord my God, I will give thanks unto Thee for ever.

LESSON XXI.

PSALM LXVI.

MAKE a joyful noise unto GOD, all the earth :
Sing forth the honor of his name ; make his praise glorious.
Say unto GOD, How terrible art Thou in thy works !
Through the greatness of thy power shall thine enemies submit themselves unto Thee.
All the earth shall worship Thee, and sing unto Thee :
They shall sing unto thy name.
Come and see the works of GOD :
He is terrible in his doing toward the children of men.

He turned the sea into dry land; they went through the flood
    on foot:
There did we rejoice in Him.
He ruleth by his power for ever; his eyes behold the nations:
Let not the rebellious exalt themselves.
O bless our GOD, ye people;
And make the voice of his praise to be heard:
Who holdeth our soul in life;
And suffereth not our feet to be moved.
For Thou, O GOD, hast proved us:
Thou hast tried us, as silver is tried.
Thou broughtest us into the net;
Thou laidst affliction upon our loins.
Thou hast caused men to ride over our heads; we went through
    fire and through water:
But Thou broughtest us out into a place of abundance.
I will go into thy house with burnt offerings:
*I will pay Thee my vows, which my lips have uttered, and my
    mouth hath spoken, when I was in trouble.*
I will offer unto Thee burnt sacrifices of fatlings, with the incense of rams:
I will offer bullocks with goats.
Come and hear, all ye that fear GOD;
And I will declare what He hath done for my soul.
I cried unto Him with my mouth;
And He was extolled with my tongue.
If I regard iniquity in my heart, the Lord will not hear me:
*But verily God hath heard me; He hath attended to the voice of
    my prayer.*

SELECTIONS AND CHANTS.

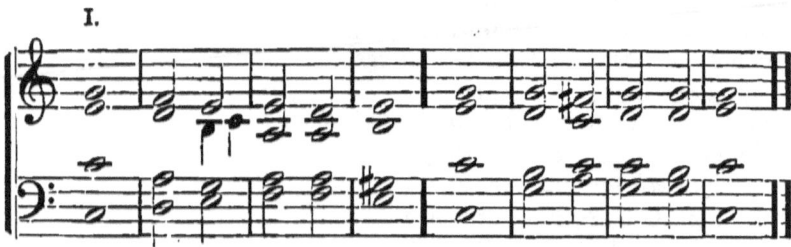

1. GIVE ear to my | words, | O | Lord;
   Con|sider my | medi|tation.

2. Hearken to the voice of my | cry, my | King · and my | God;
   For unto | Thee | will I | pray.

3. My voice shalt Thou hear in the | morning, | O | Lord:
   In the morning will I direct my prayer unto | Thee, and | will look | up.

4. For Thou art not a God that hath | pleasure in | wicked- | ness;
   Neither shall | evil | dwell with | Thee.

5. The vainglorious | shall not | stand · in thy | sight:
   Thou hatest all | workers of in|iqui|ty.

6. Thou wilt de|stroy | them · that speak | falsehood:
   The Lord will abhor the | man of | blood · and de|ceit.

7. But as for me, I will come into thy house in the | multi·tude | of thy | mercy:
   In thy fear will I worship | toward thy | holy | temple.

8. Lead me, O Lord, in thy righteousness, be|cause · of mine | ene|mies:
   Make thy way | straight be|fore my | face.   Ps. v.

II.

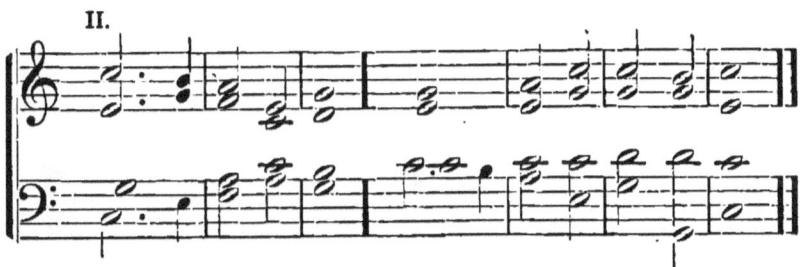

2. IT is good to give | thanks · to the | Lord,
  And to sing praises unto thy | name, O | Thou Most | High ;
  2 To show forth thy loving kindness | in the | morning,
  And thy | faithful·ness | in the | night :
  3 Upon an instrument of ten strings, and up|on the | psaltery ;
  Upon the | harp with | solemn | sound.
  4 For Thou, O Lord, hast made me | glad · through thy | work;
  I will | triumph · in the | works · of thy | hands. . . . . . .
  5 The righteous shall flourish | like the | palm-tree :
  He shall grow like a | cedar in | Leba|non.
  6 Those that be planted in the | house · of the | Lord,
  Shall flourish in the | courts | of our | God.
  7 They shall still bring forth | fruit · in old | age ;
  They shall be | fat and | flourish|ing :
  8 To show that the | Lord is | upright ;
  My Rock, and there is | no un|righteous·ness | in Him.
  Ps. xcii.

III.

3. BEHOLD, how good and how | pleasant it | is,
  For brethren to | dwell to|gether in | unity.
  2 It is like the precious ointment up|on the | head,
  That ran | down up|on the | beard,
  3 Even | Aaron's | beard,
  That went down to the | border | of his | garments.
  4 It is like the | dew of | Hermon,
  That descended up on the | mountains of | Zion :
  5 For there the Lord com'manded the | blessing,
  Even | life for | ever|more.
  Ps. cxxxiii.

INTRODUCTORY. 3

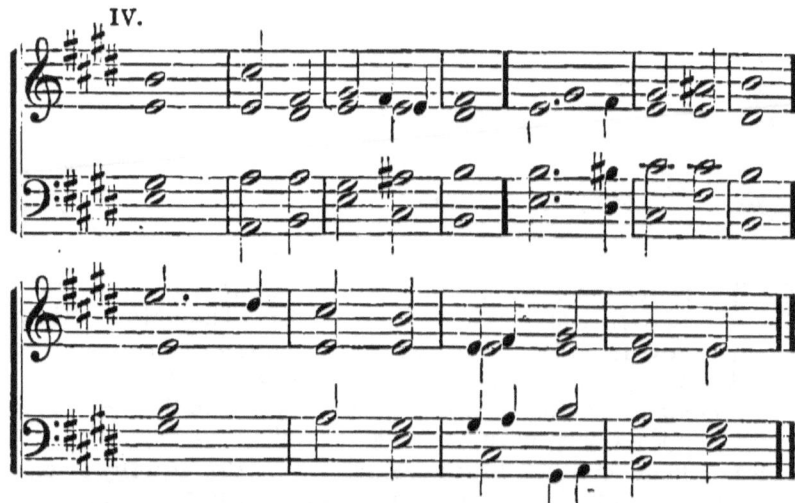

4 COMFORT ye, comfort ye my | people, | saith your | GOD :
  Speak ye comfortably to Je¡rusa¡lem ;
  And cry unto her, that her | warfare | is ac¦complished,
  2 That her in¦iqui¦ty is | pardoned :
  For she hath received from the | LORD'S | hand
  Double | for | all her | sins.
  3 The voice of him that crieth | in the | wilder¦ness,
  Prepare ye the | way · of the | LORD,
  Make straight in the desert a | highway | for our | GOD.
  4 Every | valley shall | be ex¦alted ;
  And every mountain and | hill made | low :
  And the crooked shall be made straight, and the | rough |
    places | plain.
  5 And the glory of the | LORD shall | be re¦vealed :
  And all flesh shall | see · it to¦gether :
  For the mouth of the | LORD hath | spoken | it.   Is. xl.

5 MAKE a joyful noise unto the | LORD, | all the | earth :
  Serve the | LORD with | gladness :
  Come be¦fore his | face with | singing.
  2 Know ye that the | LORD | He is | GOD :
  He hath made us, and not | we our¦selves,
  His people, and the | sheep | of his | pasture.
  3 Enter into his | gates | with thanks¦giving,
  Into his | courts with | praise :
  Give thanks unto | Him, and | bless his | name.
  4 For the | LORD | He is | good :
  His mercy is | ever¦lasting,
  And his ¦ truth to | all gener¦ations.   Ps. c.

V.

6. O GOD, my | heart is | fixed :
   I will sing and give | praise even | with my | glory.

2 Awake, | psaltery and | harp :
  I | will a|wake the | dawn.

3 I will praise Thee, O LORD, a|mong the | people ;
  And I will sing praises unto | Thee a|mong the | nations.

4 For thy mercy is great a|bove the | heavens ;
  And thy truth | reacheth | unto the | clouds.

5 Be Thou exalted, O GOD, a|bove the | heavens :
  And thy | glory a|bove all the | earth.

6 That thy beloved may | be de|livered ;
  Save with thy right | hand, and | answer | me. Ps. cviii.

VI.

7. AS the hart panteth for the | brooks of | water,
   So panteth my | soul for | Thee, O | GOD.

2 My soul thirsteth for GOD, for the | living | GOD :
  When shall I | come · and ap|pear be·fore | GOD?

3 My tears have been my meat | day and | night ;
  While they continually say unto me, | Where | is thy | GOD?

4 When I re|member · these | things,
  I pour | out my | soul with|in me.

5 For I had | gone with the | multitude :
  I went with them | to the | house of | GOD,

INTRODUCTORY. 5

6 With the voice of | joy and | praise,
With a multitude that | kept a | festi|val.

7 Why art thou cast down, | O my | soul?
And why art thou dis'quiet|ed with|in me?

8 Hope thou in GOD, for I | shall yet | praise Him
For the | help · of his | counte|nance. Ps. xlii.

VII.

8 I WAS glad when they | said unto | me,
Let us go into the | house | of the | LORD.

2 Our feet shall stand within thy gates, O Je'rusa'lem :
Jerusalem is built as a city that | is com'pact to'gether.

3 Whither the tribes go up, the | tribes of the | LORD,
A testimony to Israel, to give | thanks · to the | name · of the | LORD.

4 For there are set | thrones of | judgment,
The | thrones · of the | house of | David.

5 Pray for the peace of Je|rusa'lem :
They shall | prosper | that do | love thee.

6 Peace be with|in thy | walls ;
Prosperity with|in thy | pala|ces.

7 For my brethren and com|panions' | sakes,
I will now say, | Peace | be with|in thee.

8 For the sake of the house of the | LORD our | GOD,
I | will seek | good to | thee. Ps. cxxii.

VIII.

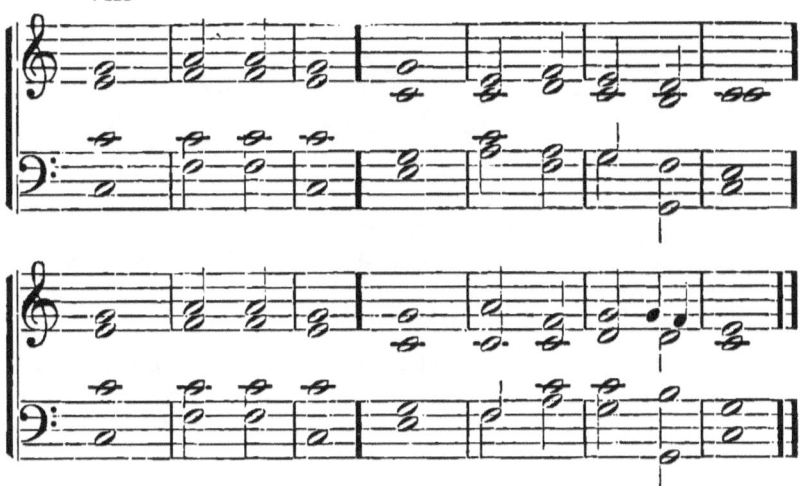

9 AND it shall come to pass | in the · last | days,
That the mountain of the | house | of the | LORD
2 Shall be established in the | top · of the | mountains,
And shall be ex|alted a|bove the | hills.
3 And all nations shall | flow unto | it ;
And many | people shall | go, and | say,
4 Come ye, and let us go up to the | mountain of the | LORD,
To the | house · of the | GOD of | Jacob.
5 And He will | teach us of his | ways,
And we will | walk | in his | paths.
6 For out of Zion shall go | forth the | law,
And the word of the LORD | from Je|rusa|lem.
7 And He shall | judge among the | nations,
And shall re|buke | many | people.
8 And they shall beat their | swords into | ploughshares,
And their | spears into | pruning|hooks.
9 Nation shall not lift up | sword against | nation ;
Neither shall they learn | war | any | more.
10 O house of | Jacob, | come ye,
And let us | walk · in the | light · of the | LORD. Is. ii. 2.

10 AND in this mountain shall the LORD of Hosts | make · to all | people
A feast of fat things, a | feast of | wines · on the | lees,
2 Of fat things | full of | marrow,
Of wines on the | lees | well re|fined.

INTRODUCTORY. 7

3 And He will de|stroy · in this | mountain
  The face of the covering | cast | over all | people,
4 And the vail that is spread | over all | nations.
  He will swallow up | death in | victo|ry.

5 And the | LORD JE|HOVIH
  Will wipe away | tears from | off all | faces :
6 And the rebuke of his people shall He take away from | off
    all the | earth ;
  For the | LORD hath | spoken | it.

7 And it shall be said in that day, Lo, | this · is our | GOD ;
  We have waited for | Him, and | He will | save us :
8 This is the LORD ; we have | waited | for Him ;
  We will be glad and re|joice in | his sal|vation.

             Is. xxv. 6.

11 COME, and let us re|turn · to the | LORD ;
    For He hath torn, and | He will | heal us ;
  He hath smitten, and | He will | bind us | up.

  2 After two days will | He re|vive us ;
    In the third day He will | raise us | up ;
    And we shall | live | in his | sight.

  3 Then | shall we | know,
    ³We shall follow | on to | know the | LORD.

  4 His going forth is pre|pared · as the | morning :
    And He shall come unto us | as the | rain ;
    As the latter and former | rain un|to the | earth.   Hos. vi.

X.

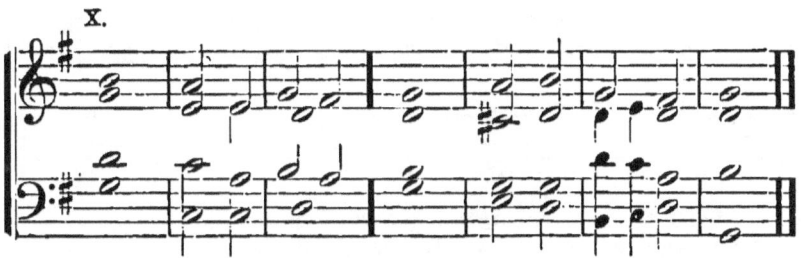

12 HOW lovely are thy | taber|nacles,
O | LORD | of | Hosts.

2 My soul longeth, yea, even fainteth for the | courts · of the | LORD :
My heart and my flesh cry | out · for the | living | GOD.

3 Yea, the sparrow hath | found an | house,
And the swallow a | nest | for her|self,

4 Where she may | lay her | young ;
Thine altars, O LORD of Hosts, my | King | and my | GOD.

5 Blessed are they that | dwell · in thy | house :
Con|tin·ual|ly they | praise Thee.

6 Blessed is the man whose | strength · is in | Thee,
In whose | heart | are the · high-|ways.

7 Passing through the valley of weeping they make it·a | place of | fountains :
The early rain also doth | cover | it with | blessings.

8 They go from | strength to | strength ;
He appeareth be|fore | GOD in | Zion.   Ps. lxxxiv.

13 O LORD, GOD of Hosts, | hear my | prayer :
Give | ear, O | GOD of | Jacob.

2 Behold, O | GOD, our | shield ;
And look upon the | face of | thine an|ointed.

3 For a day in | thy | courts
Is | better | than a | thousand.

4 I had rather stand at the door in the | house · of my | GOD,
Than to dwell in the | tents of | wicked'ness.

5 For the LORD GOD is a | sun and | shield :
The LORD | will give · grace and | glory.

6 No good will | He with·hold
From them that | walk in | upright|ness.

7 O | LORD of | Hosts,
Blessed is the | man that | trusteth in | Thee.   Ps. lxxxiv. 8.

XI.

14 GOD be merciful unto | us, and | bless us,
   And cause his | face to | shine up|on us ;
2 That thy way may be | known upon | earth,
   Thy saving | health a|mong all | nations.
3 Let the people | praise · Thee, O | GOD ;
   Let | all the | people | praise Thee.
4 O let the nations be glad and | sing for | joy :
   For Thou shalt judge the people righteously, and govern the | nations | upon | earth.
5 Let the people | praise · Thee, O | GOD ;
   Let | all the | people | praise Thee.
6 The earth shall | yield her | increase :
   GOD, | our own | GOD, shall | bless us.
7 GOD shall | bless | us,
   And all the | ends· of the | earth shall | fear Him.   Ps. lxvii.

XII.

15 THE LORD is gracious, and | full · of com|passion ;
   Slow to | anger and | great in | mercy.
2 The LORD is | good to | all ;
   And his mercies are | over | all his | works.
3 All thy works shall | praise Thee, O | LORD ;
   And thy | saints shall | bless | Thee.
4 They shall speak of the | glory of thy | kingdom,
   And | talk of | thy | might.
5 To make known to the sons of men his | mighty | acts,
   And the glorious | majes·ty | of his | kingdom.
6 Thy kingdom is an ever|lasting | kingdom ;
   And thy dominion through|out all | gener|ations.   Ps. cxlv. 8.

XIII.

16 JUDGE me, O God, and | plead my | cause,
A | gainst ・ an un|godly | nation.

2 O de|liver | me
From the man of de|ceit ・ and in|iqui|ty.

3 For Thou art the | God ・ of my | strength :
Why | dost Thou | cast me | off ?

4 Why | go I | mourning,
Because of the op|pression | of the | enemy ?

5 O send | out thy | light,
And thy | truth ; | let them | lead me :

6 Let them bring me unto thy | holy | hill,
And | to thy | taber|nacles.

7 Then will I go unto the | altar of | God ;
Unto God the | gladness | of my | joy :

8 And | I will | praise Thee
Upon the | harp, O | God, my | God.

9 Why art thou bowed down, | O my | soul ?
And why art thou dis|quiet|ed with|in me ?

10 Hope in God, for I | yet shall | praise Him ;
Who is the health of my | counte|nance, | and my | God.

Ps. xliii.

XIV.

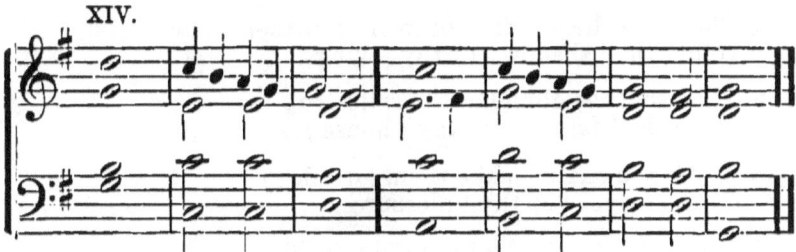

17 O GOD, Thou | art my | God ;
Early will I | seek | Thee.

2 My soul thirsteth for Thee, my flesh | longeth for | Thee,
In a dry and thirsty land, | where no | water | is :

INTRODUCTORY. 11

3 To see thy | power and thy | glory,
So as I have seen Thee | in the | sanctu|ary.

4 Because thy loving kindness is | better than | life,
My | lips shall | praise | Thee.

5 Thus will I bless Thee | while I | live :
I will lift | up my | hands · in thy | name.

6 My soul shall be satisfied as with | marrow and | fatness ;
And my mouth shall | praise · Thee with | joyful | lips ;

7 When I remember Thee up|on my | bed,
And meditate on Thee | in the | night-|watches.   Ps. lxiii.

Dox. Salvation belongeth | to the | Lord ;
Thy blessing | is up|on thy | people.   Ps. iii. 8.

XV.

18 THY mercy, O Lord, is | in the | heavens :
Thy faithfulness | reacheth | unto the | clouds.

2 Thy righteousness is like the | mountains of | God ;
Thy | judgments | are a · great | deep :

3 O Lord, Thou preservest | man and | beast.
How precious is thy | loving-|kindness, O | God !

4 Therefore the children of men | put their | trust
Under the | shadow | of thy | wings.

5 They shall be abundantly | satis|fied
With the | fatness | of thy | house ;

6 And Thou shalt | make them | drink
Of the | river | of thy | pleasures.

7 For with Thee is the | fountain of | life :
In thy | light shall | we see | light.

8 O continue thy loving-kindness unto | them that | know Thee ;
And thy righteousness | to the | upright in | heart.
                                        Ps. xxxvi. 5.

XVI.

19 THE LORD | is my | light
  And my sal|vation ; | whom · shall I | fear?
2 The LORD is the | strength · of my | life ;
  Of | whom · shall I | be a|fraid? . . . .
3 One thing have I desired of the LORD, | that · will I | seek ;
  That I may dwell in the house of the LORD | all the | days ·
    of my | life,
4 To behold the | beauty of the | LORD,
  And to in|quire | in his | temple.
5 For in the | day of | trouble
  He shall | hide · me in | his pa|vilion :
6 In the secret of his tabernacle | shall He | hide me ;
  He shall set me | up up|on a | rock.
7 And now shall mine head be | lifted | up
  Above mine | ene·mies | round a|bout me :
8 Therefore will I offer in his tabernacle sacri|fices of | joy ;
  I will sing, yea, I will sing | praises | to the | LORD.
                                            Ps. xxvii.

XVII.

20 BLESSED | is the | man
  That walketh not in the | counsel | of · the un|godly,

INTRODUCTORY. 13

2 Nor standeth in the | way of | sinners,
 Nor sitteth in the | seat | of the | scornful.

3 But his delight is in the | law · of the | LORD ;
 And in his law doth he | medi·tate | day and | night.

4 And he shall be like a tree planted by the | rivers · of | waters,
 That bringeth forth his | fruit | in his | season :

5 His leaf also | shall not | wither ;
 And whatsoever he | doeth | shall | prosper.

6 The ungodly | are not | so :
 But are like the chaff which the | wind doth | drive a|way.

7 Therefore the ungodly shall not | stand · in the | judgment,
 Nor sinners in the congre|gation | of the | righteous.

8 For the LORD knoweth the | way · of the | righteous ;
 But the way of the un|godly | shall | perish.   Ps. i.

* *This note is sung only when two syllables fall to this measure.*

21 COME, and let us go up to the mountain of the | LORD,
 And to the house of the | GOD of | Jacob.

2 And He will teach us of his | ways ;
 And we will | walk · in his | paths.

3 For the law shall go forth from | Zion,
 And the word of the LORD | from Je|rusalem.

4 And He shall judge among many | people,
 And rebuke strong | na·tions a|far off.

5 And they shall beat their swords into | ploughshares,
 And their | spears into | pruning-hooks.

6 Nation shall not lift up sword against | nation,
 Neither shall they learn | war | any more.

7 But they shall sit, | every man,
 Under his vine and | un·der his | fig-tree :

8 And none shall make a|fraid :
 For the mouth of the LORD of | Hosts hath | spoken it.
                                         Mic. iv.

XIX.

22 O GIVE thanks unto the LORD ; for | He is | good :
For his | mercy | is for | ever. . . . .

2 Open to me the gates of | righteous|ness :
I will go into them : | I will | praise the | LORD.

3 This is the | gate · of the | LORD ;
The righteous shall | enter | into | it.

4 I will praise Thee ; for | Thou hast | heard me,
And art be|come | my sal|vation.

5 The stone which the | builders re|fused,
Is become the | head-stone | of the | corner.

6 This is | from the | LORD :
It is | marvel·lous | in our | eyes.

7 This is the day which the | LORD hath | made :
We will re|joice · and be | glad in | it.

8 Save now, I beseech Thee, | O | LORD :
O LORD, I beseech Thee, | send | now pros|perity.

9 Blessed be he that cometh in the | name · of the | LORD :
We have blessed you | from the | house · of the | LORD.

10 GOD is the LORD, Who hath | showed us | light :
Bind the sacrifice with | cords · to the | horns · of the | altar.

11 Thou art my GOD, and | I will | praise Thee ;
My | GOD, I | will ex|alt Thee.

12 O give thanks unto the LORD, for | He is | good :
For his | mercy | is for | ever. Ps. cxviii. 1, 19.

INTRODUCTORY. 15

XX.

23 I WILL bless the LORD | at all | times :
Continually shall his | praise be | in my | mouth.

2 My soul shall make her | boast · in the | LORD :
The humble shall | hear, | and be | glad.

3 O magnify the | LORD | with me,
And let us ex|alt his | name to|gether.

4 I sought the LORD, | and He | heard me,
And de|livered · me from | all my | fears.

5 They looked unto | Him, and were | lightened :
And their | faces were | not a|shamed.

6 This poor man cried, and the | LORD | heard ;
And saved him | out of | all his | troubles.

7 The angel of the | LORD en|campeth
Around them that fear Him, | and de|liv·ereth | them.

8 O taste and see that the | LORD is | good :
Blessed is the | man that | trusteth · in | Him.

9 O fear the LORD, | ye his | saints ;
For there is no | want to | them that | fear Him.

10 The young lions do lack, and | suffer | hunger :
But they that seek the LORD shall not | want | any | good.

Ps. xxxiv.

XXI.

24 COME, ye children, | hearken unto | me :
   I will | teach · you the | fear · of the | LORD.

 2 What man de|sireth | life,
   And loveth many | days, that | he may · see | good?

 3 Keep thy | tongue from | evil,
   And thy | lips from | speaking | guile.

 4 Depart from evil, | and do | good :
   Seek | peace, | and pur|sue it.

 5 The eyes of the LORD are up|on the | righteous,
   And his ears are | open | to their | cry.

 6 The face of the LORD is against | them that · do | evil,
   To cut off the re|membrance · of them | from the | earth.

 7 The righteous cry, and the | LORD | heareth ;
   And delivereth them | out of | all their | troubles.

 8 The LORD is nigh unto the | broken in | heart :
   And saveth such as | be · of a | contrite | spirit.

 9 Many are the afflictions | of the | righteous :
   But the LORD doth de|liver him | from them | all.

10 He keepeth | all his | bones :
   Not | one of | them is | broken.   Ps. xxxiv. 11.

XXII.

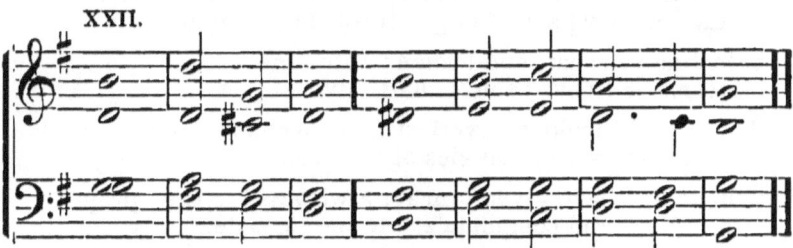

25 O COME, let us | sing · to the | LORD ;
     Let us make a joyful noise to the | Rock of | our sal|va-
   tion.

 2 Let us come before his presence with | thanks|giving,
   And make a joyful | noise unto | Him with | psalms.

INTRODUCTORY. 17

3 For a great | God is the | Lord,
  And a great | King a,bove all | gods.

4 In his hand are the | depths · of the | earth ;
  And the | heights · of the | mountains are | his.

5 The sea is | his, · and He | made it ;
  And his | hands did | form the · dry | land.

6 O come, let us | worship and bow | down ;
  Let us kneel be;fore the | Lord our | Maker.

7 For | He is · our | God ;
  And we are the people of his | pasture, and the | sheep · of
  his | hand.   Ps. xcv.

XXIII.

26 HO, every one that thirsteth, come | ye · to the | waters ;
    And he that hath no | money, | come ye, | buy and | eat.

2 Yea, come, buy | wine and | milk,
  Without | money, | and with,out | price.

3 Wherefore do ye spend money for that which | is not | bread ?
  And your labor for | that which | satis;fieth | not ?

4 Hearken diligently unto me, and eat ye | that · which is | good;
  And let your | soul de;light it;self in | fatness.

5 Incline your ear, and | come · unto | me :
  Hear, | and your | soul | shall | live.

6 And I will make an everlasting | cove·nant | with you.
  Even the | sure | mer·cies of | Da;vid.

7 Behold, I have given him for a witness | to the | people,
  A leader | and com;mander | to the | people.

8 Behold, thou shalt call a nation that thou | knowest | not ;
  And nations that | knew not | thee shall | run unto | thee ;

9 Because of the | Lord thy | God ;
  And for the Holy One of Israel ; for | He hath | glori|fied |
  thee.   Is. lv.

XXIV.

This note is sung only when two syllables fall to this measure.

27 SEEK ye the Lord, while He may be | found ;
　　Call ye upon Him, | while · He is | near.
2 Let the wicked forsake his | way,
　　And the unrighteous | man his | thoughts :
3 And let him return unto the | Lord,
　　And He will have | mercy up|on him ;
4 And unto our | God,
　　For He will a|bun·dantly | pardon.
5 For my thoughts are not | your thoughts,
　　Neither are my ways your ways, | saith the | Lord.
6 For as the heavens are higher than the | earth,
　　So are my ways higher than your ways, and my | thoughts than | your thoughts.
7 For as the rain cometh down, and the snow from | heaven,
　　And returneth not thither, but | watereth the | earth ;
8 And maketh it bring forth and | bud,
　　That it may give seed to the sower, and | bread · to the | eater :
9 So shall my word be, that goeth forth out of my | mouth :
　　It shall not re|turn · to Me | void ;
10 But it shall accomplish that which I | please,
　　And it shall prosper in the thing where|to I | sent it.

---

11 For ye shall go out with | joy,
　　And be led | forth with | peace.
12 The mountains and the hills shall break forth before you into | singing ;
　　And all the trees of the field shall | clap their | hands.
13 Instead of the thorn shall come up the | fir-tree ;
　　And instead of the brier shall come | up the | myrtle :
14 And it shall be to the Lord for a | name ;
　　For an everlasting sign that shall | not · be cut | off.
　　　　　　　　　　　　　　　　　Is. lv. 6.

XXV.

28 **T**EACH me thy | way, O | Lord;
　　I will | walk · in thy | truth :
　　Unite my | heart to | fear thy | name.

　2 I will praise Thee, O | Lord my | God,
　　With | all my | heart ;
　　And I will glorify thy | name for | ever-|more.

　3 For great is thy | mercy | toward me :
　　And Thou | hast de livered
　　My | soul · from the | lowest | hell.

　4 O God, the proud are | risen a|gainst me,
　　And the assemblies of violent men have sought | after my |
　　　　soul ;
　　And have | not set | Thee be|fore them.

　5 But | Thou, O | Lord,
　　Art a God full of com passion and | gracious,
　　Long suffering, and plenteous in | mercy | and in | truth.

　6 O turn unto me, and have mercy up on me :
　　Give thy strength unto thy servant,
　　And | save the | son · of thine handmaid.

　7 Show me a | token for | good,
　　That they who hate me may | see and · be a|shamed :
　　Because Thou, O Lord, hast | holpen · me, and | com-
　　　　fort·ed | me.　　　　　　　　　　　　Ps. lxxxvi. 11.

XXVI.

29 HEAR my | prayer, · O | LORD :
Give | ear · to my | suppli|cations.

2 In thy faithfulness | answer | me,
And | in thy | righteous|ness.

3 And enter not into | judgment with thy | servant :
For in thy sight shall no man | living be | justi|fied.

4 For the enemy hath pursued | after my | soul :
He hath smitten my | life | down · to the | ground.

5 He hath made me to | dwell in | darkness,
As | those · that have | been long | dead.

6 Therefore is my spirit over|whelmed with | in me :
My heart with|in · me is | deso|late.

7 I remember the days of old : I meditate on | all thy | works ;
I muse upon the | work | of thy | hands.

8 I stretch forth my | hands unto | Thee :
My soul thirsteth after | Thee, as a | thirsty | land.

Ps. cxliii.

XXVII.

30 BOW down thine ear, O | LORD, | hear me ;
For | I am | poor and | needy.

2 Preserve my soul, for | I am | holy :
O Thou my GOD, save thy | servant that | trusteth in | Thee.

3 Be merciful unto | me, O | LORD ;
For I cry unto | Thee | all the | day.

PENITENTIAL. 21

4 Rejoice the | soul · of thy | servant :
 For unto Thee, O Lord, do , I lift , up my soul.

5 For Thou, O Lord, art good, and ready to for give ;
 And plenteous in mercy to all that , call up on Thee.

6 Give ear, O Lord, to my ' prayer ;
 And attend to the , voice · of my suppli cations.

7 In the day of my trouble I will call up on Thee ;
 For , Thou wilt | answer , me.   Ps. lxxxvi.

XXVIII.

31 O LORD, | who · shall a bide
   In thy ' taber nacle ?
 Who shall dwell in the | mountain | of thy | holiness ?

2 He that walketh upright ly
 And worketh righteous ness,
 And speaketh the truth in his ' heart.

3 He that slandereth ' not · with his tongue,
 Nor doeth evil to his com panion,
 Nor taketh up a re proach a gainst his ' neighbor.

4 In whose eyes a vile person ! is con temned ;
 But he honoreth them that | fear the ' Lord :
 He that sweareth to his own hurt, and changeth | not.

5 He that putteth not out his ' money to usury,
 Nor taketh reward a gainst the innocent :
 He that doeth | these · things shall | never be | moved.
                                        Ps. xv.

XXIX.

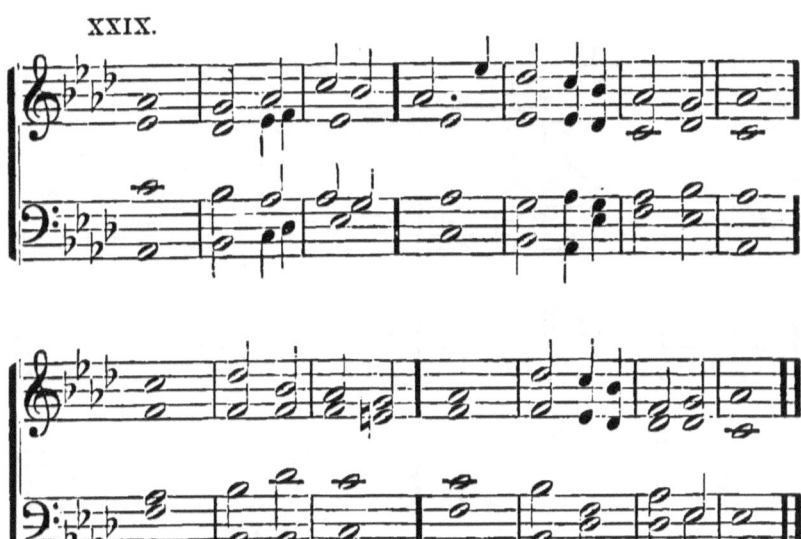

32 GIVE ear to my | prayer, O | God ;
   And hide not Thy|self · from my | suppli|cation.

 2 Attend unto | me, and | hear me :
   I mourn in my com|plaint, and | make a | noise :

 3 Because of the | voice · of the | enemy ;
   Because of the op|pression | of the | wicked :

 4 For they cast in|iqui·ty up|on me ;
   And in | anger | do they | hate me.

 5 My heart is sore | pained with|in me :
   And the terrors of | death are | fallen up|on me.

 6 Fearfulness and trembling are | come up|on me ;
   And | horror hath | over|whelmed me.

 7 And I said, O that I had | wings · like a | dove ;
   I would fly a|way and | be at | rest.

 8 Lo, I would | wander far | off,
   And re|main · in the | wilder|ness.

 9 I would hasten | my es|cape
   From the | windy | storm and | tempest.

10 O that I had | wings · like a | dove ;
   I would fly a|way and | be at | rest.   Ps. lv.

PENITENTIAL. 23

33 IN Thee, O Lord, do I | put my | trust :
   Let me never be a shamed.
2 Deliver me in thy | righteous ness :
   Bow down thine ear to me ; de|liver me | speedi|ly.
3 Be Thou to me a | rock of ' strength,
   For an house · of de,fence to | save me :
4 For Thou art my | rock · and my | fortress ;
   Therefore for thy | name's sake, lead · me and | guide me.
5 Pull me out of the net that they have privily | laid for | me ;
   For Thou | art my strength.
6 Into thine hand I com mit my | spirit :
   Thou hast redeemed me, O Lord, | God of | truth.
7 I have hated them that regard | lying | vanities ;
   But I have trusted in the | Lord.
8 I will be glad and re joice · in thy | mercy :
   For Thou | hast con|sidered my | trouble :
9 Thou hast known my | soul in ad|versities :
   And hast not shut me | up
10 Into the | hand of the | enemy :
    Thou hast set my | feet · in a | large | place.   Ps. xxxi.

Dox. O bless our | God, ye | people,
   And make the voice · of his | praise · to be | heard ;
   Who holdeth our | soul in life,
   And suffereth not our feet · to be | moved.   Ps. lxvi. 8.

XXXI.

34 HEAR, O Lord ; I | cry · with my | voice :
Have mercy also up|on · me, and | answer | me.

2 When Thou saidst, | Seek ye my | face ;
My heart said unto Thee, Thy | face, O | Lord, will I | seek.

3 Hide not thy | face from | me ;
Put not thy | ser·vant a|way in | anger.

4 Thou hast been my help ; | leave me | not,
Neither forsake me, O | God of | my sal|vation.

5 When my father and | mother for|sake me,
Then the | Lord will | take me | up.

6 Teach me thy | way, O | Lord ;
And lead me | in a | path of | plainness.   Ps. xxvii. 7.

XXXII.

35 UNTO Thee, O Lord, do I lift | up my | soul :
O my | God, I | trust in | Thee :

2 Let me | not be a|shamed :
Let not mine enemies | triumph | over | me.

3 Yea, let none that wait on | Thee be a|shamed :
Let them be ashamed who trans gress with|out a | cause.

4 Show me thy | ways, O | Lord ;
Teach | Thou me | thy | paths.

5 Lead me in thy | truth, and | teach me :
For Thou art the God of my salvation : on Thee do I | wait | all the | day.

PENITENTIAL. 25

6 Remember, O Lord, thy tender mercies and thy | loving | kindnesses ;
For they | are from | ever|lasting.

7 Remember not the | sins · of my | youth,
Nor | my trans|gres|sions.

8 According to thy mercy re|member Thou | me,
For thy | goodness' | sake, O | Lord.   Ps. xxv.

XXXIII.

36 HEAR my cry, O God ; at|tend · to my | prayer :
From the end of the earth will I | cry | unto | Thee,
2 When mine heart is | over|whelmed :
Lead me to the | Rock · that is | higher than | I.

3 For Thou hast been a | shelter | for me,
A strong | tower from the | ene|my.
4 I will abide for ever in thy | taber|nacle :
I will trust in the | covert | of thy | wings.

5 For Thou, O God, hast | heard my | vows :
Thou hast given me the heritage of | those that | fear thy | name.
6 Thou wilt add days to the | days · of the | king ;
His years as gener|ation and | gener|ation.

7 He shall abide before | God for | ever :
O prepare mercy and | truth ; let | them pre|serve him.
8 So will I sing praise unto thy | name for | ever,
That I may | daily per|form my | vows.   Ps. lxi.

XXXIV.

37 THE days of our years are threescore | years and | ten ;
And if by reason of | strength they be | fourscore | years,

2 Yet is their strength | labor and | sorrow ;
For it is soon cut | off, and we | fly a|way.

3 Who knoweth the | power of thine | anger?
Even according to thy | fear, | so · is thy | wrath.

4 So teach us to | number our | days,
That we may apply our | hearts | unto | wisdom.

5 Return, O | Lord, how | long?
And let it re|pent · Thee con,cerning thy | servants.

6 Oh, satisfy us early | with thy | kindness ;
That we may rejoice and be | glad | all our | days.

7 Make us glad according to the days wherein Thou hast af- | flicted | us,
And the | years wherein | we have · seen | evil.

8 Let thy work ap'pear · to thy | servants,
And thy | glory | unto their | children.

9 And let the beauty of the Lord our | God · be up'on us ;
And establish Thou the | work · of our | hands up'on us :

10 Yea, the | work · of our | hands
Es|tablish | Thou | it.   Ps. xc. 10.

PENITENTIAL. 27

XXXV.

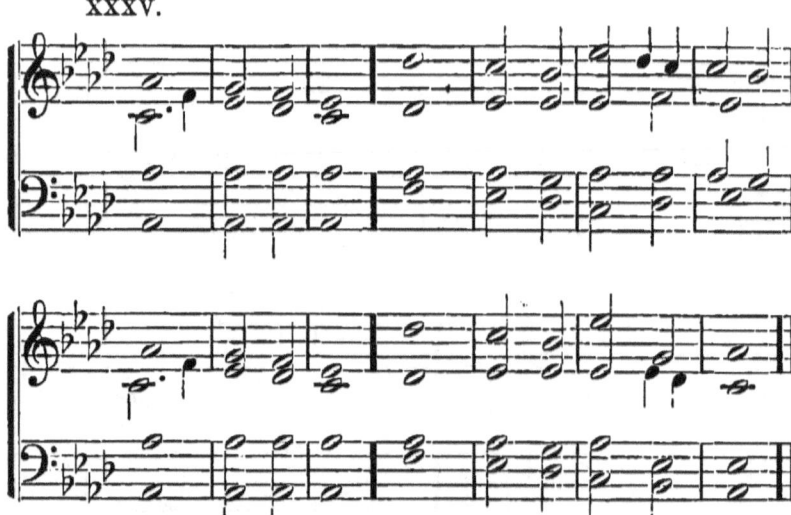

38 **M**Y days are like a shadow | that de|clineth,
   And I am | withered | like the | grass.
  2 But Thou, O LORD, shalt en|dure for | ever ;
    And thy remembrance to gener|ation and | gener|ation.

  3 Thou shalt arise, and have | mercy on | Zion :
    For the time to favor her, yea, the | set | time is | come.
  4 For thy servants take pleasure | in her | stones,
    And | favor the | dust there|of.

  5 And the nations shall fear the | name · of the | LORD,
    And all the | kings · of the | earth thy | glory.
  6 When the LORD shall | build up | Zion,
    He shall ap|pear | in his | glory.

  7 He will regard the prayer of the | desti|tute,
    And | not des|pise their | prayer.
  8 This shall be written for the gener|ation to | come ; [LORD.
    And the people which shall be cre|ated shall |praise the |

  9 For He hath looked down from the height of his | sanctu|ary :
    From heaven did the | LORD be|hold the | earth.
 10 To hear the groaning of the | prison|er ;
    To re|lease the | sons of | death ;

 11 To declare the name of the | LORD in | Zion,
    And his | praise · in Je|rusa|lem ;
 12 When the people are | gath·ered to|gether,
    And the | king·doms to | serve the | LORD.   Ps. cii. 11.

XXXVI.

39 WHO is a God | like to | Thee,
   That pardoneth in|iqui|ty.
 2 And passeth | by · the trans|gression
   Of the remnant of his | heri|tage ?
 3 He retaineth not his | anger for | ever ;
   Because He de|lighteth in | mercy.
 4 He will | turn a|gain ;
   He will have com|pas·sion up|on us :
 5 He will subdue our in|iqui|ties :
   And Thou wilt cast all their sins into the | depths · of the | sea.
 6 Thou wilt perform the | truth unto | Jacob,
   The mercy unto | Abra|ham,
 7 Which Thou hast sworn | unto our | fathers,
   From the | days of | old.   Mic. vii. 18.

XXXVII.

40 O LORD, Thou hast | searched · me and | known me ;
   Thou knowest my down-sitting and mine up-rising,
   Thou under|standest my | thoughts a|far off.
 2 Thou compassest my path and my | lying | down,
   And art ac|quainted with | all my | ways.
 3 For there is not a | word · in my | tongue,
   But, lo, O LORD, Thou | knowest it | alto|gether.
 4 Thou hast beset me be|hind · and be|fore,
   And hast | laid thine | hand up|on me.
 5 Such knowledge is too | wonder·ful | for me : ·
   It is high ; I | can·not at|tain · unto | it.

PENITENTIAL. 29

6 Whither shall I | go · from thy | Spirit?
Or whither | shall I | flee · from thy | presence?

7 If I ascend up into | heaven, Thou art | there:
If I make my bed in | hell, be|hold, Thou art | there.

8 If I take the | wings · of the | morning,
And dwell in the | utter·most | parts · of the | sea;

9 Even there thy | hand shall | lead me.
And | thy right | hand shall | hold me.

10 If I say, Surely the | darkness shall | cover me;
Even the | night · shall be | light a|bout me.

11 Yea, the darkness hideth not from Thee; but the night |
shineth | as the day:
The darkness and the light are | both a|like to | Thee.
Ps. cxxxix.

XXXVIII.

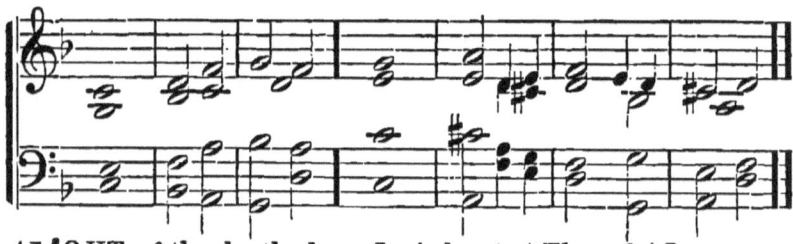

41 **O**UT of the depths have I cried unto | Thee, O | Lord;
O Lord, | hearken | to my | voice.

2 Let thine | ears be at|tentive
Unto the | voice · of my | suppli|cations.

3 If Thou, O Lord, shouldst | mark in|iquities,
O | Lord, | who shall | stand?

4 But with | Thee · is for|giveness,
That | Thou | mayst be | feared.

5 I wait for the Lord, my | soul doth | wait;
And in his | word | do I | hope.

6 My soul waiteth for the Lord more than | watchers for the |
morning:
Than | watchers | for the | morning.

7 Let Israel | hope · in the | Lord;
For with the | Lord | there is | mercy:

8 And with Him is | plen·teous re|demption;
And He shall redeem | Israel from | all · his in|iqui·ties.
Ps. cxxx.

42 O LORD, rebuke me | not · in thine | anger,
    Neither chasten me | in thy | hot dis|pleasure.

2 Have mercy upon me, O LORD ; for | I am | weak :
   O LORD, heal me ; | for my | bones are | vexed :

3 My soul is also | sorely | vexed :
   But | Thou, O | LORD, how | long ?

4 Return, O LORD, de|liver my | soul :
   O save me | for thy | mercies' | sake.

5 For in death there is no re|mem·brance of | Thee :
   In the grave | who shall | give Thee | thanks ?

6 I am weary | with my | groaning ;
   All the night make I my bed to swim ; I | water my | couch with my | tears.

7 Mine eye is consumed be|cause of | grief ;
   It waxeth old because of | all mine | ene|mies.

8 Depart from me, all ye workers of in'iqui|ty :
   For the LORD hath | heard the | voice · of my | weeping.

9 The LORD hath heard my | suppli|cation ;
   The LORD | will re|ceive my | prayer.

10 Let all mine enemies be ashamed and | sorely | vexed :
   Let them return and be | sudden|ly a|shamed.   Ps. vi.

PENITENTIAL. 31

XL.

43 BLESSED is the man whom Thou dost | chasten, O | LORD;
And dost | teach him | out · of thy | law:
2 That Thou mayest give him rest from the | days of | evil,
Until the | pit be | digged · for the | wicked.

3 For the LORD will not cast | off his | people,
Neither will He for'sake · his in heri tance.
4 But judgment shall return unto | righteous'ness;
And all the upright in | heart shall | follow | it.

5 Who will rise up for me against the | evil'doers?
Who will stand up for me against the | workers · of in|iqui|ty?
6 Unless the LORD had | been my | help,
My soul had | almost | dwelt in | silence.

7 When I said, my | foot | slippeth,
Thy mercy, O | LORD, | held me | up.
8 In the multitude of my | thoughts with|in me,
Thy comforts | do de|light my | soul.

9 Shall the throne of iniquity be | joined to | Thee,
Which frameth | mischief | by a | law?
10 They gather themselves together against the | soul · of the righteous,
And con|demn the | inno·cent | blood.

11 But the LORD is | my de|fence;
And my | GOD · is the | Rock of my | refuge:
12 And He shall bring upon them their | own in|iquity,
And shall cut them off in their own wickedness: The LORD
our | GOD shall | cut them | off. Ps. xciv. 12.

XLI.

44 JUDGE me, O LORD; for I have walked in mine in-|tegri|ty :
I have trusted also in the | LORD ; I | shall not | slide.

2 Examine me, O | LORD, and | prove me ;
Try my | reins | and my | heart.

3 For thy loving kindness is be|fore mine | eyes :
And I have | walked | in thy | truth.

4 I have not | sat with · vain | persons,
Neither will | I go | in · with dis|semblers.

5 I have hated the congregation of | evil'doers ;
And | will not | sit · with the | wicked.

6 I will wash mine | hands in | innocence :
So will I | compass thine | altar, O | LORD :

7 That I may publish with the voice of | thanks|giving,
And tell of | all thy | wondrous | works.

8 O LORD, I have loved the habi'tation of thy | house,
And the place | where thine | honor | dwelleth.

9 Gather not my | soul with | sinners,
Nor my | life with | men of | blood :

10 In whose | hands is | mischief,
And their right | hand is | full of | bribes.

11 But as for me, I will walk in mine in'tegri|ty :
Redeem me, and be | merciful | unto | me.

12 My foot standeth in an | even | place :
In the congregations | will I | bless the | LORD.   Ps. xxvi.

PENITENTIAL. 33

XLII.

45 I CRIED by reason of | mine af fliction,
Unto the | Lord, | and He | heard me:
2 Out of the belly of | hell cried | I,
And | Thou didst | hear my | voice.

3 For Thou hadst cast me | into the | deep,
In the | midst | of the | seas:
4 And the floods | compassed me a|bout:
All thy billows and thy | waves passed | over | me.

5 Then I said, I am cast | out · of thy | sight;
Yet I will look again toward the | temple | of thy | holiness.
6 The waters compassed me a|bout · to the | soul:
The depth closed me around; the weeds were | wrapped a|bout my | head.

7 I went down to the | bottoms · of the | mountains:
The earth with her | bars · was a|bout · me for | ever:
8 Yet hast Thou brought | up my | life
From cor|ruption, O | Lord, my | God.

---

9 When my soul did | faint with|in me,
I re|mem|bered the | Lord;
10 And my prayer came | in · unto | Thee,
Into the | temple | of thy | holiness.

11 They that observe lying vanities for|sake · their own | mercy;
But I will sacrifice unto | Thee · with the | voice · of thanks-|
12 I will pay | that · I have | vowed.   [giving:
Sal|vation is | of the | Lord.   Jonah ii. 2.

XLIII.

46 WHEREWITH shall I | come be|fore the | LORD,
And bow myself be|fore the | High | GOD?

2 Shall I come be|fore Him | with burnt-|offer·ings,
With | calves · of a | year | old?

3 Will the LORD be | pleased with | thousands of | rams,
With ten | thousands of | rivers of | oil?

4 Shall I give my | first-born | for · my trans|gression,
The fruit of my body | for the | sins · of my | soul?

5 He hath showed thee, O | man, | what is | good;
And what doth the | LORD re|quire of | thee,

6 But to do justly, | and to | love | mercy,
And to walk | humbly | with thy | GOD.   Mic. vi. 6.

XLIV.

47 HEAR me | when I | call,
O | GOD · of my | righteous|ness.

2 Thou hast enlarged me | when · in dis|tress;
Have mercy up|on · me, and | hear my | prayer.

3 O ye sons of men, how long shall my | glory be for | shame?
How long will ye love vanity, and | seek | after | falsehood?

4 But know that the LORD hath set apart him that is godly | for Him'self:
The LORD will | hear · when I | call unto | Him.

5 Stand in | awe, · and sin | not:
Commune with your own heart up|on your | bed, and be | still.

PENITENTIAL. 35

6 Offer the sacrifices of | righteous'ness,
And put your | trust | in the | LORD.

7 There be many that say, Who will | show us | good?
O LORD, lift up the light of thy | counte͵nance up͵on us.

8 Thou hast put | gladness in my | heart,
More than in the time their | corn · and their | wine in|creased.

9 I will both lay me down in | peace, and | sleep ;
For Thou only, O LORD, dost | make me | dwell in | safety.
                                          Ps. iv.

XLV.

48 HAVE mercy up|on me, O | GOD,
    According | to thy | loving | kindness.

2 According to the multitude | of thy | mercies,
Blot | out | my trans gressions.

3 Wash me thoroughly from mine in|iqui|ty,
And | cleanse me | from my | sin.

4 For I acknowledge | my trans'gressions ;
And my | sin is | ever be|fore me.

5 Against Thee, Thee only, | have I | sinned,
And done | evil | in thy | sight.

6 That Thou mightest be justified | when Thou | speakest,
And be | clear | when Thou | judgest.

7 Behold, I was shapen in in|iqui|ty ;
And in | sin did my | mother con|ceive me.

8 Behold, Thou desirest truth in the | inward | parts ;
And in the hidden part Thou shalt | make · me to | know | wisdom.

9 Purge me with hyssop, and | I · shall be | clean :
Wash me, and I | shall be | whiter than | snow.

10 Make me to hear | joy and | gladness,
That the bones which Thou hast | broken | may re|joice.

11 Hide thy | face · from my | sins,
And | blot out | all · mine in|iquities.   Ps. li.

XLVI.

49 BLESSED are the perfect | in the | way,
    Who | walk · in the ' law · of the | Lord.
2 Blessed are they that keep his | testi|monies,
  That | seek · Him with | all the | heart.

3 They also do no in|iqui|ty :
  They | walk | in his | ways.
4 Thou | hast com|manded
  To keep thy | precepts | dili·gent'|ly.

5 O | that my | ways
  Were di|rected to | keep thy | statutes.
6 Then shall I | not · be a|shamed,
  When I have re|spect unto | all · thy com|mandments.

7 I will praise Thee with upright|ness of | heart,
  When I shall have learned the | judgments | of thy | justice.
8 I will | keep thy | statutes :
  O do not for|sake me | utter|ly.   Ps. cxix.

XLVII.

50 DEAL bountifully | with thy | servant,
    That I may | live, and | keep thy | word.

PENITENTIAL. 37

2 Open | Thou mine | eyes,
That I may behold wondrous | things | out of · thy | law.

3 I am a stranger | in the | earth :
Hide not | thy com|mandments | from me.

4 My soul breaketh | for the | longing,
That it hath unto thy | judgments | at all | times.

5 Thou hast rebuked the | proud · that are | cursed,
Who do | err from | thy com|mandments.

6 Remove from me re'proach · and con'tempt ;
For I have | kept thy | testi|monies.

7 Princes also did sit and | speak a|gainst me :
Thy servant did | medi·tate | in thy | statutes.

8 Thy testimonies also are | my de|light,
And | my | counsel'lors.   Ps. cxix. 17.

XLVIII.

51 MY soul cleaveth | unto the | dust :
Quicken Thou me ac'cording | to thy | word.

2 I have declared my ways, and | Thou hast | heard me :
O | teach Thou | me thy | statutes.

3 Make me to understand the | way · of thy | precepts :
So shall I | talk · of thy | wondrous | works.

4 My soul doth | melt for | grief :
Strengthen Thou me ac|cording | to thy | word.

5 Remove from me the | way of | lying ;
And grant me thy | law | gracious|ly.

6 I have chosen the | way of | truth :
Thy judgments | have I | laid be|fore me.

7 I cleave unto thy | testi'monies :
O Lord, | put me | not to | shame.

8 I will run the way of | thy com|mandments,
When | Thou · shalt en'large my | heart.   Ps. cxix. 25.

XLIX.

52 WHEREWITH shall a young man | cleanse his | way ?
By taking heed ac|cording | to thy | word.

2 With my whole | heart have I sought Thee :
O let me not | wander from | thy com|mandments.

3 Thy word have I | hid · in mine | heart,
That I might not | sin a|gainst | Thee.

4 Blessed art | Thou, O | Lord :
O | teach Thou | me thy | statutes.

5 With my lips have | I de|clared
All the | judgments | of thy | mouth.

6 I have rejoiced in the way of thy | testi|monies,
As | much · as in | all | riches.

7 I will meditate | in thy | precepts,
And | have re'spect · to thy | ways.

8 I will delight myself | in thy | statutes :
I will | not for|get thy | word.   Ps. cxix. 9.

PENITENTIAL.

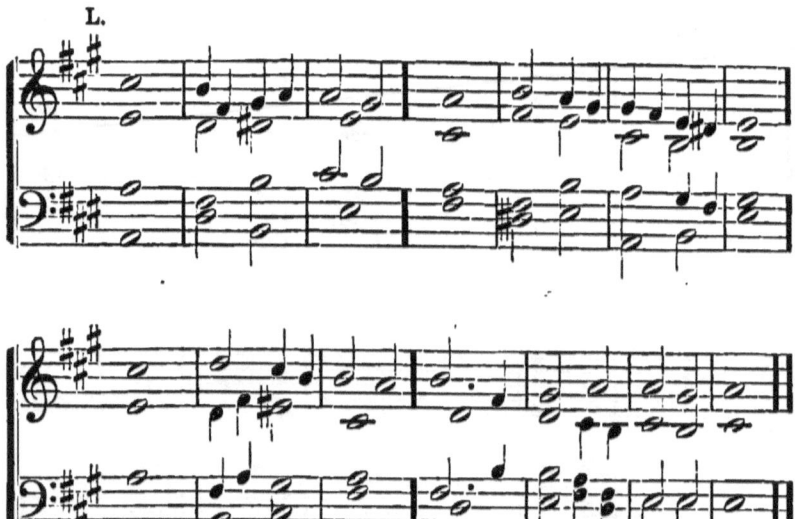

53 TEACH me, O Lord, the | way · of thy | statutes ;
And I shall | keep it | unto the | end.

2 Make me to understand, and I shall | keep thy | law ;
And I shall observe it | with the | whole | heart.

3 Make me to go in the path of | thy com|mandments ;
For there|in do | I de|light.

4 Incline my heart unto thy | testi|monies,
And not | unto | covet·ous|ness.

5 Turn away mine eyes from be|holding | vanity :
Quicken | Thou me | in thy | way.

6 Establish thy word | unto thy | servant,
Who is de|voted | to thy | fear.

7 Turn away my re|proach · which I | fear ;
For thy | judgments | are | good.

8 Behold, I have | longed · for thy | precepts :
Quicken me | in thy | righteous|ness.   Ps. cxix. 33.

LI.

54 THOU art my | portion, O | Lord :
   I have said that | I would | keep thy | words.

2 I entreated thy favor with | all the | heart :
  Be merciful unto me ac¦cording | to thy | word.

3 I | thought up·on my | ways,
  And turned my | feet · to thy | testi|monies.

4 I made haste, and de¦layed | not,
  To | keep | thy com|mandments.

5 The bands of the | wicked have | robbed me :
  I have | not for|gotten thy | law.

6 At midnight I will rise to give | thanks unto | Thee,
  Because of the | judgments | of thy | justice.

7 I am a companion of all | them that | fear Thee,
  And of | them that | keep thy | precepts.

8 The earth, O Lord, is | full · of thy | mercy :
  O | teach Thou | me thy |.statutes.   Ps. cxix. 57.

LII.

55 THY hands have made me and | fashioned | me:
  Make me to understand, that | I may | learn · thy com-| mandments.

  2 They that fear Thee will be | glad · when they | see me,
  Because I have | hoped | in thy | word.

  3 I know, O LORD, that thy | judg·ments are | justice;
  And that Thou in faithfulness | hast af|flicted | me.

  4 Let, I pray Thee, thy merciful kindness | be · for my | comfort,
  According to thy | word | to thy | servant.

  5 Let thy tender mercies come unto me, that | I may | live;
  For thy | law is | my de|light.

  6 Let the proud be ashamed; for they dealt perversely with me with|out a | cause:
  I will | medi·tate | in thy | precepts.

  7 Let those that fear Thee | turn unto | me;
  And those that | know thy | testi|monies.

  8 Let my heart be | sound · in thy | statutes,
  That I | may not | be a|shamed.   Ps. cxix. 73.

LIII.

56 O HOW I | love thy | law :
It is my medi,tation | all the | day.

2 Thou hast made me wiser | than mine | enemies,
Through thy commandments, for | they are | ever | with me.

3 I have more understanding than | all my | teachers ;
For thy testimonies | are my | medi|tation.

4 I understand | more · than the | ancients,
Be|cause I | keep thy | precepts.

5 I have refrained my feet from | every evil | way,
That | I might | keep thy | word.

6 I have not departed | from thy | judgments ;
For | Thou hast | taught | me.

7 How sweet are thy | words to my | taste :
Sweeter than | honey | unto my | mouth.

.8 Through thy precepts I get | under,standing ;
Therefore I hate | every | path of | falsehood.

Ps. cxix. 97.

PENITENTIAL. 43

LIV.

57 THY word is a | lamp · to my | feet,
  And a | light un|to my | path.

2 I have sworn, and I | will per|form,
  That I will keep the | judgments | of thy | justice.

3 I am afflicted | very | much :
  Quicken me, O LORD, ac|cording | to thy | word.

4 Accept, I beseech Thee, the free-will offerings of my | mouth, O | LORD ;
  And | teach Thou | me thy | judgments.

5 My soul is continually | in my | hand :
  Yet do I | not for|get thy | law.

6 The wicked have laid a | snare for | me :
  Yet I have not | wandered | from thy | precepts.

7 Thy testimonies have I taken as an | heri·tage for | ever ;
  For they are the re|joicing | of my | heart.

8 I have in|clined my | heart,
  To perform thy statutes | always, | to the | end.

Ps. cxix. 105.

LV.

58 I HAVE done | judgment and | justice :
    Leave me | not to | mine op|pressors.

2 Be surety for thy | servant for | good :
  Let | not the | proud op|press me.

3 Mine eyes fail for | thy sal'vation,
  And for the | word · of thy | righteous|ness.

4 Deal with thy servant ac|cording · to thy | mercy,
  And | teach Thou | me thy | statutes.

5 I am thy servant ; give me | under'standing,
  That I may | know thy | testi|monies.

6 It is time for Thee, O | LORD, to | work ;
  For they | have made | void thy | law.

7 Therefore I love thy commandments | more than | gold,
  And | more than | fine | gold.

8 Therefore all thy precepts concerning all things do | I es·teem | right ;
  And every | false way | do I | hate.   Ps. cxix. 121.

PENITENTIAL. 45

LVI.

59 THY testimonies are | wonder|ful ;
  Therefore ¦ doth my | soul ¦ keep them.

2 The entrance of thy ¦ words giveth ¦ light ;
  It giveth under standing | to the ¦ simple.

3 I opened my ¦ mouth, and | panted ;
  For I | longed for ¦ thy com¦mandments.

4 Look Thou upon me, and be merciful | unto | me ;
  As Thou usest to do unto | those that ¦ love thy | name.

5 Order my | steps · in thy | word :
  And let not any iniquity have do|minion | over | me.

6 Deliver me from the op¦pression of | man ;
  So | will I | keep thy ¦ precepts.

7 Make thy face to shine up¦on thy ¦ servant ;
  And | teach Thou | me thy | statutes.

8 Rivers of waters run | down mine | eyes,
  Because they | do not | keep thy | law.   Ps. cxix. 129.

LVII.

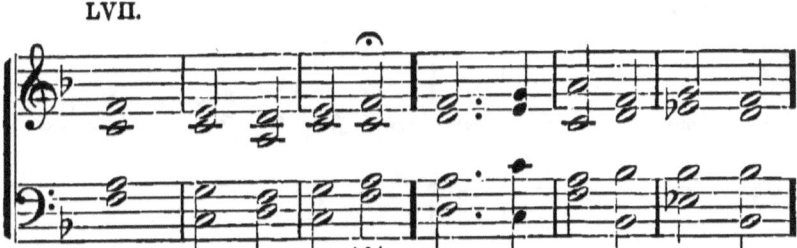

60 1 CRIED with all the heart ; | Hear me, O | LORD :
I will | keep thy | statutes.

2 I cried unto | Thee : O | save me ;
And I shall keep thy | testi͵monies.

3 I prevented the | dawn, and | cried :
I | hoped in | thy word.

4 Mine eyes pre|vent the · night | watches,
That I might | medi·tate in | thy word.

5 Hear my voice according unto thy | loving-|kindness :
O LORD, quicken me ac|cording to thy | judgment.

6 They draw near that | follow | mischief :
They are | far from | thy law.

7 Thou art | near, O | LORD ;
And all thy com|mandments | are truth.

8 Concerning thy testimonies, I have | known of | old,
That Thou hast | founded them for|ever.   Ps. cxix. 145.

PENITENTIAL. 47

LVIII.

61 PRINCES have persecuted me with out a | cause ;
But my heart doth | tremble ; at thy | word.

2 I re'joice at thy | word,
As one that | findeth | great | spoil.

3 Falsehood do I | hate · and ab,hor ;
But thy | law | do I | love.

4 Seven times a | day · do I | praise Thee,
Because of the | judgments | of thy justice.

5 Great peace have they who | love thy | law ;
And no ' stumbling | block have | they.

6 O LORD, I have hoped for ' thy sal vation ;
And thy com|mandments | have I | done.

7 My soul hath kept thy | testi|monies ;
And I do | love · them ex|ceeding ly.

8 I have kept thy precepts and thy | testi|monies ;
For all my | ways | are be|fore Thee.   Ps. cxix. 161.

SELECTIONS AND CHANTS.

LIX.

[musical notation]

62 LET thy mercies come also unto | me, O | LORD;
Thy salvation, ac|cording | to thy | word.

2 So shall I have wherewith to answer him that re|proacheth | me:
For I | trust | in thy | word.

3 And take not the word of truth utterly | out · of my | mouth;
For I have | hoped | in thy | judgments.

4 So shall I keep thy law con|tin·ual|ly,
For | ever | and | ever.

5 And I will walk at | liber|ty;
For | I do | seek thy | precepts.

6 I will speak of thy testimonies also be|fore | kings,
And | will not | be a|shamed.

7 And I will de|light my|self
In thy com|mand·ments which | I have | loved.

8 My hands also will I lift up unto thy commandments, which | I have | loved;
And I will | medi·tate | in thy | statutes.   Ps. cxix. 41.

LX.

[musical notation]

63 RIGHTEOUS art | Thou, O | LORD;
And | upright | are thy | judgments.

2 Thy testimonies, that | Thou · hast com|manded,
Are | righteous and | very | faithful.

3 My zeal hath con|sumed | me,
Because mine enemies | have for|gotten thy | words.

PENITENTIAL. 49

4 Thy word is | very | pure ;
Therefore thy | servant | loveth | it.

5 I am | small · and des|pised :
I do | not for|get thy | precepts.

6 Thy righteousness is an everlasting | righteous|ness ;
And thy | law | is the | truth.

7 Trouble and anguish have taken | hold on | me :
Yet thy com:mandments are | my de|lights.

8 The righteousness of thy testimonies is | ever|lasting :
Make me to under|stand, and | I shall | live.   Ps. cxix. 137.

LXI.

64 CREATE in me a clean | heart, O | GOD ;
And renew a | right | spirit with|in me.

2 Cast me not a|way · from thy | presence ;
And take not thy | Holy | Spirit | from me.

3 Restore unto me the joy of | thy sal | vation ;
And up|hold · me with | thy free | Spirit.

4 I will teach trans|gressors thy | way ;
And sinners shall be con|verted | unto | Thee.

5 Deliver me from blood, O GOD, Thou GOD of | my sal|vation :
My tongue shall sing a|loud · of thy | righteous|ness.

6 O LORD, open | Thou my | lips ;
And my mouth shall | show | forth thy | praise.

7 For Thou desirest not sacrifice, | else · would I | give :
Thou delightest | not · in burnt-|offer|ing.

8 The sacrifices of GOD are a | broken | spirit :
A broken and contrite heart, O GOD, | Thou wilt | not des-|
[pise.

9 Do good in thy good pleasure | unto | Zion :
Build Thou the | walls · of Je|rusa|lem.

10 Then shalt | Thou be | pleased
With the sacri|fices of | righteous|ness.

11 With burnt-offering and | whole burnt-|offering :
Then shall they offer | bullocks up|on thine | altar.
Ps. li. 10.

SELECTIONS AND CHANTS.

LXII.

65 LOOK down from heaven, | and be|hold,
From the habitation of thy | holi·ness | and thy | glory.

2 Where is thy | zeal · and thy | strength,
The sounding of thy bowels and of thy mercies | toward me ? | are · they re|strained ?

3 Doubtless, | Thou · art our | Father,
Though Abraham be ignorant of us, and | Israel ac|knowl-edge us | not.

4 Thou, O LORD, | art our | Father,
Our Redeemer ; thy | name · is from | ever|lasting.

5 O LORD, why hast Thou made us to | err · from thy | ways,
And hardened our | heart | from thy | fear ?

6 Return for thy | servants' | sake,
The tribes of | thine in|heri|tance.   [while :

7 The people of thy holiness have possessed it but a | little
Our adversaries have trodden | down thy | sanctu|ary.

8 We are thine : Thou never barest | rule over | them ;
They | were not | called by thy | name.   Is. lxiii. 15.

LXIII.

66 TRUST in the LORD, | and do | good ;   [be | fed.
So shalt thou dwell in the land, and | veri·ly thou | shalt

2 Delight thyself also | in the | LORD ;
And He shall give thee the de|sires | of thine | heart.

3 Commit thy way | unto the | LORD ;
Trust also in Him ; and | He shall | bring · it to | pass.

4 And He shall bring forth thy righteousness | as the | light,
And thy | judgment | as the | noonday.

PENITENTIAL. 51

5 Rest | in the | Lord,
And wait | patient,ly for | Him.
6 Fret not thyself because of him who prospereth | in his | [way,
Because of the man who bringeth | wicked · de|vices to | pass.
7 Cease from anger, and for'sake | wrath :
Fret not thyself in | any | wise · to do | evil.
8 For evildoers shall | be cut | off : [earth.
But those that wait on the Lord, | they · shall in|herit the |
9 For yet a little while, and the wicked | shall not | be :
Yea, thou shalt diligently consider his | place, and it | shall not | be.
10 But the meek shall in'herit the | earth ;
And shall delight themselves | in · the a|bun·dance of | peace.
Ps. xxxvii. 3.

LXIV.

67 THE steps of a good man are | ordered by the | Lord,
And He de,lighteth | in his | way.
2 Though he fall, he shall not be | wholly cast | down ;
For the Lord doth up|hold him | with his | hand.
3 I have been young, and | now am | old ;
Yet have I not seen the righteous for'saken, nor his | seed begging | bread.
4 He is gracious all the | day, and | lendeth ;
And his | seed is | bless,ed.
5 Depart from evil, ' and do | good ;
And | dwell for | ever'more.
6 For the Lord ' loveth ' judgment,
And for'saketh | not his | saints.
7 They are pre'served for|ever :
But the seed of the | wicked shall | be cut | off.
8 The righteous shall in'herit the | land,
And | dwell there|in for|ever.
9 The mouth of the righteous | speaketh | wisdom,
And his | tongue doth | talk of | judgment.
10 The law of his God is | in his | heart ;
None of his | steps | shall | slide. Ps. xxxvii. 23.

SELECTIONS AND CHANTS.

LXV.

68 THE law of the | Lord is | perfect,
Con|verting the | soul :
2 The testimony of the | Lord is | sure,
Making | wise the | simple.
3 The precepts of the | Lord are | right,
Re|joicing the | heart :
4 The commandment of the | Lord is | pure,
En,lighten·ing the | eyes.
5 The fear of the | Lord is | clean,
En|during for|ever :
6 The judgments of the | Lord are | truth ;
They are righteous | alto|gether.
7 More to be desired | are they · than | gold ;
Yea, than | much fine | gold ;
8 Sweeter | also than | honey,
And the | honey-|comb.

Ps. xix. 7.

LXVI.

69 THE LORD | is my | Shepherd ;
I | shall | not | want.

PRAISE AND THANKSGIVING.   53

2 He maketh me to lie | down in · green | pastures ;
  He leadeth me be|side the | still | waters.
3 He re|storeth my | soul ;
  He leadeth me in the paths of righteousness | for his | name's | sake.
4 Yea, though I walk through the valley of the | shadow of | [death,
  I will | fear | no | evil :
5 For | Thou art | with me ;
  Thy rod and thy | staff they | comfort | me.
6 Thou preparest a | table be|fore me
  In the | presence | of mine | enemies :
7 Thou anointest my | head with | oil ;
  My | cup | runneth | over.
8 Surely goodness and mercy shall | follow | me
  All the | days | of my | life ;
9 And | I shall | dwell
  In the house of the | LORD | for|ever.   Ps. xxiii.

LXVII.

70 BLESS the LORD, | O my | soul ;
     And all that is within me, | bless his | holy | name.
2 Bless the LORD, | O my | soul ;
  And for|get not.| all his | benefits.
3 Who forgiveth | all thine in|iquities ;
  Who | healeth | all · thy dis|eases ;
4 Who redeemeth thy | life · from de'struction ;
  Who crowneth thee with | kindness | and with | mercies ;
5 Who satisfieth thy | mouth with | good :
  Thy youth is re|newed | like the | eagle's.
6 The LORD doeth | righteous|ness,
  And judgment for | all that | are op|pressed.
7 He made known his | ways unto | Moses,
  His deeds unto the | chil·dren of | Isra|el.   Ps. ciii.

SELECTIONS AND CHANTS.

LXVIII.

71 I WILL lift up mine | eyes · to the | mountains,
From | whence doth | come my | help.
2 My help is | from the | LORD,
Who made the | heavens | and the | earth.
3 He will not suffer thy | foot · to be | moved :
He that doth | keep thee | will not | slumber.
4 Behold, He that keepeth | Isra el,
Shall neither | slumber | nor | sleep.
5 The LORD | is thy | keeper :
The LORD is thy | shade on | thy right | hand.
6 The sun shall not | smite · thee by | day,
Neither the | moon | by | night.
7 The LORD shall keep thee from | all | evil :
He shall | keep | thy | soul.
8 The LORD shall keep thy going out and thy | coming | in,
From this time forth, and | even for | ever|more.
Ps. cxxi.

LXIX.

72 THE LORD is | merci·ful and | gracious ;
Slow to | anger, and | great in | mercy.

PRAISE AND THANKSGIVING. 55

2 He will not | always | chide ;
Neither will He | keep his | anger for | ever.
3 He hath not dealt with us | after our | sins ;
Nor rewarded us according to | our in|iqui|ties.
4 For as the heaven is high a|bove the | earth,
So great is his | mercy toward | them that | fear Him.
5 As far as the east | is from the | west,
So far hath He re|moved our trans gressions | from us.
6 Like as a father | piti·eth his | children,
So the Lord | piti·eth | them that | fear Him.
7 For He knoweth our | frame ;
He re|membereth that | we are | dust.
8 As for man, his | days · are as | grass :
As a flower of the | field, so he | flourish|eth.
9 For the wind passeth over it, and | it is | not ;
And the place there of shall | know · it no | more.
10 But the mercy of the Lord is from everlasting to everlasting upon | them that | fear Him,
And his righteousness | unto | children's | children :
11 To such as | keep his | covenant,
And to those that re|member his com|mand·ments to | do them.   Ps. ciii. 8.

LXX.

73 THE LORD hath prepared his | throne · in the | heavens ;
And his kingdom | ruleth | over | all.
  2 Bless the Lord, | ye his | angels,
That ex|cel | in | strength :
  3 That | do his | word,
Hearkening to the | voice | of his | word.
  4 Bless ye the Lord, | all his | hosts ;
Ye ministers of | his that | do his | pleasure.
  5 Bless the Lord, all his works, in all places of | his do|-minion :
Bless the | Lord, | O my | soul.   Ps. ciii. 19.

LXXI.

74 AND in the same country were shepherds a|biding in the | field,
Keeping watch | over their | flock by | night.

2 And, lo, the angel of the | LORD came up'on them,
And the glory of the | LORD shone | round a,bout them.

3 And they were | sore a'fraid :
And the angel | said unto | them, Fear | not :

4 For, behold, I bring you good | tidings ˙ of great | joy,
Which shall | be to | all | people.

5 For to you in the city of David is | born this | day
A Saviour, | Who is | CHRIST the | LORD.

6 And this shall be a | sign unto | you :
Ye shall find the Babe, wrapped in swaddling clothes, | lying | in a | manger.

7 And suddenly there | was ˙ with the | angel
A multitude of the heavenly host, | praising | GOD, and | say-ing,

8 Glory to | GOD ˙ in the | highest :
And on earth | peace ; among | men good | will.

Luke ii. 8.

PRAISE AND THANKSGIVING.

LXXII.

75 MY soul doth | magni·fy the | LORD,
And my spirit hath re|joiced in | GOD my | Saviour :

2 For He hath regarded the low es|tate · of his | handmaid ;
For, behold, from henceforth all gener|ations shall | call me | blessed.

3 ³For He that is mighty hath done to | me great | things,
And | holy | is his | name.

4 And his mercy is on | them that | fear Him,
To gener|ations and | gener,ations.

5 He hath showed | strength · with his | arm ;
He hath scattered the proud in the imagin|ation | of their | heart.

6 He hath put down the mighty | from their | seats,
And ex,alted them of | low de|gree.

7 He hath filled the hungry with | good | things,
And the rich He hath | sent | empty a,way.

8 He hath holpen his servant | Isra'el,
In re|membrance | of his | mercy :

9 As He | spake to our | fathers,
To Abraham, and | to his | seed for | ever.

Luke i. 46.

58 SELECTIONS AND CHANTS.

LXXIII.

76 BLESSED be the Lord God of | Isra|el ;
      For He hath visited | and re‚deemed his | people ;
  2 And hath raised up an horn of sal‚vation | for us,
    In the | house · of his | servant | David.
  3 As He spake by the mouth of his | holy | prophets,
    Who have | been since the | world be|gan :
  4 That we should be saved from our | ene|mies,
    And from the | hand of | all that | hate us.
  5 To perform the mercy | promised to our | fathers,
    And to remember his | holy | cove|nant ;
  6 The oath which He sware to our father | Abra|ham,
    That He would | grant | unto | us ;
  7 That we, being delivered from the hand of our | ene|mies,
    Might | serve Him | without | fear,
  8 In holiness and | righteous|ness,
    Be|fore Him, | all our | days.   Luke i. 68.

LXXIV.

77 LORD, now lettest Thou thy servant de|part in | peace,
     Ac|cording | to thy | word.

PRAISE AND THANKSGIVING. 59

2 For mine eyes have seen | thy sal|vation,
Which Thou hast prepared before the | face of | all | people ;
3 A light to | lighten the | Gentiles,
And the | glory of thy | people | Israel. Luke ii. 29.

LXXV.

78 HOLY, Holy, Holy, LORD | GOD Al|mighty,
Who was, and Who | is, and Who | is to | come. . . . . .
2 Thou art | worthy, O | LORD,
To receive | glory, and | honor, and | power :
3 For Thou hast cre|ated all | things ;
And for thy pleasure they | are, and | were cre|ated.
Rev. iv.
4 Great and marvellous are thy works, LORD | GOD Al|mighty ;
Just and true are thy | ways, Thou | King of | saints.
5 Who shall not | fear Thee, O | LORD,
And glorify thy name ? for | Thou a|lone art | holy.
6 For all nations shall come and | worship be|fore Thee ;
For thy judgments | are made | mani|fest. Rev. xv.

79 THE kingdoms of this world are become our | LORD'S · and
his | CHRIST'S ;
And He shall | reign for | ever and | ever. . . .
2 We give Thee thanks, O LORD | GOD Al|mighty,
Who art, and Who | wast, and Who | art to | come ;
3 Because Thou hast | taken to | Thee
Thy great | power, | and hast | reigned. Rev. xi.
4 Salvation | to our | GOD,
Who sitteth upon the | throne, and | to the | LAMB. . . . . .
5 Amen : Blessing, and | glory, and | wisdom,
And thanksgiving, and | honor, and | power, and | might,
6 Be | unto our | GOD,
For | ever and | ever : A|men. Rev. vii.

LXXVI.

80 A**LLE|LU|IA :**
For the L ORD | G OD om|nipo·tent | reigneth.

2 Let us be | glad, and re'joice,
And give the | glory | unto | Him :

3 For the marriage of the | L AMB is | come ;
And his | Wife hath | made · herself | ready.

4 And to her was granted that she should | be ar|rayed
In fine | linen | bright and | clean :

5 For the | fine | linen
Is the | righteous'ness of | saints.

6 Blessed are | they · that are | called
Unto the marriage | supper | of the | L AMB.   Rev. xix. 6.

Dox. Amen : Blessing, and | glory, and | wisdom,
And thanksgiving, and | honor, and | power, and | might,
Be | unto our | G OD,
For | ever and | ever : A|men.   Rev. vii. 12.

LXXVII.

81 H**OW** | great is thy | goodness,
Which Thou hast laid | up for | them that | fear Thee ;

2 Which Thou hast | wrought for | them,
That trust in Thee be'fore the | sons of | men.

3 Thou shalt hide them in the secret of thy presence, from
the | pride of | man :
Thou shalt secrete them in a pavilion, | from the | strife of |
tongues.

4 Blessed | be the | LORD;
  For He hath showed me his marvellous | kindness | in a
    strong | city.

5 For I | said · in my | haste,
  I am cut | off · from be|fore thine | eyes.

6 But Thou heardest the voice of my | suppli|cations,
  When I | cried | unto | Thee.

7 Oh | love the | LORD,
  All | ye his | godly | ones.

8 The LORD pre|serveth the | faithful,
  And plentifully re|wardeth the | proud | doer.

9 Be of good courage, and He shall | strengthen your | heart,
  All | ye that | hope · in the | LORD.   Ps. xxxi. 19.

LXXVIII.

82 THE LORD upholdeth | all that | fall,
     And raiseth up | all the | bowed | down.

2 The eyes of all | wait on | Thee;
  And Thou givest them their | meat | in its | season.

3 Thou dost | open thine | hand,
  And satisfy the desire of | ev·ery | living | thing.

4 The LORD is righteous in | all his | ways,
  And | kind in | all his | works.

5 The LORD is nigh unto all that | call up|on Him,
  To all that | call upon | Him in | truth.

6 He will fulfil the desire of | them that | fear Him:
  He also will | hear their | cry, and will | save them.

7 The LORD preserveth | all that | love Him;
  But all the | wicked will | He de'stroy.

8 My mouth shall speak the | praise · of the | LORD:
  And let all flesh bless his holy | name for | ever and | ever.
                                              Ps. cxlv. 14.

LXXIX.

83 I WILL extol Thee, my | GOD, O | King ;
And I will bless thy | name for | ever and | ever.

2 Every | day · will I | bless Thee ;
And I will praise thy | name for | ever and | ever.

3 Great is the LORD, and | greatly to be | praised ;
And un|searcha·ble | is his | greatness.

4 Generation to generation shall ' praise thy | works,
And shall de,clare thy | mighty | acts.

5 I will speak of the glorious honor of thy | majes'ty,
And | of thy | wondrous | works.

6 And men shall speak of the might of thy | terrible | acts :
And | I · will de,clare thy | greatness.

7 The memory of thy great goodness shall | they pro|claim ;
And shall sing a|loud · of thy | righteous,ness.

Ps. cxlv.

LXXX.

84 THOU hast been favorable, O LORD, ' to thy | land ;
Thou hast brought back the cap|tivi,ty of | Jacob.

2 Thou hast forgiven the iniquity | of thy | people ;
Thou hast | covered | all their | sin.

3 Thou hast taken away | all thy | wrath ;
Thou hast turned away from the | burning | of thine | anger.

4 Restore us, O GOD of | our sal vation,
And turn a,way thine | anger | from us.

PRAISE AND THANKSGIVING. 63

5 Wilt Thou be angry with | us for'ever?
Wilt Thou prolong thine anger to | all | gener ations?

6 Wilt Thou not re vive · us a gain.
That thy people | may re joice in | Thee?

7 Make us to see thy mercy, | O | Lord,
And | grant us | thy sal vation.

Ps. lxxxv.

LXXXI.

85 MY heart rejoiceth | in the | Lord;
Mine horn is ex alted | in the | Lord:

2 My mouth is enlarged over mine | ene mies;
Because I re joice in | thy sal vation.

3 None is holy as the Lord; for there is | none but | Thee;
Neither is there any | rock like | unto our | God.

4 Talk no more so ex ceeding | proudly;
Let not arrogancy | come out | of your | mouth:

5 For the Lord is a | God of | knowledge,
And by | Him are | actions | weighed.

6 The bows of the mighty | men are | broken,
And they that stumbled | are be girt with | strength.

7 The full have hired out them'selves for | bread;
And the | hungry | they have | ceased:

8 So that the barren | hath borne | seven;
And she that hath many | children is | waxed | feeble.

1 Sam. ii.

LXXXII.

86 I WILL hear what God the | Lord will | speak :
For He will speak | peace un|to his | people,

2 And | to his | saints :
But let them not | turn a|gain to | folly.

3 Surely his salvation is near | them that | fear Him ;
That | glory may | dwell in our | land.

4 Mercy and truth are | met to|gether ;
Righteousness and | peace have | kissed each | other.

5 Truth shall spring | out · of the | earth ;
And righteousness shall | look | down · from the | heavens.

6 Yea, the Lord shall | give | good :
And our | land shall | yield her | increase.

7 Righteousness shall | go be|fore Him,
And shall set us in the | way | of his | steps.   Ps. lxxxv. 8.

LXXXIII.

* *This note is sung only when two syllables fall to this measure.*

87 ALTHOUGH the fig-tree shall not | blossom,
And there shall be no | fruit | in the | vines ;

2 The produce of the olive shall | fail,
And the | fields shall | yield no | food ;

3 The flock shall be cut off from the | fold,
And there shall be no | herd | in the | stalls ;

PRAISE AND THANKSGIVING. 65

4 Yet will I rejoice in the | LORD,
I will joy in the | GOD of | my sal|vation.

5 The LORD JEHOVIH is my | strength,
And He will | make my | feet like | hinds';

6 And He will make me to | walk
Up|on mine | high | places.

Hab. iii. 17.

LXXXIV.

88 THE LORD is the portion of mine inheritance and | of my | cup :
Thou | dost main|tain my | lot.

2 The lines are fallen to me in | pleasant | places ;
Yea, I have a | goodly | heri|tage.

3 I will bless the LORD, Who hath | given me | counsel :
My reins also in|struct me | in the | nights.

4 I have set the LORD | always be|fore me :
Because He is at my right | hand, I shall | not be | moved.

5 Therefore my heart is glad, and my | glory re|joiceth :
My flesh shall | also | rest in | hope.

6 For Thou wilt not leave my | soul in | hell :
Neither wilt Thou suffer thine | Holy One to | see cor|ruption.

7 Thou wilt show me the | path of | life :
In thy | presence is | fulness of | joy ;

8 At | thy right | hand
Are | pleasures for|ever|more.

Ps. xvi. 5.

LXXXV.

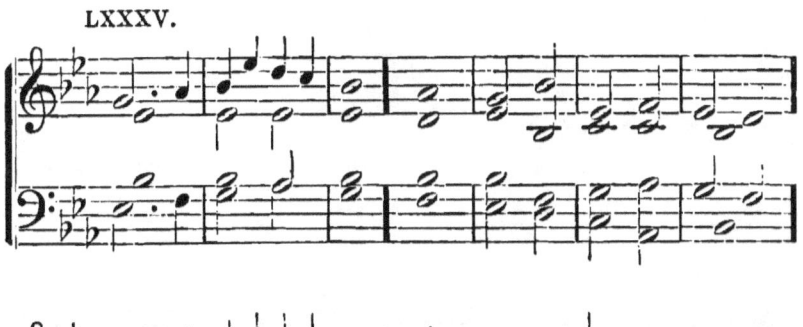

89 FOR Thou, O Lord, | art my | refuge ;
　The Most High hast thou | made thy | habi|tation ;

2 There shall no | evil be|fall thee,
　Neither shall any | plague come | nigh thy | dwelling.

3 For He shall give his angels | charge over | thee,
　To | keep · thee in | all thy | ways.

4 They shall bear thee | up · in their | hands,
　Lest thou dash thy | foot a|gainst a | stone.

5 Thou shalt tread upon the | lion and | adder :
　The young lion and the dragon shalt thou trample | under | feet.

6 Because he hath set his | love up|on Me,
　Therefore will | I de|liver | him :

7 I will | set him · on | high,
　Because he hath | known | my | name.

8 He shall | call up|on Me,
　And | I will | answer | him :

9 I will be | with him · in | trouble ;
　I will de|liver · him, and | honor | him.

10 With length of days will I | satis·fy | him,
　And will | show him | my sal|vation.　　Ps. xci. 9.

PRAISE AND THANKSGIVING. 67

LXXXVI.

90 1 I | LOVE the | Lord,
Because He hath heard my | voice, my | suppli|cations.

2 Because He hath inclined his | ear unto | me,
Therefore will I call up|on · Him as | long · as I | live.

3 The sorrows of death | compassed | me ;
And the pains of hell gat hold upon me ; I | found dis|tress and | sorrow.

4 Then called I upon the | name · of the | Lord :
O Lord, I be|seech · Thee, de|liver my | soul.

5 Gracious is the | Lord, and | righteous ;
Yea, our | God is | merci.ful.

6 The Lord pre'serveth the | simple :
I was brought | low, and He | helped | me.

7 Return unto thy rest, | O my | soul ;
For the Lord hath | dealt | bountifully | with thee.

8 For Thou hast delivered my | soul from | death,
Mine eyes from | tears, my | feet from | falling.

9 3 I will walk be|fore the | Lord
In the | land · of the | liv|ing.   Ps. cxvi.

Dox. O bless our | God, ye | people,
And make the | voice · of his | praise · to be | heard ;
Who holdeth our | soul in | life,
And suffereth | not our | feet · to be | moved. Ps. lxvi. 8.

LXXXVII.

91 O SING unto the Lord a | new | song :
  Sing unto the | Lord | all the | earth.

2 Sing unto the Lord, | bless his | name :
  Proclaim his sal|vation from | day to | day.

3 Declare his glory a|mong the | nations,
  His | wonders a|mong all the | people.

4 For the Lord is great, and | greatly to be | praised ;
  He is to be | feared a|bove all | gods.

5 For all the gods of the | people are | idols ;
  But the | Lord | made the | heavens.

6 Honor and majesty are be|fore his | face ;
  Strength and beauty are | in his | sanctu|ary.

7 Give unto the Lord, O ye kindreds | of the | people,
  Give unto the | Lord | glory and | strength.

8 Give unto the Lord the glory | of his | name :
  Bring an offering, and | come in|to his | courts.

9 ³O worship the Lord in the | beauty of | holiness :
  Tremble be|fore Him, | all the | earth. Ps. xcvi.

PRAISE AND THANKSGIVING.

LXXXVIII.

92   I WILL sing of the mercies of the | Lord for | ever :
   With my mouth will I make known thy | faithful·ness to | all gener|ations.

 2 For I have said, Mercy shall be built | up for | ever :
   Thy faithfulness shalt Thou es|tablish in the | very | heavens.

 3 I have made a covenant | with my | chosen ;
   I have | sworn unto | David my | servant :

 4 Thy seed will I es|tablish for | ever,
   And build up thy | throne to | all gener|ations.

 5 And the heavens shall praise thy | wonders, O | Lord !
   Thy faithfulness also in the congre|gation | of the | saints :

 6 For who in heaven can be com'pared · to the | Lord?
   Who among the sons of the Gods can be | likened | to the | Lord?

 7 God is greatly to be feared in the as|sembly of the | saints,
   And to be reverenced by | all that | are a|bout Him.

 8 O Lord, God of Hosts, who is like unto Thee, | mighty | Lord?
   Or to thy | faith·fulness | round a|bout Thee?

                                                    Ps. lxxxix.

LXXXIX.

93 HE that dwelleth in the secret place | of the · Most | High,
Shall abide under the | shadow | of the · Al|mighty.

2 I will say of the LORD, He is my | refuge and my | fortress ;
My GOD, in | Him | will I | trust.

3 Surely He shall deliver thee from the | snare · of the | fowler,
And from the | noisome | pesti,lence.

4 He shall cover thee with his feathers, and under his | wings ·
shalt thou | trust,
His , truth thy | shield and | buckler.

5 Thou shalt not be afraid for the | terror by | night ;
Nor for the | arrow that | flieth by | day ;

6 Nor for the pestilence that | walketh in | darkness ;
Nor for the destruction | that doth | waste at | noonday.

7 A thousand shall fall at thy side, and ten thousand at | thy
right | hand ;
But it | shall not | come nigh | thee.

8 Only with thine eyes shalt | thou be,hold,
And | see · the re,ward · of the | wicked.   Ps. xci.

XC.

94 WHAT shall I | render to the | LORD,
For all his | bene·fits | toward | me ?

2 I will take the | cup · of sal,vation,
And call upon the | name | of the | LORD.

3 I will pay my | vows · to the | LORD,
Now in the | presence of | all his | people.

PRAISE AND THANKSGIVING. 71

4 Precious in the | sight · of the | Lord
Is the | death | of his | saints.

5 O Lord, truly | I · am thy | servant;
I am thy servant, the son of thine handmaid : | Thou hast | loosed my | bonds.

6 I will offer to Thee the sacrifice of | thanks'giving,
And will call upon the | name | of the | Lord.

7 I will pay my | vows · to the | Lord,
Now in the | presence of | all his | people;

8 In the courts of the | house · of the | Lord;
In the midst of | thee, O Je|rusa|lem.   Ps. cxvi. 12.

XCI.

95 MAKE a joyful noise unto | God, all the | earth :
Sing forth the | honor | of his | name;

2 Make his | praise | glorious.
Say unto God, How terrible | art Thou | in thy | works:

3 Through the greatness | of thy | power,
Shall thine enemies sub|mit them|selves unto | Thee.

4 All the earth shall worship Thee, and | sing unto | Thee:
They shall | sing | unto thy | name.

5 Come and see the | works of | God:
He is terrible in his doing | toward the | chil·dren of | men.

6 He turned the sea into | dry | land:
They went | through the | flood on | foot:

7 There did we re|joice in | Him.
He ruleth by his | power | for|ever:

8 His eyes be|hold the | nations:
Let not the re|bellious · ex|alt them|selves.

9 O bless our | God, ye | people;
And make the | voice · of his | praise · to be | heard:

10 Who holdeth our | soul in | life;
And suffereth | not our | feet · to be | moved.   Ps. lxvi.

XCII.

96 THE heavens are thine, the earth is | also | thine :
The world and the fulness thereof, | Thou hast | founded | them.

2 The north and the south, Thou hast cre'ated | them :
Tabor and Hermon shall re|joice | in thy | name.

3 Thou hast a | mighty | arm :
Strong is thy hand, | high is | thy right | hand.

4 Justice and judgment are the foundation | of thy | throne :
Mercy and truth shall | go be|fore thy | face.

5 Blessed is the people that know the | joyful | sound :
They shall walk, O LORD, in the | light · of thy | counte-| nance.

6 In thy name shall they re'joice · all the | day ;
And in thy righteousness | shall they | be ex|alted.

7 For Thou art the glory | of their | strength :
And in thy favor our | horn shall | be ex|alted.

8 For the LORD is | our de|fence ;
And the HOLY ONE of | Israel | our | King. Ps. lxxxix. 11.

XCIII.

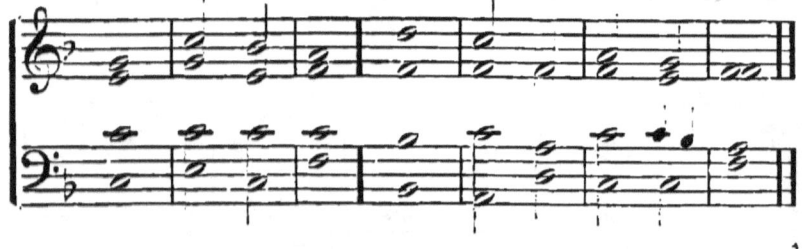

97 O GIVE thanks unto the LORD ; ' call up·on his | name :
Make known his deeds a mong the | people.

2 Sing unto Him, sing psalms unto Him :
Talk ye of | all his | wondrous works.

3 Glory ye in his ' holy ' name :
Let the heart of them re joice that ' seek the ' LORD.

4 Seek the LORD, and ' his strength :
Seek his face for ever more.

5 Remember his marvellous works that ' He hath ' done ;
His wonders, and the judgments of his mouth ;

6 O ye seed of ' Abra·ham his ' servant,
Ye children of ' Jacob his chosen.

7 He is the ' LORD our ' GOD :
His judgments are in ' all the | earth.

8 He hath remembered his ' cove·nant for ' ever ;
The word He commanded, to a | thousand gener·ations.

Ps. cv.

XCIV.

98 GOD is our | refuge and | strength ;
A very | present | help in | trouble.

2 Therefore will not we fear though the | earth · be re|moved,
And though the mountains be cast into the | midst | of the | seas :

3 Though the waters thereof | roar · and be | troubled,
Though the mountains | shake · with the | swelling there|of.

4 There is a river whose streams shall make glad the | city of | GOD,
The holy place of the | tabernacles | of the · Most | High.

5 GOD is in the midst of her, she | shall · not be |moved :
GOD will help her at the | dawn | of the | morning.

6 The heathen raged, the | kingdoms were | moved :
He uttered his | voice, the | earth did | melt.

7 The LORD of | Hosts is | with us ;
The GOD of | Jacob | is our | refuge.   Ps. xlvi.

99 IN GOD will I | praise his | word ;
In the LORD | will I | praise his | word.

2 In GOD do I put my trust ; I | will not | fear :
What can | man | do unto | me.

3 Thy vows are up|on me, O | GOD :
I will render | praises | unto | Thee.

4 For Thou hast delivered my | soul from | death :
Wilt not Thou de|liver my | feet from | falling ?

5 That I may | walk be· fore | GOD
In the | light | of the | living.   Ps. lvi. 10.

PRAISE AND THANKSGIVING.

XCV.

100 O GIVE thanks to the LORD ; for | He is | good :
⁴For his | mercy | is for | ever.

  2 Thus shall the redeemed of the | LORD | say,
    Whom He hath redeemed from the | hand · of the | ene|my ;

  3 And hath gathered them | out · of the | lands,
    From the east, and from the west, from the | north, and | from the | south.

  4 They wandered in the wilderness in a | deso·late | way :
    They found no | city of | habi|tation.

  5 They were | hungry and | thirsty,
    Their | soul did | faint with|in them.

  6 Then they cried unto the | LORD in their | trouble,
    He delivered them | out of | their dis'tresses.

  7 And He led them forth by a | straight | way,
    To go to a | city of | habi|tation.

  8 Let them confess to the | LORD his | mercy,
    And his wonderful | works · to the | chil·dren of | men.

  9 For He satisfieth the | longing | soul,
    And filleth the | hungry | soul with | good   Ps. cvii.

101 PRAISE ye the | Lord.
    Praise ye the Lord | from the | heavens :
Praise ye | Him | in the | heights.

2 Praise ye Him, | all his | angels :
Praise | ye Him, | all his | hosts.

3 Praise ye Him, | sun and | moon :
Praise Him, | all ye | stars of | light.

4 Praise Him, ye | heavens of | heavens ;
And ye waters that | are a|bove the | heavens.

5 Let them praise the | name · of the | Lord ;
For He com|manded, and | they · were cre|ated.

6 He hath also established them for | ever and | ever :
He hath made a de|cree, and it | shall not | pass.

7 He also exalteth the | horn · of his | people,
The | praise of | all his | saints ;

8 Of the | children of | Israel.
   A people | near | unto | Him.
   Praise ye the | LORD.

Ps. cxlviii.

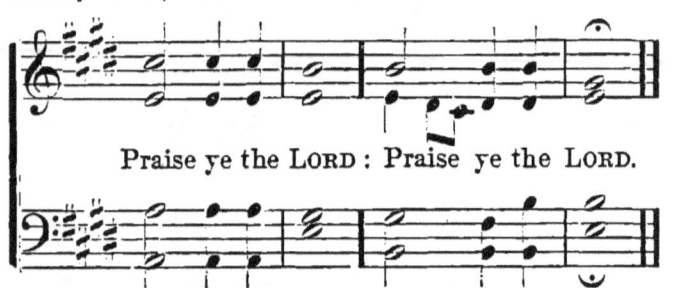

Praise ye the LORD : Praise ye the LORD.

XCVII.

102 O LORD, how are they increased that | trouble | me :
        Many are they that | rise | up a'gainst me.

  2 Many there be who | say · of my | soul,
     There is no | help for | him in | GOD.

  3 But Thou, O LORD, art a | shield for | me ;
     My glory, and the | lifter | up · of my | head.

  4 I cried unto the | LORD · with my | voice,
     And He heard me from the   mountain | of his | holiness.

  5 I laid me | down and | slept :
     I awaked ; for the   LORD | did sus'tain me.

  6 I will not be afraid of ten | thousands of | people,
     That have set themselves a gainst me | round a bout.

  7 A rise, O | LORD ;
     Save | me, | O my | GOD :

  8 For Thou hast smitten all mine enemies up'on the · cheek-|
        bone ;
     Thou hast broken the | teeth | of the · un'godly.

  9 Salvation belongeth | to the | LORD :
     Thy blessing | is up on thy | people.

Ps. iii.

XCVIII.

103 I WILL praise Thee, O | Lord, with | all my | heart ;
 I will declare | all thy | wondrous | works.

2 I will be | glad · and re'joice in | Thee :
 I will sing praise to thy | name, O | Thou Most | High.

3 When mine | ene·mies are | turned | back,
 They shall fall and | perish | at thy | presence.

4 For Thou hast main|tained my | right · and my | cause ;
 Thou sattest in the | throne | judging | right.

5 Thou hast rebuked the heathen, | Thou · hast de|stroyed the | wicked,
 Thou hast put out their | name for'ever and | ever.

6 The enemy, their deso'lations are | ended for|ever :
 And Thou hast destroyed their cities ; their me|mori·al is | perished | with them.

7 But the | Lord shall en'dure for|ever :
 He hath pre'pared his | throne for | judgment ;

8 And He shall judge the | world in | righteous'ness,
 He shall minister judgment to the | people in | upright|ness.

9 The Lord also will be a | refuge | for the · op'pressed,
 A | refuge in | times of | trouble.

10 And they that know thy name will | put their | trust in | Thee :
 For Thou, O Lord, hast not for|saken | them that | seek Thee.   Ps. ix.

PRAISE AND THANKSGIVING.

XCIX.

104 O GIVE thanks unto the Lord ; for | He is | good ;
For his | mercy | is for | ever.

2 They that go down to the | sea in | ships,
That do | business | in great | waters ;

3 These see the | works · of the | Lord,
And his | wonders | in the | deep.

4 For He commandeth, and raiseth the | stormy | wind,
Which lifteth | up the | waves there of.

5 They mount up to heaven, they go | down · to the | depths :
Their soul is | melted be|cause of | trouble.

6 They reel and stagger like a | drunken | man ;
And all their | wisdom is | brought to | naught.

7 Then they cry unto the | Lord · in their | trouble,
And He bringeth them | out of | their dis|tresses.

8 He maketh the | storm a | calm,
And the | waves there of are | still.

9 Then are they glad be'cause · they are | quiet :
And He bringeth them unto the | haven of | their de|sire.

10 Let them confess to the | Lord his | mercy,
And his wonderful | works · to the | chil·dren of | men.

Ps. cvii. 1, 23.

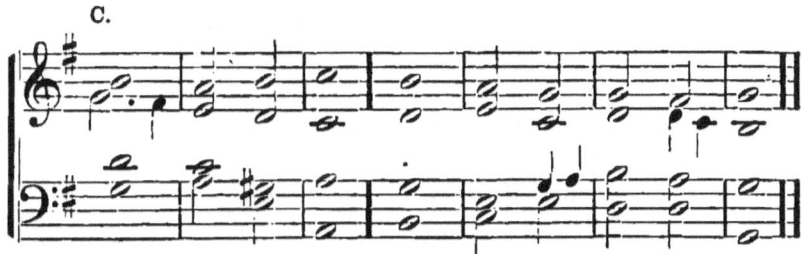

105 MANY, O | Lord, my | God,
   Are thy wonderful | works which | Thou hast | done,

2 And thy | thoughts toward | us :
  They cannot be reckoned up in | order | unto | Thee.

3 If I would declare and | speak of | them,
  They are | more than | can be | numbered.

4 Sacrifice and offering Thou didst | not de|sire :
  Mine | ears | hast Thou | opened.

5 Burnt-offering and | sin-'offering
  Hast | Thou | not re|quired.

6 Then said I, | lo, I | come :
  In the volume of the | book · it is | written of | me,

7 I delight to do thy will, | O my | God :
  Yea, thy | law · is with,in my | heart.

8 I have preached righteousness in the | great congre'gation :
  Lo, I have not refrained my | lips, O | Lord, Thou | knowest.

9 I have not hid thy righteousness with'in my | heart ;
  I have declared thy | faithful·ness and | thy sal|vation.

10 I have not concealed thy | loving-|kindness
   And thy | truth · from the | great congre|gation. Ps. xl. 5.

* *This note is sung only when two syllables fall to this measure.*

106 PRAISE ye the Lord. O give thanks to the Lord, for
   He is | good ;
   For his | mercy | is for | ever.

2 Who can utter the mighty acts of the | LORD?
  Who can | show forth | all his | praise?

3 Blessed are they that keep | judgment,
  And he that doeth | righteous'ness | at all | times.

4 Remember me, O | LORD,
  With the favor that Thou | bearest | to thy | people.

5 O visit me with thy sal'vation;
  That I may | see the | good · of thy | chosen;

6 That I may rejoice in the joy of thy | nation;
  That I may | glory with | thine in|heritance.   Ps. cvi.

CII.

107 THE LORD hear thee in the | day of | trouble;
    The name of the | GOD of | Jacob de|fend thee.

2 Send thee help from the | sanctu|ary,
  And sus'tain thee | out of | Zion.

3 Remember all thy | offer'ings,
  And accept thy | burnt | sacri|fice.

4 Grant thee according to | thine own | heart,
  And ful'fil | all thy | counsel.

5 We will rejoice in | thy sal|vation,
  And in the | name · of our | GOD · will we | triumph.

6 The LORD fulfil | all · thy pe|titions.
  Now know I that the LORD | saveth | his an|ointed:

7 He will hear him from his | holy | heaven,
  With the saving | strength of | his right | hand.

8 Some trust in chariots, and | some in | horses:
  But we will remember the | name of the | LORD our | GOD.

9 They are brought | down and | fallen:
  But we are | risen, and | stand | upright.

10 Save, | O | LORD!
   Let the King | hear us | when we | call.   Ps. xx.

CIII.

108 LET them exalt Him in the congre|gation of the | people,
And praise Him in the as|sembly | of the | elders.

2 He turneth rivers into a | wilder'ness,
Springs of | water | into dry | ground ;

3 A fruitful land into ' barren|ness,
For the wickedness of | them that | dwell there|in.

4 He turneth the wilderness into a | pool of | waters,
And dry | land into | water-|springs.

5 And there He maketh the | hungry to | dwell,
That they may prepare a | city for | habi|tation ;

6 And sow the fields, and | plant | vineyards,
Which may | yield | fruits of | increase.

7 He blesseth them also, and they are | multi·plied | greatly ;
And He suffereth not their | cattle | to de|crease.

8 Again, they are minished and | brought | low,
Through op|pression, af|fliction, and | sorrow.

9 He poureth con'tempt upon | princes,
And causeth them to wander | in a | pathless | waste.

10 Yet setteth He the poor on | high · from af|fliction,
And maketh him | families | like a | flock.

PRAISE AND THANKSGIVING. 83

11 The righteous shall | see, and re|joice;
And all in,iqui·ty shall | stop her | mouth.

12 Whoso is wise, and will ob|serve these | things,
Even they shall understand the loving-|kindness | of the | LORD.   Ps. cvii. 32.

CIV.

109 O SING unto the LORD a | new | song;
    For | He hath · done | wondrous | things:

2 His right hand, and his | holy | arm,
Hath gotten | Him the | victo|ry.

3 The LORD hath made | known · his sal|vation:
His righteousness hath He openly | showed · in the | sight · of the | nations.

4 He hath remembered his mercy | and his | truth
Toward the | house of | Isra|el.

5 All the | ends · of the | earth
Have seen the sal|vation | of our | GOD.

6 Make a joyful noise unto the | LORD, all the | earth;
Make a loud noise, and re|joice, and | sing | praise.

7 Sing unto the | LORD with the | harp,
With the | harp, and the | voice · of a | psalm.

8 With trumpets and | sound of | cornet,
Make a joyful noise be|fore the | LORD, the | King.

9 Let the sea roar, and the | fulness there|of;
The world, and | they that | dwell there|in.

10 Let the floods | clap their | hands:
Let the·| mountains be | joyful to|gether.

11 Before the LORD; for He cometh to | judge the | earth:
He shall judge the world in righteousness, and the | people in | upright|ness.   Ps. xcviii.

CV.

110 PRAISE ye the | LORD.
  Praise GOD in his | sanctu|ary :
Praise Him in the | firma·ment | of his | power.

2 Praise Him for his | mighty | acts :
  Praise Him ac|cording to his | excel·lent | greatness.

3 Praise Him with the | sound · of the | trumpet :
  Praise Him with the | psal·tery | and the | harp.

4 Praise Him with the | tim·brel and | dance :
  Praise Him with | stringed instru|ments and | organs.

5 Praise Him up|on the · loud | cymbals :
  Praise Him up|on the | high-sounding | cymbals.

6 Let | every | thing
  That hath | breath | praise the | LORD.
  Praise ye the | LORD.   Ps. cl.

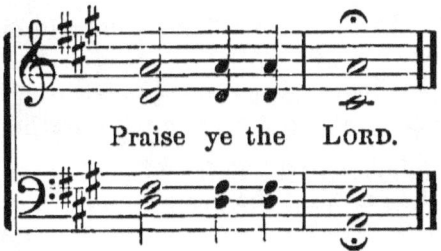

PROPHECY AND PROMISE. 85

CVI.

111 O ZION, that | bringest | good | tidings,
Get thee up | into the | high | mountain.

2 O Jerusalem, that | bringest | good | tidings,
Lift | up thy | voice with | strength.

3 Lift it | up, be | not a|fraid :
Say unto the cities of | Judah, Be|hold your | GOD.

4 Behold, the LORD JE'HOVIH will | come in | strength ;
And his | arm shall | rule for | Him.

5 Behold, his re|ward is | with | Him,
And his | work be fore | Him.

6 He shall | feed his | flock · like a | shepherd ;
He shall | gather the | lambs · with his | arm ;

7 And shall | carry | them · in his | bosom :
And shall gently | lead · those that | are with | young.

         Is. xl. 9.

112 REJOICE | greatly, O | daughter of | Zion ;
Shout, O | daughter of Je|rusa|lem.

2 Behold, thy | King | cometh unto | thee :
He is | just, and | having sal|vation ;

3 Lowly, and | rid·ing up|on an ' ass ;
And upon a | colt, the | foal · of an | ass.

4 And I will cut | off the ' chari·ot from | Ephraim,
And the | horse · from Je|rusa,lem.

5 And the battle-|bow shall | be cut ' off :
And He shall speak | peace un to the | heathen.-

6 And his dominion shall | be from | sea to | sea,
And from the | river to the | ends · of the | earth.

         Zech. ix. 9.

SELECTIONS AND CHANTS.

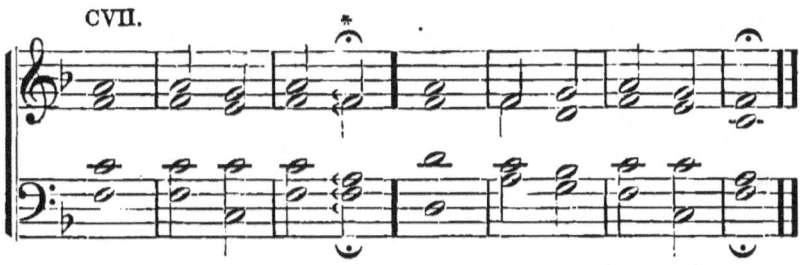

CVII.

* *This note is sung only when two syllables fall to this measure.*

113 OH that Thou wouldst rend the heavens, that Thou | wouldst come | down,
That the mountains | might flow | down · at thy | presence;

2 As when the melting | fire | burneth,
The fire doth | cause the | waters to | boil;

3 To make thy name known to thine | adver|saries,
That the nations may | tremble | at thy | presence.

4 When Thou didst terrible things we | looked not | for,
Thou camest down; the mountains | flowed | down · at thy | [presence.

5 For | from of | old,
They have not | heard · nor per|ceived · by the | ear;

6 Neither hath the eye seen, O GOD, a|side from | Thee,
What He hath prepared for | him that | waiteth | for Him.

7 Thou meetest him that rejoiceth and worketh | righteous|ness,
Those that re|member | Thee · in thy | ways.   Is. lxiv.

CVIII.

114 THE people that | walked in | darkness,
Have | seen a | great | light:

2 They that dwell in the land of the | shadow of | death,
Upon | them hath the | light | shined. . . . .

3 For unto us a | CHILD is | born,
Unto | us a | SON is | given:

4 And the government shall be up|on his | shoulder;
And his | name | shall be | called,

PROPHECY AND PROMISE.

5 Wonderful, Counsellor, the | mighty | God,
Father of e|terni·ty, | Prince of | Peace.

6 Of the increase of his government and peace there shall | be no | end,
Upon the throne of David, | and up|on his | kingdom;

7 To order it, and to es|tablish | it,
With | judgment | and with | justice.

8 From henceforth | even for | ever:
The zeal of the Lord of | Hosts will per|form | this.
Is. ix.

CIX.

115 THE Spirit of the Lord Je|hovih is up|on me;
Because the Lord hath an|ointed | me,
To preach glad | tidings | to the | meek.

2 He hath sent me to bind up the | broken-|hearted,
To proclaim liberty | to the | captives,
And the opening of the | prison | to the | bound:

3 To proclaim the acceptable | year · of the | Lord,
And the day of vengeance | of our | God:
To | comfort | all that | mourn:

4 To appoint unto them that | mourn in | Zion;
To give unto them | beauty for | ashes,
The | oil of | joy for | mourning:

5 The garment of praise for the | spirit of | heavi·ness;
That they may be called | trees of | righteous·ness;
The planting of the Lord, that He | might be | glori'fied.
Is. lxi.

116 THERE shall come forth a Rod out of the | stem of | Jesse,
And a Branch shall | grow out | of his | roots.

2 And the Spirit of the LORD shall | rest up on him,
The Spirit of | wis·dom and | under|standing,

3 The Spirit of counsel | and of | might,
The Spirit of knowledge and of the | fear | of the | LORD ;

4 And shall make him quick of | under|standing,
In the | fear | of the | LORD.

5 And he shall not judge after the | sight · of his | eyes,
Neither reprove after the | hearing | of his | ears.

6 But with righteousness shall he judge the | poor,
And reprove with equity | for the | meek · of the | earth.

7 And he shall smite the earth with the | rod · of his | mouth ;
And with the breath of his | lips · shall he | slay the | wicked.

8 And righteousness shall be the girdle | of his | loins,
And faithfulness the | girdle | of his | reins.   Is. xi.

117 THE wolf shall | dwell · with the | lamb ;
And the leopard | shall lie | down · with the | kid :

2 And the calf, and the young lion, and the | fat·ling to|gether ;
And a | little | child shall | lead them.

3 And the cow and the | bear shall | feed :
¹Their young ones shall lie down to gether ;
And the | lion shall eat | straw · like the | ox.

4 And the sucking child shall play on the | hole · of the | asp ;
  And the weaned child shall put his | hand up·on the | cocka·- [trice' | den.
5 They shall not | hurt · nor de|stroy,
  In all the | mountain of my | holi|ness :
6 For the earth shall be full of the | knowledge of the | LORD,
  As the | waters | cover the | seas.   Is. xi. 6.

CXII.

118 HOW beautiful up|on the | mountains
      Are the feet of | him that | bringeth good | tidings,
  2 That pro|claimeth | peace,
    That | bringeth good | tidings of | good,
  3 ³That pro|claimeth sal|vation ;
    That saith to | Zion, | Thy GOD | reigneth.
  4 Thy watchmen shall lift | up the | voice :
    With the voice to|gether | shall they | sing.
  5 For they shall see | eye to | eye,
    When the | LORD shall | bring a·gain | Zion.
  6 Break | forth into | joy ;
    Sing together, ye waste | places of Je|rusa|lem :
  7 For the LORD hath | comfort·ed his | people ;
    He hath re|deemed Je|rusa|lem.
  8 The LORD hath made bare his | holy | arm,
    In the | eyes of | all the | nations ;
  9 And all the | ends · of the | earth
    Shall see the sal|vation | of our | GOD.   Is. lii. 7.

CXIII.

119 BEHOLD, the tabernacle of | GOD | is with | men,
 And He will | dwell with | them,

2 And they shall | be his | people,
 And GOD Himself shall be | with them, | their | GOD.

3 And GOD shall wipe a|way all | tears · from their | eyes;
 And death shall | be no | more;

4 Neither shall there be mourning, nor crying, nor | pain any | more;
 For the former | things are | passed a|way.   Rev. xxi.

CXIV.

120 THE bread of GOD is He that cometh | down from | heaven,
 And giveth | life un|to the | world. . . . .

2 He that cometh to Me shall | never | hunger,
 And he that believeth on | Me shall | never | thirst. . . . .

3 This is the bread that cometh | down from | heaven,
 That one may | eat there,of, and not | die.

PROPHECY AND PROMISE. 91

4 I am the living bread that came | down from | heaven :
If any one eat of this | bread, he shall | live for | ever.

5 And the bread that I will give | is my | flesh,
Which I will | give · for the | life · of the | world.

6 And the Spirit and the | Bride say, | Come :
And let him that | heareth | say, | Come :

7 And let him that | thirsteth | come :
And let him that willeth take | water of | life | freely.
John vi. 33, 35, 50, 51 : Rev. xxii. 17.

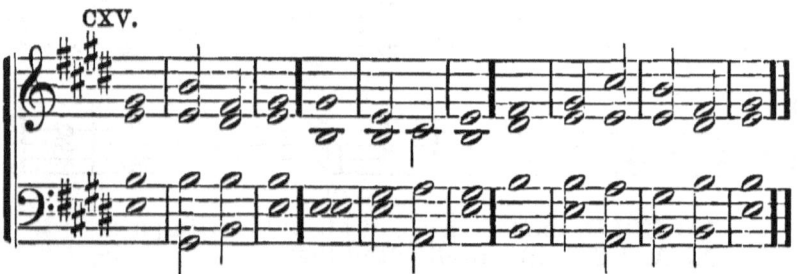

CXV.

121 HEAR ye this, O | house of | Jacob,
That are called by the name of | Isra|el,
And are come forth | out · of the | waters of | Judah :

2 Who swear by the | name · of the | LORD,
And make mention of the GOD of | Isra|el ;
But not in | truth, nor in | righteous|ness.

3 For they call themselves of the | holy | city,
And stay themselves upon the GOD of | Isra|el :
The | LORD of | Hosts · is his | name.

4 I have declared the former things | from · the be|ginning ;
And they went out of my | mouth, and I | showed them :
I did them suddenly, | and they | came to | pass. . . . .

5 Thus saith the LORD, thy Redeemer, the HOLY ONE of | Isra|el ;
I am the LORD thy GOD, Who teacheth | thee to | profit,
Who leadeth thee by the | way that | thou shou|dst | go.

6 O that thou hadst hearkened to | my com|mandments ;
Then had thy peace | been · as a | river,
And thy righteousness | as the | waves · of the | sea :

7 Thy seed also had | been · as the | sand,
And the offspring of thy bowels as the | gravel there|of :
His name should not have been cut | off · nor de|stroyed
from be|fore Me.
Is. xlviii.

CXVI.

122 I WILL | heal their back|sliding;
I will | love them | freely:
For mine anger is turned a|way | from him

2 I will be as the dew unto | Isra|el:
He shall | grow · as the | lily,
And cast forth his roots as | Leba|non.

3 His | branches shall | spread,
And his beauty shall be as the | olive-|tree,
And his smell shall be as | Leba|non.

4 They that dwell under his shadow | shall re|turn;
They shall revive as the corn, and | grow · as the | vine;
The scent thereof shall be as the wine of | Leba|non. . . . .

5 Who'so is | wise,
And he shall under'stand these | things;
Prudent, and | he shall | know them.

6 For the ways of the | LORD are | right;
And the just shall | walk in | them:
But the transgressors shall | fall there|in.

Hos. xiv. 4–7, 9.

CXVII.

123 GOOD and upright | is the | LORD;
Therefore will He teach | sinners | in the | way.

2 The meek will He | guide in | judgment:
And the | meek will He | teach his | way.

3 All the paths of the LORD are | mercy and | truth,
To those that keep his covenant | and his | testi|monies.

PROPHECY AND PROMISE. 93

4 For thy name's sake, O Lord,
Pardon mine iniquity, for · it is great.

5 What man is he that feareth the Lord?
Him shall He teach in the way that He shall choose.

6 His soul shall dwell in good;
And his seed shall inherit the earth.

7 The secret of the Lord is with them that fear Him,
And his covenant; to give them knowledge.
Ps. xxv. 8.

CXVIII.

124 BLESSED is the nation whose God · is the Lord;
The people He hath chosen for his own inheritance.

2 The Lord looketh from the heavens;
He beholdeth all the sons of men.

3 From the place of his habitation He looketh
Upon all the inhabitants of the earth.

4 He fashioneth their hearts alike;
He considereth all their works. . . . .

5 Behold, the eye of the Lord is upon them that fear Him,
Upon them that hope · in his mercy.

6 To deliver their soul from · death,
And to keep · them alive in famine.

7 Our soul waiteth for the Lord:
He is our help and our shield.

8 For our heart shall rejoice in Him:
Because we have trusted in his holy name.

9 Let thy mercy, O Lord, be upon us,
According as we hope in Thee.
Ps. xxxiii. 12.

CXIX.

125 1 IF thou take away from the | midst of thee the | yoke,
    The putting forth of the finger, and | speaking | vani|ty ;

2 And if thou draw out thy | soul · to the | hungry,
   And | satis·fy th' af|flicted | soul ;

3 Then shall thy light | rise · in ob'scurity,
   And thy | darkness shall be | as the | noonday.

4 And the Lord shall | guide thee con|tinually,
   And satisfy thy soul in | drought, and make | fat thy | bones.

5 And thou shalt be like a | watered | garden ;
   And like a spring of water, whose | waters | do not | fail.

6 And they that shall be of thee shall build the | old waste | places :
   Thou shalt raise up the foundations of | many | gener|ations.

7 And thou shalt be called, the re|pairer of the | breach,
   The re|storer of | paths to | dwell in.

---

8 If thou turn away thy | foot · from the | sabbath,
   From doing thy pleasure | on my | holy | day ;

9 And call the | sabbath a de|light,
   The | holy of the | Lord, | honorable ;

10 And shalt honor Him, not doing | thine own | ways,
    Nor finding thine own pleasure, nor | speaking | thine own | words ;

11 Then shalt thou delight thy|self · in the | Lord ;
    And I will cause thee to ride upon the high | places | of the | earth ;

12 And feed thee with the heritage of | Jacob thy | father :
    For the mouth of the | Lord hath | spoken | it.

                                                Is. lviii. 9.

PROPHECY AND PROMISE.

CXX.—*This Chant may be sung in unison.*

126 FOR Zion's sake will I not | hold my | peace,
And for Jerusalem's | sake I | will not | rest;

2 Until the righteousness thereof go | forth as | brightness,
And the salvation there|of · as a | lamp that | burneth.

3 And the Gentiles shall | see thy | righteous·ness,
And | all | kings thy | glory:

4 And thou shalt be | called by a | new name,
Which the | mouth of the | LORD shall | name.

5 Thou shalt be a crown of glory in the | hand · of the | LORD,
And a royal diadem in the | hand | of thy | GOD.

6 Thou shalt no more be | termed, For|saken;
Neither shall thy land any | more be | termed, | Deso·late.

7 But thou shalt be called, My de|light is | in her ·
And | thy | land, the | Married:

8 For the LORD de|lighteth | in thee;
And thy | land | shall be | married.

9 For as a young man doth | mar·ry a | virgin,
So shall thy | sons | marry | thee:

10 And as the bridegroom rejoiceth | o·ver the | bride,
So shall thy GOD re|joice | over | thee.   Is. lxii.

CXXI. *Unison Chant.*

127 SING, O barren, thou that | didst not | bear ;
Break forth into singing, and cry aloud, thou that didst not | travail with | child ;

2 For more are the children of the | deso|late,
Than the children of the married | wife, saith the | LORD.

3 Enlarge the | place · of thy | tent,
And let them stretch forth the curtains of thine | habi|tations :

4 Spare not ; | lengthen thy | cords,
And | strengthen thy | stakes.

5 For thou shalt | break | forth,
On the right hand and | on the | left :

6 And thy seed shall in|herit the | Gentiles,
And make the desolate cities to be in|habit|ed.

7 Fear not ; for thou shalt | not be a|shamed :
Neither be thou confounded ; for thou shalt not be | put to | shame :

8 For thou shalt forget the | shame · of thy | youth,
And shalt not remember the reproach of thy widowhood | any | more.

9 For thy | Maker is thy | husband ;
The LORD of | Hosts is his | name ;

10 And thy Redeemer the HOLY ONE of | Isra|el ;
The GOD of the whole earth shall | He be | called.

Is. liv.

PROPHECY AND PROMISE. 97

CXXII.

128 AND in that day thou shalt say, O LORD, | I will | praise
    Thee,
    Though | Thou wast | angry | with me.

2 Thine anger is | turned a|way.
  And | Thou hast | comfort·ed | me.

3 Behold, GOD is | my sal·vation ;
  I will | trust, and | not · be a fraid :

4 For the LORD JEHOVAH is my | strength and | song ;
  He also is be come | my sal vation.

5 Therefore with joy shall | ye draw | water,
  Out of the | wells | of sal vation.

6 And in that | day shall ye | say,
  Praise the LORD, | call up|on his | name ;

7 Declare his doings a mong the | people ;
  Make mention that his | name | is ex alted.

8 Sing unto the | LORD ;
  For He | hath done | excel·lent | things :

9 This is made known in | all the | earth :
  Cry out and shout, thou in habi tant of | Zion :

10 For great in the | midst of | thee
   Is the HOLY | ONE of | Isra|el.   Is. xii.

CXXIII.

129 THE wilderness and the | barren | place
　　　Shall | be | glad | for them;

2 And the desert | shall re|joice,
　And | blossom | as the | rose.

3 It shall blossom a|bundant|ly,
　And rejoice | even with | joy and | singing.

4 The glory of Lebanon shall be | given | to it,
　The excellency of | Carmel | and of | Sharon.

5 They shall see the | glory of the | LORD,
　The | excel·lency | of our | GOD.

6 Strengthen | ye the · weak | hands,
　And con|firm the | feeble | knees.

7 Say to them of | fearful | heart,
　Be | strong, | fear | not.

8 Behold, your GOD will | come with | vengeance,
　GOD with a recompense; | He will | come and | save you.

9 Then the eyes of the | blind · shall be | opened,
　And the ears of the | deaf shall | be un|stopped.

10 Then shall the lame | leap · as an | hart,
　And the | tongue · of the | dumb shall | sing.　Is. xxxv.

CXXIV.

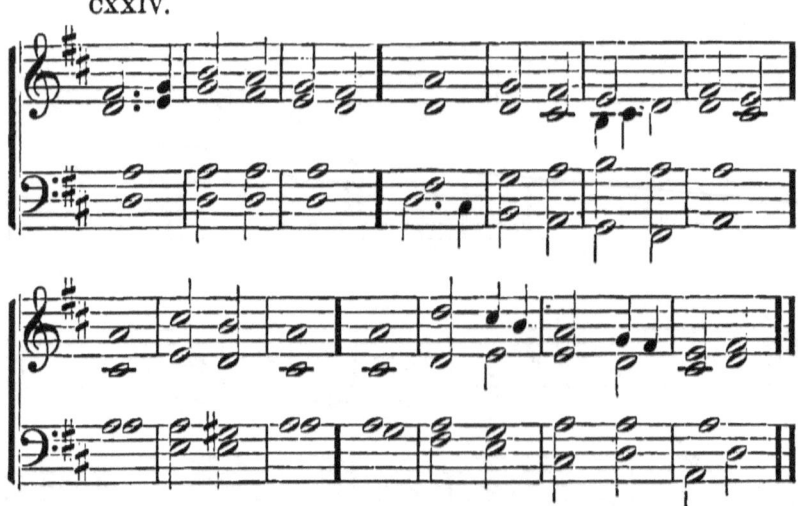

130 THEN shall the eyes of the | blind be | opened,
And the ears of the | deaf shall | be un͵stopped.

2 Then shall the lame | leap · as an | hart,
And the | tongue · of the | dumb shall | sing.

3 For in the wilderness shall | waters break | out,
And | streams | in the | desert :

4 And the parched ground shall be|come a | pool,
And the thirsty | land | springs of | water.

5 In the habitation of dragons, | where each | lay,
Shall be | grass for | reeds and | rushes.

6 And an highway shall be | there, and a | way ;
And it shall be | called the | way of | holi·ness :

7 The unclean shall not | pass | over it,
But | it shall | be for | those :

8 The | wayfaring | men,
Though | fools, | shall not | err.

9 No lion | shall be | there,
Nor any ravenous | beast · shall go | up there|on :

10 It shall not be | found | there ;
But the re|deemed shall | walk | there.

11 And the ransomed of the LORD shall return, and | come to | Zion,
With songs, and everlasting | joy up|on their | heads.

12 They shall obtain | joy and | gladness,
And sorrow and | sigh·ing shall | flee a|way.   Is. xxxv. 5.

CXXV. *The 1st and 2d strains may be sung in unison.*

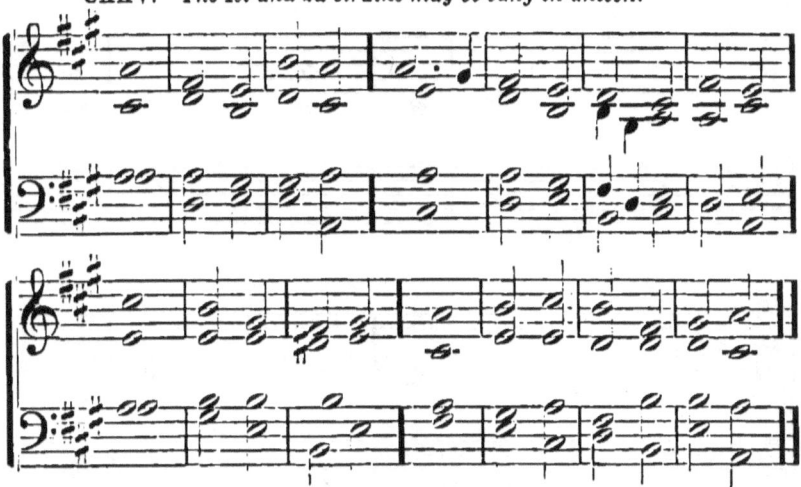

131 BUT now thus saith the LORD, that cre|ated thee, O |
     And He that formed thee, O | Isra·el ; [Jacob ;
  2 Fear not ; for | I · have re|deemed thee :
    I have called thee by thy | name, | thou art | mine.
  3 When thou passest through the waters, | I · will be | with thee ;
    And through the rivers, they | shall not ' over|flow thee :
  4 When thou walkest through the fire, thou shalt not be |
    Neither shall the | flame | kindle up|on thee.   [burned ;
  5 For I am the | LORD, thy GOD,
    The Holy One of | Isra el, thy | Saviour :
  6 I gave | Egypt for thy ' ransom,
    Ethi opi·a and | Seba | for thee.
  7 Since thou wast precious | in my | sight,
    Thou hast been | honored, and | I have | loved thee :
  8 Therefore will I give ' men for | thee,
    And | people for thy life.
  9 Fear not thou ; for | I am | with thee :
    I will bring thy seed from the east, and | gather | thee · from
 10 I will say to the | north, Give ' up ;   [the | west :
    And to the | south, Keep not back :
 11 Bring my sons from far, and my daughters from the | ends
       of the ' earth :
    Every one that is called ' by my | name ;
 12 For I have created him for my | glory :
    I have | formed him ; | yea, I have | made him. Is. xliii.

CXXVI.

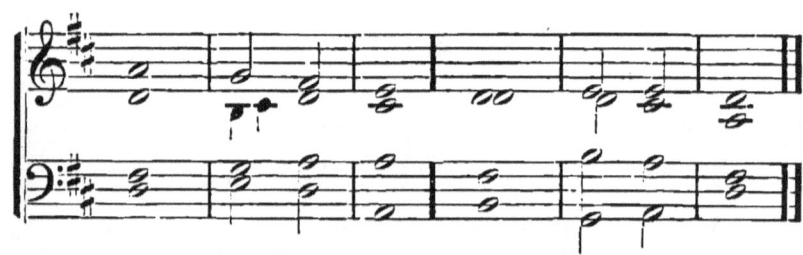

132 YET now hear, O | Jacob, my | servant ;
     And Israel, whom | I have | chosen :

2 Thus saith the LORD Who ˙ made thee,
  And formed thee from the womb, , Who will | help thee :

3 Fear not, O | Jacob, my | servant ;
  And thou, Jesurun, whom | I have | chosen :

4 For I will pour water upon ˈ him · that is | thirsty,
  And floods up on the · dry | ground.

5 I will pour my Spirit up on thy | seed,
  And my blessing up on thine | offspring :

6 And they shall spring up as a mong the | grass,
  As willows by the | water- courses.

7 One shall say, ˈ I · am the ˈ LORD's ;
  And another shall call himself by the | name of | Jacob : ·

8 And another shall subscribe with his ˈ hand · to the | LORD,
  And surname himself by the name of | Isra el.

9 Thus saith the LORD, the King of ˈ Isra el ;
  And his Redeemer, the   LORD of | Hosts ;

10 I am the First, and | I the | Last ;
   And beside Me there | is no | GOD.   Is. xliv.

CXXVII.

133 FOR thy | Maker is thy | husband ;
The | LORD of | Hosts ᐧ is his | name :
2 And thy Redeemer, the HOLY ONE of | Isra|el ;
The GOD of the whole | earth shall | He be | called.

3 For the | LORD hath | called thee,
As a woman for,sa·ken and | grieved in | spirit,
4 And a | wife of | youth,
When thou wast re|fused, | saith thy | GOD.

5 For a small moment have I for'saken | thee ;
But with great mercies | will I | gather | thee.
6 In a little wrath I hid my face from thee | for a | moment ;
But with everlasting kindness will I have mercy on thee, |
saith the ᐧ LORD | thy Re|deemer.

7 For this is as the waters of | Noah unto | me :
For as I have sworn that the waters of Noah should no |
more go | o·ver the | earth ;
8 So | have I | sworn
That I would not be | wroth with | thee, nor re|buke thee.

9 For the mountains shall depart, and the ᐧ hills ᐧ be re'moved ;
But my kindness shall | not de|part from | thee,
10 Neither shall the covenant of my | peace ᐧ be re|moved,
Saith the LORD | That hath | mer·cy up|on thee.

Is. liv. 5.

134 O | THOU af'flicted,
Tossed with | tempest, and not | comfort|ed,
2 Behold, I will lay thy | stones with ᐧ fair | colors,
And | lay ᐧ thy foun|dations with | sapphires.

PROPHECY AND PROMISE. 103

3 And I will make thy windows of agates, and thy gates of |
 And all thy | bor·ders of precious stones. [carbuncles,
4 And all thy children shall be | taught · of the | LORD ;
 And | great shall be the | peace · of thy | children.
5 In righteousness | shalt thou be es·tablished :
 Thou | shalt be | far · from op|pression,
6 For thou shalt not | fear ;
 And from terror, | for it shall | not come | near thee.
7 Behold, they shall surely | gath·er to|gether,
 But | not | by | Me :
8 Whosoever shall gather to|gether a|gainst thee,
 Shall | fall | for thy | sake.
9 Behold, I have cre|ated the | smith,
 That | bloweth the | coals in the fire,
10 And that bringeth forth an instrument | for his | work ;
 And I have created the | waster | to de·stroy.
11 No weapon that is formed against thee shall prosper ;
 And every tongue that shall rise against thee in judgment |
  thou · shalt con·demn.
12 This is the heritage of the | servants of the LORD ;
 And their righteousness | is of | Me, saith the | LORD. 11.

CXXVIII.

135 BLESSED is every one that | feareth the | LORD ;
    That walketh | in his | ways.
 2 For thou shalt eat the labor | of thine | hands :
  Happy shalt thou be, and it shall be | well with | thee.
 3 Thy wife shall be as a | fruitful | vine
  By the sides | of thy | house :
 4 Thy children like | olive | plants
  Round a|bout thy | table.
 5 Behold that thus shall the | man be | blessed
  That | feareth the LORD.
 6 The LORD shall bless thee | out of | Zion :   [thy | life.
  And thou shalt see the good of Jerusalem all the | days · of
 7 Yea, thou shalt see thy | children's | children,
  And | peace upon | Israel.   Ps. cxxviii.

CXXIX.

136 ARISE, shine, for thy | light is | come;
  And the glory of the | LORD is | risen up | on thee :
2 For, behold, darkness shall | cover the | earth,
  And | gross | dark·ness the | people.
3 But the LORD shall a'rise upon | thee ;
  And his | glory shall be | seen up'on thee.
4 And the Gentiles shall | come · to thy | light,
  And kings to the | brightness ˏ of thy ˏ rising.
5 Lift up thine eyes round a'bout, and | see :
  All they gather themselves to gether, they | come to | thee.
6 Thy sons shall | come from | far,
  And thy | daughters shall be ˏ nursed at thy | side.
7 Then thou shalt see, and ' flow to'gether ;
  And thy heart shall | fear, and | be en|larged :
8 Because the abundance of the sea shall be con|verted unto | thee ;
  The forces of the | Gentiles shall | come unto | thee.
9 The multitude of camels shall | cover | thee,
  The dromedaries of | Mid·ian ˏ and of ˏ Ephah.
10 All they from Sheba shall come ; they shall bring | gold and | incense ;
  And they shall show forth the | praises | of the | LORD.
11 All the flocks of Kedar shall be gathered | unto | thee ;
  The rams of Nebaioth shall | minis·ter | unto | thee.
12 They shall come up with acceptance | on mine | altar ;
  And I will glorify the | house | of my | glory.   Is. lx.

PROPHECY AND PROMISE. 105

CXXX.

137 VIOLENCE shall no more be | heard · in thy | land,
Wasting nor de|struction with|in thy | borders :

2 But thou shalt call thy | walls, Sal|vation,
And | thy | gates, | Praise.

3 The sun shall be no more thy | light by | day ;
Neither for brightness shall the | moon give | light unto | thee :

4 But the LORD shall be unto thee an ever|lasting | light,
And thy | GOD thy | glo|ry.

5 Thy sun shall no | more go | down ;
Neither shall thy | moon with|draw it|self :

6 For the LORD shall be thine ever|lasting | light ;
And the days of thy | mourning | shall be | ended.

7 Thy people also shall | be all | righteous :
They shall in|herit the | land for|ever :

8 The | branch · of my | planting,
The work of my hands, that | I · may be | glori|fied.

9 A little one shall be|come a | thousand,
And a | small · one a | strong | nation :

10 I | the | LORD
Will | hasten it | in his | time.

Is. lx. 18.

CXXXI.

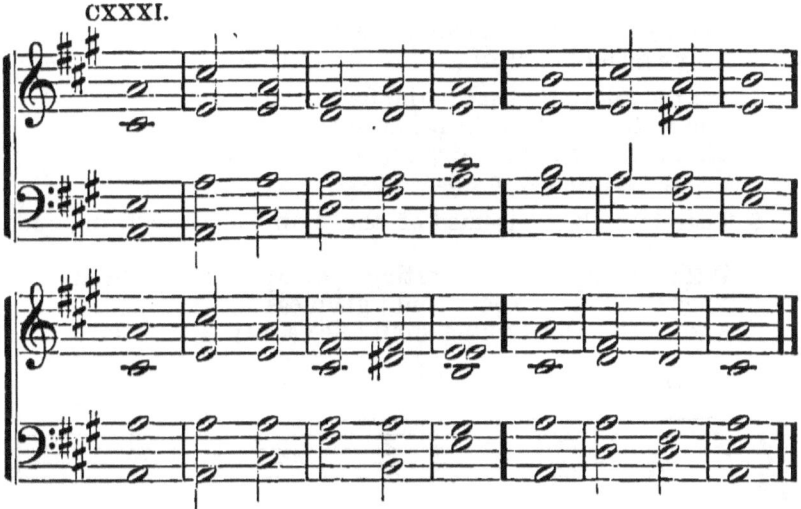

138 AND they shall build | houses, | and in|habit;
  They shall plant vineyards, and eat the | fruit | of them.
2 They shall not | build, and an|other in|habit;
  They shall not plant, and an|other | eat.
3 For as the days of a | tree · are the | days · of my | people;
  And mine elect shall long enjoy the | work · of their | hands.
4 They | shall not | labor in | vain,
  Nor bring | forth for | trouble:
5 For they are the seed of the | blessed | of the | LORD,
  And their | offspring | with them.
6 And it shall come to pass, that be|fore they | call, I will | answer;
  And while they are yet speaking, | I will | hear. [answer;
7 The wolf and the | lamb shall | feed to|gether;
  And the lion shall eat | straw · like the | bullock;
8 And | dust shall be the | serpent's | meat:
  They shall not hurt nor destroy in all my holy mountain, | saith the | LORD.   Is. lxv. 21.

139 HEARKEN unto me, ye that | know | righteous|ness;
  The people in whose | heart · is my | law:
2 Fear ye | not · the re|proach of | men,
  Neither be ye afraid of | their re|vilings.
3 For the moth shall | eat them | up · like a | garment,
  And the worm shall eat them | up like | wool.
4 But my righteousness | shall en|dure for | ever.
  And my salvation from generation to | gener|ation.
5 Awake, a|wake, | put on | strength,
  O | arm · of the | LORD:

PROPHECY AND PROMISE. 107

6 Awake as | in the | ancient | days,
 In the gener|ations of | old. . . . .
7 Art thou not | it · that hath | dried the | sea,
 The waters of the | great | deep?
8 That hath made the | depths · of the | sea a |way
 For the ransomed to | pass | over?
9 Therefore the redeemed of the LORD shall re|turn, and |
  come to | Zion,
 With singing, and everlasting | joy up·on their | head :
10 They shall ob|tain joy | and | gladness ;
 And sorrow and sighing shall | flee a|way.   Is. li. 7.

CXXXII.

* *This note is sung only when two syllables fall to this measure.*

140 GOD is not a man, that He should | lie ;
     Neither the son of man, that | He · should re|pent
 2 Hath He said, and shall He not | do?
  Or hath He spoken, and shall He not | make it | good?
 3 Behold, I have received command to | bless ;
  And He hath blessed, and I can not re|verse it.
 4 He hath not beheld iniquity in | Jacob ;
  Neither hath He seen per|verse·ness in | Is·rael.
 5 The LORD his GOD is | with him,
  And the shout of a | king is a|mong them.
 6 GOD brought them out of | Egypt :
  He hath as it were the | strength · of an | u·nicorn.
 7 Surely there is no enchantment against | Jacob ;
  Neither is there any divination a|gainst | Is·rael.
 8 According to this time it shall be said of | Jacob,
  And of Israel, | What hath GOD wrought?
 9 Behold, the people shall rise up as a great | lion,
  And lift up himself as a | young | lion :
10 He shall not lie down until he eat of the | prey,
 And drink the | blood | of · the slain.   Num. xxiii. 19.

CXXXIII.

141 GIVE the king thy | judg'ments, O | GOD ;
And thy | righteous'ness | to the · king's | son.
2 He shall judge thy people with | righteous ness,
And thy | poor | with | judgment.
3 The mountains shall bring | peace · to the | people,
And the little | hills by | righteous'ness.
4 He shall judge the | poor · of the | people,
He shall save the children of the | needy, and | crush · the [op|pressor.
5 They shall fear Thee while sun and | moon en|dure,
Through|out all | gener|ations.
6 He shall come down like rain up'on the · mown | grass ;
As | showers that | water the | earth.
7 In his days shall the | righteous | flourish,
And abundance of | peace · till the | moon · be no | more.
8 He shall have dominion also from | sea to | sea ;
And from the river | to the | ends · of the | earth.
Ps. lxxii.

142 YEA, all kings shall bow | down to | him ;
All | nations | shall | serve him :
2 For he shall deliver the needy | when he | crieth :
The poor also, and | him that | hath no | helper.
3 He shall spare the | poor and | needy,
And shall | save the | souls · of the | needy.
4 He shall redeem their soul from deceit and | vio'lence :
And precious shall their | blood be | in his | sight.
5 And | he shall | live ;
And to him shall be | given of the | gold of | Sheba :

PROPHECY AND PROMISE.   109

6 Prayer also shall be made for him con|tin·ual|ly ;
  And | daily shall | he be | praised.
7 There shall be an handful of | corn · in the | earth,
  Up on the | top · of the | mountains :
8 The fruit thereof shall shake like | Leba'non ;   [earth.
  And they of the city shall flourish like | grass · of the |
9 His name shall en|dure for|ever :
  His name shall be con'tin·ued as | long · as the | sun :
10 And they shall be [blessed in | him ;
   All | nations shall | call him | blessed.
11 Blessed be the LORD GOD, the GOD of | Isra|el,
   Who only | doeth | wondrous | things :
12 And blessed be his glorious | name for'ever ;
   And let the whole | earth be | filled · with his | glory.
                                          Ps. lxxii. 11.

CXXXIV.

* *This note is sung only when two syllables fall to this measure.*

143 HOW goodly are thy tents, O | Jacob ;
    Thy tabernacles, | O | Is'rael.
 2 As the valleys are they | spread forth,
   As gardens | by the | riv·er's side.
 3 As the trees of lign-aloes which the LORD hath | planted,
   As cedar trees be|side the | waters.
 4 He shall pour the water out of his | buckets ;
   And his seed shall be in | many | waters :
 5 And his king shall be higher than | Agag ;
   And his kingdom shall | be ex|alted.
 6 GOD brought him forth out of | Egypt :
   He hath as it were the | strength · of an | u·nicorn.
 7 He shall eat up the nations his | en·emies ;
   And break their bones, and pierce them | with his | arrows.
 8 He couched, he lay down as a | lion,
   And as a great lion ; | who shall | stir · him up ?
 9 Blessed is he that blesseth | thee ;
   And cursed is | he that | curs·eth thee.   Num. xxiv. 5.

SELECTIONS AND CHANTS.

CXXXV.

144 GIVE ear, O ye heavens, and | I will | speak ;
    And hear, O | earth, the | words · of my | mouth.

2 My doctrine shall | drop · as the | rain ;
  My | speech · shall dis¦til · as the | dew ;

3 As the small rain upon the | tender | herb,
  And as the | showers up¦on the | grass :

4 Because I will publish the | name · of the | LORD :
  Ascribe ye | greatness | to our | GOD.

5 He is the Rock, his | work is | perfect ;
  For | all his | ways are | judgment :

6 A GOD of truth, and without in|iqui|ty ;
  Both | just and | right is | He.

7 They have cor¦rupted them|selves :
  Their spot is | not the | spot · of his | children :

8 They | are · a per|verse
  And a | crooked | gener|ation.

9 Do ye thus re|quite the | LORD,
  O foolish | people | and un|wise ?

10 Is not He thy | father that hath | bought thee ?
   Hath He not | made thee, and es¦tablished | thee ?

Deut. xxxii.

PROPHECY AND PROMISE. 111

CXXXVI.

145 **A**ND they shall | build the · old | wastes ;
They shall raise up the | former | deso|lations :

2 And they shall re|pair the · waste | cities,
The desolations of | many | gener|ations.

3 And strangers shall stand, and | feed your | flocks ;
And the sons of the alien shall be your ploughmen | and your | vine-|dressers.

4 But ye shall be named the | priests · of the | LORD :
They shall call you the | minis·ters | of our | GOD.

5 Ye shall eat of the | riches of the | Gentiles ;
And in their | glory shall ye | boast your|selves.

6 For your shame ye shall re|ceive | double ;
And for confusion they shall re|joice | in their | portion.

7 Therefore in their land they shall pos|sess the | double :
Everlasting | joy shall | be · unto | them.

8 For I the LORD | love | judgment :
I hate | robbery | for burnt-|offering.

9 And I will direct their | work in | truth ;
And I will make an ever|lasting | cove·nant | with them.

10 And their seed shall be | known a·mong the | nations,
And their | off·spring a|mong the | people.

11 All that see them shall ac|knowledge | them,
That they are the | seed the | LORD hath | blessed.

Is. lxi. 4.

CXXXVII.

146 THOU dost visit the earth, and | water | it ;
Thou greatly enrichest it with the river of | GOD, which is | full of | water.

2 Thou dost pre|pare them | corn,
When Thou hast | so pro|vided | for it.

3 Thou waterest the ridges thereof a|bundant|ly ;
Thou | set·tlest the | furrows there|of.

4 Thou makest it | soft with | showers ;
Thou | blessest the | springing there|of.

5 Thou crownest the | year · with thy | goodness ;
And thy | paths | drop | fatness :

6 They drop upon the pastures of the | wilder|ness ;
And the little hills re|joice on | every | side.

7 The pastures are | clothed with | flocks :
The valleys also are | covered | over with | corn :

8 They | shout for | joy :
They | do | also | sing.

Ps. lxv. 9.

CXXXVIII.

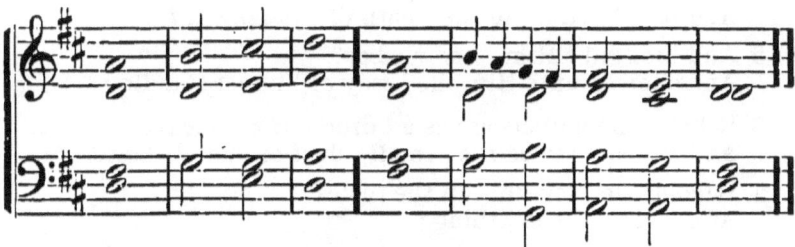

147 HE sendeth forth | springs into | brooks :
They | run a,mong the | mountains.

2 They give drink to every | beast · of the | field :
The wild | asses | quench their | thirst.

3 By them shall the fowls of the | heavens | dwell :
They shall | sing a|mong the | branches.

DESCRIPTIVE. 113

4 He watereth the mountains | from his | chambers :
  The earth is , filled · with the | fruit · of thy | works.
5 He causeth the grass to | grow · for the | cattle,
  And | herb for the | service of | man :
6 That He may bring forth food | out · of the | earth ;
  And wine that maketh | glad the , heart of | man :
7 With oil to make his | face to shine,
  And bread which doth sus.tain the | heart of | man. . . . . .
8 Bless thou the LORD, | O my , soul :
  Halle,lujah : | Praise ye the | LORD.   Ps. civ. 10.

CXXXIX.

148 WHO hath measured the waters in the | hollow | of his |
    And meted out | heaven | with a | span ?   [hand ?
  2 And comprehended the dust of the | earth | in a | measure ?
    And weighed the mountains in | scales, and the | hills · in a | balance ?
  3 Who hath directed the | Spirit | of the | LORD ?
    Or, being his counsel,lor, hath | taught Him ?
  4 With whom took He counsel, and | who in'structed | Him ?
    And taught Him | in the | path of , judgment ?
  5 And ' taught | Him knowledge ?
    And showed unto Him the | way of | under'standing ?
  6 Behold, the nations are as a | drop | of a ' bucket ;
    And are counted as the | small | dust of the | balance.
  7 Behold, He | taketh ' up the | isles
    As a | very | little | .thing :
  8 And Lebanon is | not suf'ficient to ' burn,
    Nor the beasts thereof sufficient | for a | burnt-'offering.
  9 All nations be fore Him | are as ' nothing ;
    And they are counted to Him | less than | nothing, and |
 10 To whom then ' will ye | liken | GOD ?   [vanity.
    Or what likeness | will · ye com pare unto | Him ?
                                                Is. xl. 12.

CXL.

149 **T**O whom then will ye | liken | Me,
Or shall I be equal? saith the | Holy | One.

2 Lift up your eyes round a|bout and | see,
Who hath cre|ated | these?

3 That bringeth out their | host by | number:
He calleth them | all by | names:

4 By the greatness of his power, and the | might of his | [strength,
Not | one doth | fail.

5 Why sayest | thou, O | Jacob,
And speakest, O | Isra|el.

6 My way is | hid · from the | Lord,
And my judgment is passed over | from my | God?

7 Hast thou not known? hast | thou not | heard?
That the everlasting | God, the | Lord,

8 The Creator of the ends of the earth, fainteth not, | neither is | weary?
There is no searching of his | under|standing.

9 He giveth | power to the | faint;
And to them that have no might He in'creaseth | strength.

10 Even the youths shall faint · and be | weary,
And the young men shall | ut·terly | fall.

11 But they that wait for the Lord | shall re·new | strength;
They shall mount up with | wings as | eagles;

12 They shall run, and | not be | weary;
They shall | walk, and not | faint.   Is. xl. 25.

CXLI.

150 PRAISE the LORD, O Je|rusa|lem :
      Praise ¦ thou thy | GOD, O ¦ Zion.

2 For He hath strengthened the ¦ bars · of thy | gates ;
  He hath | blessed thy chil·dren with¸in thee.

3 He maketh thy ¦ border ' peace :
  He filleth thee with the ' finest | of the | wheat.

4 He sendeth forth his commandment ¦ to the | earth :
  His word runneth | very ¦ swiftly

5 He giveth ' snow like wool :
  He ┃ scatter·eth the ¦ hoar · frost like ¦ ashes.

6 He casteth forth his · ice like ¦ morsels :
  Who can | stand be¦fore his | cold?

7 He sendeth out his word, and ¦ melteth | them :
  He causeth his wind to ¦ blow ; the | waters | flow.

8 He declareth his word unto ' Jacob,
  His statutes and his | judg·ments to | Isra|el.

9 He hath not dealt so with | any | nation :
  And his ¦ judg·ments, they ¦ have not | known them.
  Praise ye the ¦ LORD.   Ps. cxlvii. 12.

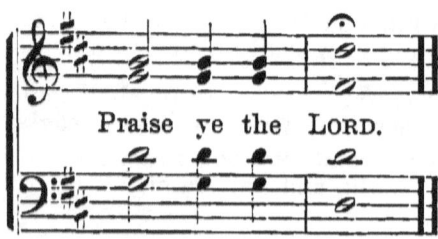

Praise ye the LORD.

CXLII.

151 THY way, O God, is in the | sanctu|ary :
Who is so great a | god as | God?
Thou art the | God that | doest | wonders.

2 Thou hast declared thy strength a|mong the | people :
Thou hast with thine arm re|deemed thy | people,
The sons of | Jacob | and of | Joseph.

3 The waters | saw · Thee, O | God ;
The waters saw Thee ; they | were a|fraid :
The | depths were | also | troubled.

4 The clouds | poured out | water ;
The skies sent | out a | sound :
Thine arrows | also | went a|broad.

5 The voice of thy thunder was | in the | whirlwind ;
Thy lightnings | lightened the | world ;
The | earth did | tremble and | shake.

6 Thy way is | in the | sea ;
And thy path in | many | waters ;
And thy | footsteps | are not | known.

7 Thou didst | lead thy | people,
Like | un·to a | flock,
By the hand of | Moses | and of | Aaron.   Ps. lxxvii. 13.

CXLIII.

152 PRAISE waiteth for Thee, O | God, in | Zion ;
And unto | Thee shall the | vow be per|formed.

2 O Thou that | hearest | prayer,
Unto | Thee shall | all flesh | come.

DESCRIPTIVE. 117

3 Iniquities pre|vail a|gainst me :
Our transgressions, | Thou shalt . purge · them a|way.
4 Blessed is the man whom | Thou dost | choose,
And cause to approach, that | he may | dwell · in thy | courts.
5 We shall be satisfied with the goodness | of thy | house,
Even of | thy | holy | temple.
6 By terrible things in righteousness wilt Thou | answer | us,
O | GOD of | our sal,vation :
7 The confidence of all the | ends · of the | earth,
And of them that are afar | off up on the | sea.
8 Who by his strength setteth | fast the | mountains,
Being | girded | with | power.
9 Who stilleth the noise of the seas, the | noise · of their | waves,
And the | tumult | of the | people.
10 They also that dwell in the uttermost parts are a|fraid · at thy | tokens ;
Thou makest the outgoings of the morning and | evening | to re|joice.   Ps. lxv.

CXLIV.

153 THE LORD reigneth ; He is | clothed with | majesty ;
The LORD is clothed with | strength, He hath | girded
[Him|self.
2 The world also | is es tablished,
That it | can,not be | moved.
3 Thy throne is es|tablished of | old :
Thou | art from | ever|lasting.
4 The floods have lifted | up, O | LORD ;
¹The floods have lifted | up their | voice ;
The floods | shall lift | up their | waves.
5 Than the voices of ' many | waters,
¹Than the mighty | waves · of the | sea,
Mightier | is the | LORD on | high.
6 Thy testimonies are | very | sure :
Holiness becometh thine | house, O | LORD, for | ever.
Ps. xciii.

CXLV.

Praise ye the LORD.

154 PRAISE ye the | LORD :
For it is good to sing | praises to our | GOD ;
For it is | pleasant ; and | praise is | comely.
2 The LORD doth build up Je'rusa|lem :
He gathereth together the | out·casts of | Isra|el.
3 He healeth the | broken in | heart,
And | bindeth | up their | wounds.
4 He telleth the | number of the | stars :
He calleth them | all | by their | names.
5 Great is our LORD, and | great in | power :
His under|stand·ing is | infi'nite.
6 The LORD lifteth | up the meek ·
He casteth the | wicked | down · to the | ground.
7 Sing unto the LORD with | thanks|giving :
Sing praise upon the | harp | unto our | GOD ;
8 Who covereth the | heaven with | clouds ;
Who prepareth | rain | for the | earth :
9 Who | mak·eth the | grass
To | grow up|on the | mountains.

10 He giveth to the | beast his | food,
   To the young | ravens | which do | cry.
11 He delighteth not in the | strength · of the | horse :
   He taketh not | pleasure in the | legs · of a | man.
12 The LORD taketh pleasure in | them that | fear Him,
   In those that | hope | in his | mercy.
   Praise ye the | LORD.   Ps. cxlvii.

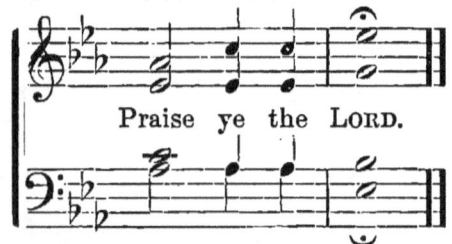

Praise ye the LORD.

CXLVI.

155 HOW manifold are thy | works, O | LORD !
        In wisdom | hast Thou | made them | all.
  2 The earth is | full · of thy | riches ;
    So is this | great and | wide | sea :
  3 Wherein are creeping | things · without | number ;
    Both | small and | great | beasts.
  4 There go the ships, and that le|via|than,
    Which Thou hast | made to | play there|in.
  5 These wait | all upon | Thee,
    That Thou mayest | give their | food · in its | season.
  6 Thou givest them ; | they do | gather :
    Thou openest thine hand ; | they are | filled with | good.
  7 Thou hidest thy face ; | they are | troubled :
    Thou takest away their breath ; they | die, and re|turn · to
       their | dust.
  8 Thou sendest forth thy spirit ; they | are cre|ated :
    And Thou dost re|new the | face · of the | ground. . . . .
  9 Bless thou the LORD, | O my | soul ;
    Halle|lujah : | Praise ye | the LORD.   Ps. civ. 24.

156 PRAISE ye the | Lord.
Happy is he that hath the God of Jacob | for his | help,
Whose hope is | in the | Lord his | God.

2 Who made | heaven and | earth,
The sea, and | all that | is there|in.

3 Who keepeth | truth for | ever :
Who executeth judgment | for · the op|pressed :

4 Who giveth | food · to the | hungry :
The Lord | looseth the prison|ers :

5 The Lord openeth the | eyes · of the | blind :
The Lord raiseth | them · that are | bowed | down :

6 The Lord | loveth the | righteous :
The Lord | doth pre|serve the | strangers :

7 He relieveth the fatherless | and the | widow :
But the way of the | wicked He | maketh | crooked.

DESCRIPTIVE. 121

8 The LORD shall | reign for | ever,
Thy GOD, O Zion, to | all gener|ations.
Praise ye the | LORD.

Ps. cxlvi. 5.

Praise ye the LORD.

CXLVIII.

157 BLESS the LORD, | O my | soul.
O LORD my | GOD, Thou art | very | great:
2 Thou art clothed with honor and | majesty.
Who coverest Thyself with | light | as a | garment:
3 Who stretchest out the | heavens like a | curtain :
Who layeth the beams of his | chambers | in the | waters:
4 Who maketh the | clouds his | chariot :
Who goeth upon | wings | of the | wind :
5 Who maketh | spirits his | angels,
The flaming | fire his | minis,ters.
6 He hath founded the earth up|on its | bases :
That it should not be re,moved | for | ever.
7 Thou coveredst it with the | deep · as a | garment:
The waters | stood a|bove the | mountains.
8 At thy re|buke they | flee :
At the voice of thy | thun·der they | hasten a|way.
9 The mountains rise, the | valleys go | down
Unto the place which | Thou hast | founded | for them.
10 Thou hast set a bound which they | may not | pass ;
That they may not re|turn to | cover the | earth.
11 Bless thou the LORD, | O my | soul :
Halle|lujah : | Praise ye the | LORD.

Ps. civ.

CXLIX.

158 WE have thought of thy | kindness, O | GOD,
In the | midst | of thy | temple.

2 According to thy | name, O | GOD,
So is thy | praise to the | ends of the | earth :

3 Thy right hand is full of | righteous|ness.
Mount | Zion | shall re|joice,

4 The daughters of | Judah shall be | glad,
Be|cause of | thy | judgments.

5 Walk about Zion, and go | round a|bout her :
Tell | ye the | towers there|of :

6 Mark ye | well her | bulwarks ;
Con|sider her | pala|ces :

7 That | ye may | tell it
To the gener|ation | follow|ing :

8 For this GOD is our GOD for ever and | ever :
He will be our | guide | unto | death.   Ps. xlviii. 9.

CL.

159 THE earth is the LORD'S, and the | fulness there|of ;
The world, and | they that | dwell there|in.

2 For He hath founded it up|on the | seas,
And es|tablished it up|on the | floods.

DESCRIPTIVE. 123

3 Who shall ascend into the | mountain of the | LORD ?
   Or who shall | stand · in his | holy | place ?

CLI.

4 He that is clean of hands, and ' pure in | heart ;
   Who hath not lifted up his soul to vanity, nor | sworn de-|ceitfully.

5 He shall receive ' blessing from the ' LORD,
   And righteousness from the GOD of his sal|vation.

6 This is the generation of | them that | seek Him,
   That seek thy | face, O | Jacob.

CLII.

7 Lift up your heads, | O ye | gates ,
   And be ye lifted up, ye ever lasting | doors ;
   And the King of glory ' shall come | in.

8 Who is this King of | glory ?
   The LORD | strong and mighty,
   The LORD might·y in | battle.

9 Lift up your heads, | O ye | gates ;
   Even lift up, ye ever lasting | doors ;
   And the King of | glory | shall come | in.

10 Who is this | King of ' glory ?
   The | LORD of ' Hosts,
   He | is the | King of | glory.

Ps. xxiv.

CLIII.

160 LOOK | upon | Zion,
The city of | our so|lemni|ties.

2 Thine eyes shall see Jerusalem a quiet | habi|tation,
A tabernacle that shall | not be | taken | down.

3 Not one of the stakes thereof shall ever | be re|moved,
Neither shall any of the | cords there|of be | broken.

4 But there the glorious LORD shall | be unto | us
A place of | broad | rivers and | streams ;

5 Wherein shall go no | galley with | oars,
Neither shall gallant | ship | pass there|by.

6 For the LORD | is our | Judge
The LORD | is our | Law|giver,

7 The LORD | is our | King,
He | will | save | us.   Is. xxxiii. 20.

CLIV.

I.

161 WHO is this that cometh from Edom with dyed | garments from | Bozrah :
¹This that is glorious in his apparel travelling in the greatness | of his | strength.
I that speak in | righteousness | mighty to | save.

2 Wherefore art thou red in | thine ap|parel,
  ¹And thy garments like him that treadeth | in the | wine-vat?
  I have trodden the wine-press alone, and of the people | there was | none with | me.

3 For the day of vengeance is | in mine | heart,
  And the year of | my re|deemed is | come.

4 And I looked and there was | none to | help;
  ¹And I wondered that there was | none to up|hold;
  Therefore mine own arm brought salvation unto Me, and my | fury | it up|held Me.

CLV.

II.

5 I will mention the loving kindness | of the | LORD;
  And the | praises | of the | LORD:

6 According to all that the LORD hath be|stowed on | us:
  And the great goodness toward the | house of | Isra|el,

7 Which He hath bestowed on them according | to his | mercies;
  And according to the multitude | of his | loving | kindnesses.

8 For He said surely they are my people, children that | will not | lie:
  So | He | was their | Saviour.

9 In all their affliction | He was af'flicted;
  And the angel | of his | presence | saved them.

10 In his love and in his pity | He re|deemed them,
  And He bare them and carried them | all the | days of | old.
                                              Is. lxiii.

CLVI.

I.

162 BEHOLD, my servant | shall deal | prudently,
He shall be ex│alted | and ex│tolled ;
2 And shall be | very | high ;
  As many | were as tonished | at thee :
3 His visage was so marred, more than | any | man,
  And his form | more · than the | sons of | men :
4 So shall he sprinkle ¹ many nations ;
  The kings shall | shut their | mouths | at him :
5 For that which had not been told them | shall they | see ;
  And that which they had not | heard shall | they con│sider.

II.

6 Who hath be│lieved our re│port ?
  And to whom is the | arm · of the | LORD re│vealed ?
7 For he shall grow up before Him as a | tender | plant,
  And as a | root out | of a · dry | ground.
8 He hath no | form nor | comeliness :
  ¹And | when we shall see him,
  There is no | beauty that | we · should de│sire him.
9 He is despised and re│jected of | men ;
  A man of | sorrows, and ac│quainted with | grief.
10 And we hid as it were our | faces | from him :
   He was despised, and | we es│teemed him | not.

III.

11 Surely he hath | borne our | griefs,
   And | carried | our | sorrows.
12 Yet we did es│teem him | stricken ;
   Smitten of | GOD, | and af│flicted.
13 But he was wounded for ¹ our trans│gressions,
   He was | bruised for | our in iquities.
14 The chastisement of our | peace was up│on him ;
   And with | his stripes | we are | healed.
15 All we like sheep have | gone a stray ;
   We have turned every | one to his | own | way :

16 And the LORD hath | laid on | him
   The in iqui·ty | of us | all.

CLVII.

IV.

17 He was oppressed, and he · was af flicted,
   Yet he | opened | not his mouth.
18 He is brought as a lamb · to the slaughter;
   ¹And as a sheep before her · shearers is dumb,
   So he openeth | not his mouth.
19 He was taken from prison and from | judgment:
   And who shall de clare his gener ation.
20 For he was cut off out of the | land · of the living:
   For the transgression of my people was he | stricken.
21 And he made his · grave · with the wicked,
   And with the rich in his death:
22 Because he had | done no violence;
   Neither was de ceit | in his mouth.
23 Yet it pleased the LORD to bruise him:
   He hath | put him to | grief.
24 When thou shalt make his soul a trespass- offering,
   He shall see his seed, he shall pro long his | days;
25 And the | pleasure of the LORD
   Shall | prosper in his | hand.
26 He shall see of the travail of his | soul,
   And | shall be | satis|fied.
27 By his knowledge shall my just servant | justi·fy | many;
   For he shall bear · their in iqui ties.
28 Therefore will I divide him a portion with the | great;
   And he shall divide the | spoil with the | strong:
29 Because he hath poured out his soul unto | death:
   And he was | numbered with the · trans gressors:
30 And he bare the | sin of many,
   And made inter cession | for the · trans gressors.

Is. lii. 13–15, and liii.

CLVIII.

163 ARISE, O Lord, | into thy | rest;
    Thou and the | ark | of thy | strength.
  2 Let thy priests be clothed with | righteous|ness;
    And let thy | saints | shout for | joy.
  3 For thy servant | David's | sake,
    Turn not away the | face of | thine an|ointed.
  4 The Lord hath sworn in | truth unto | David;
    He | will not | turn | from it;
  5 Of the fruit of thy body will I set up|on thy | throne.
    If thy | children will | keep my | covenant,
  6 And my testimony that | I shall | teach them,
    Their children also shall sit upon thy | throne for | ever|more.
  7 For the Lord hath | chosen | Zion:
    He hath desired it | for his | habi|tation.
  8 This is my | rest for | ever:
    Here will I | dwell; for | I · have de|sired it.
  9 I will abundantly | bless · her pro|vision:
    Her poor will I | satis'fy with | bread.
 10 I will also clothe her | priests · with sal|vation;
    And her saints shall | shout a|loud for | joy
 11 There will I make the horn of | David to | bud:
    I have ordained a | lamp for | mine an|ointed.
 12 His enemies will I | clothe with | shame;
    But upon him|self his | crown shall | flourish.

                                   Ps. cxxxii. 8.

ANTHEMS.

CHANT ANTHEM I.
Ps. i.

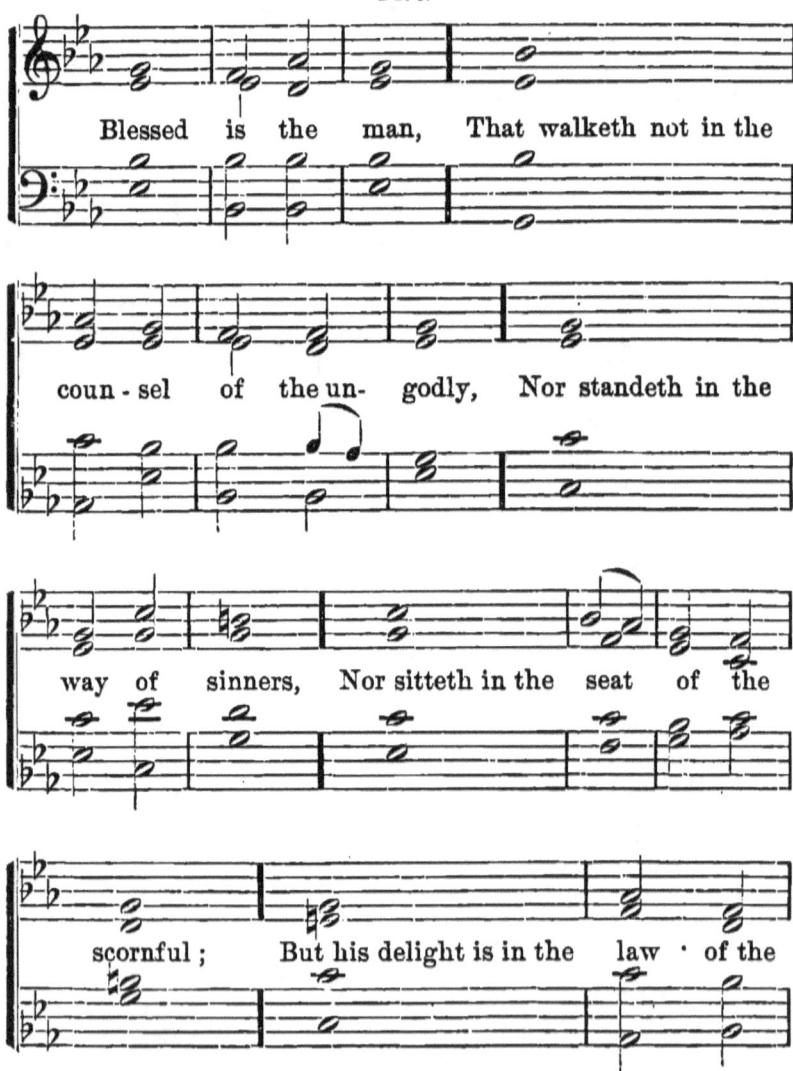

132 ANTHEMS.

way of the un- god- ly shall pe - rish.

CHANT ANTHEM II.
Ps. lxv.

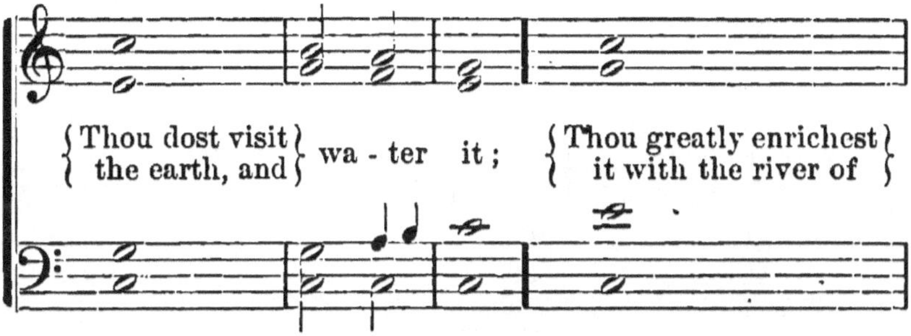

{ Thou dost visit the earth, and } wa - ter it; { Thou greatly enrichest it with the river of }

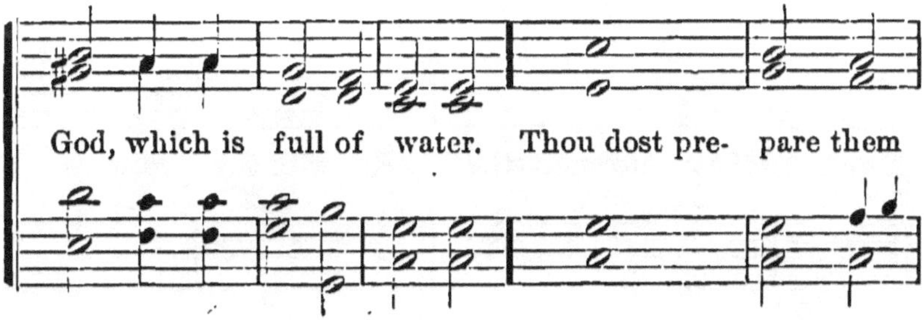

God, which is full of water. Thou dost pre- pare them

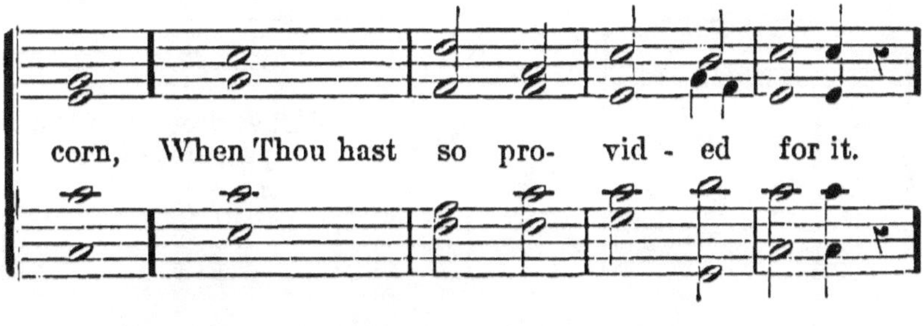

corn, When Thou hast so pro- vid - ed for it.

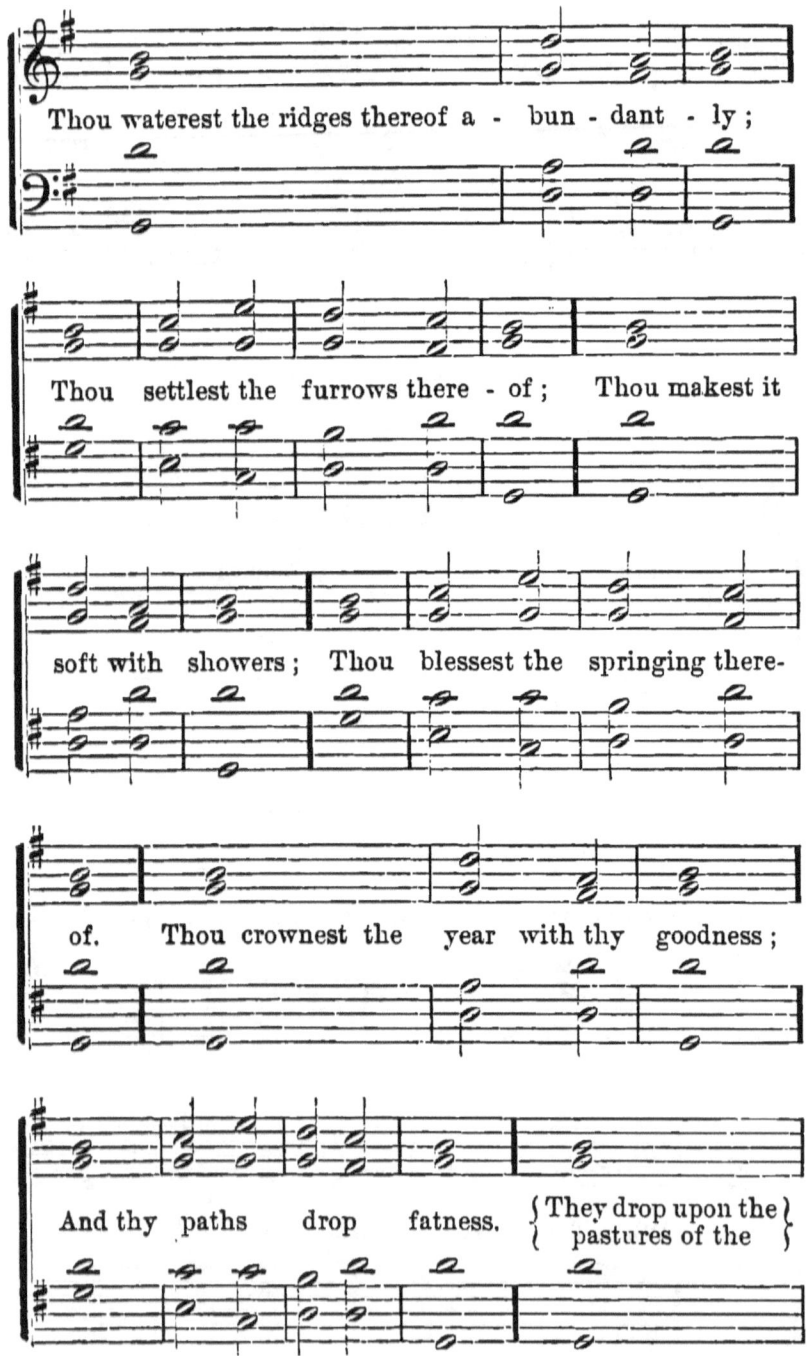

134 ANTHEMS.

CHANT ANTHEM IV.

Isaiah lx.

CHANT ANTHEM V.
Ps. cxix. 73.

CHANT ANTHEM VI.

Ps. xlii.

CHANT ANTHEMS. 147

CHANT ANTHEM VII.

Ps. lxxxv.

Thou hast been favorable, O Lord, to thy land; Thou hast brought back the cap-tiv-i-ty of Jacob. Thou hast forgiven the iniquity of thy people; Thou hast covered all their sin. Thou hast taken away all thy wrath; Thou hast turned away from the burn-ing of thine anger.

ANTHEMS.

CHANT ANTHEM VIII.
Rev. xxii.

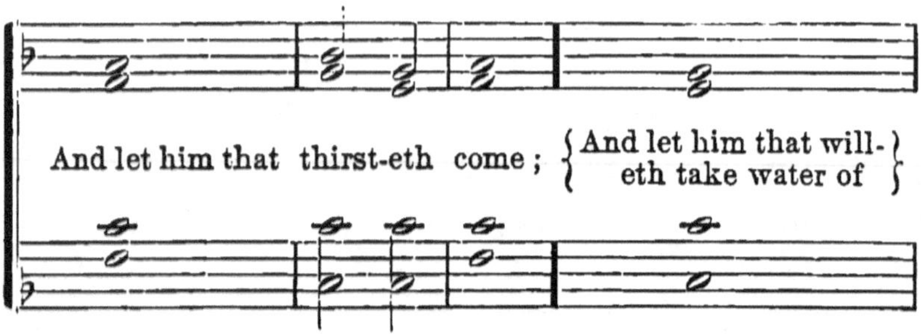

And let him that thirst-eth come; { And let him that will-eth take water of } life freely. He who testifieth these things saith, Surely, I come quickly: Amen, Yea, come, Lord Jesus.

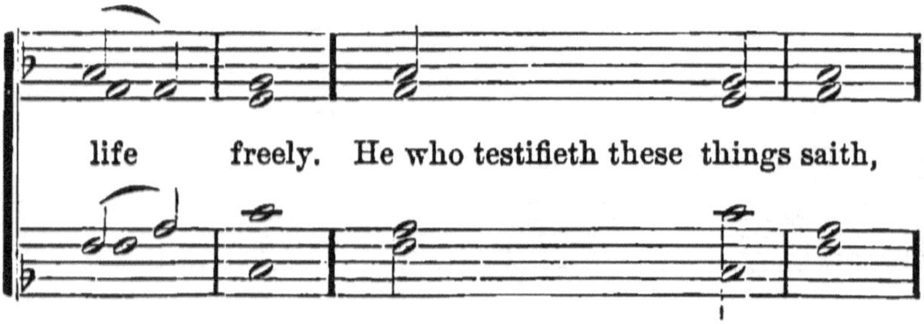

CHANT ANTHEM IX.

Ps. cl.

Praise ye the LORD. Praise GOD in his sanctuary:

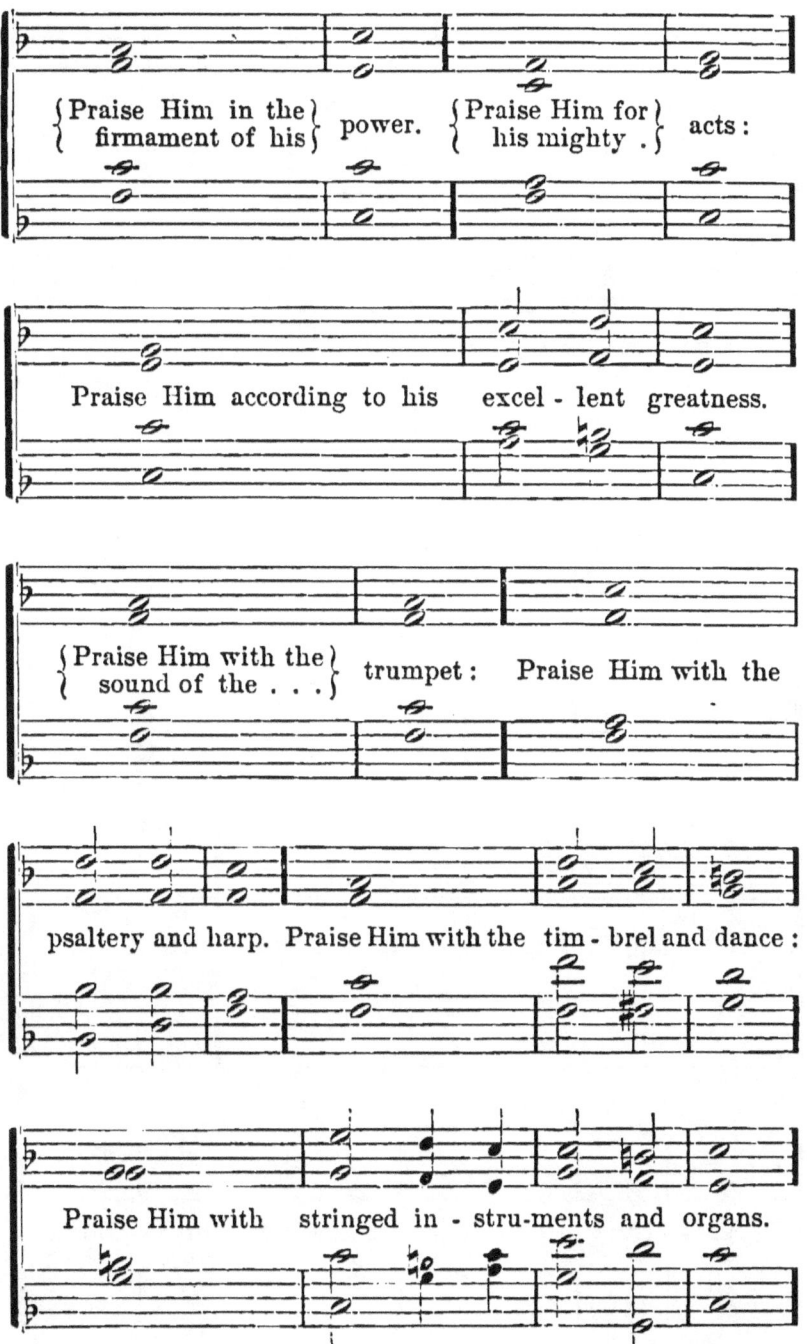

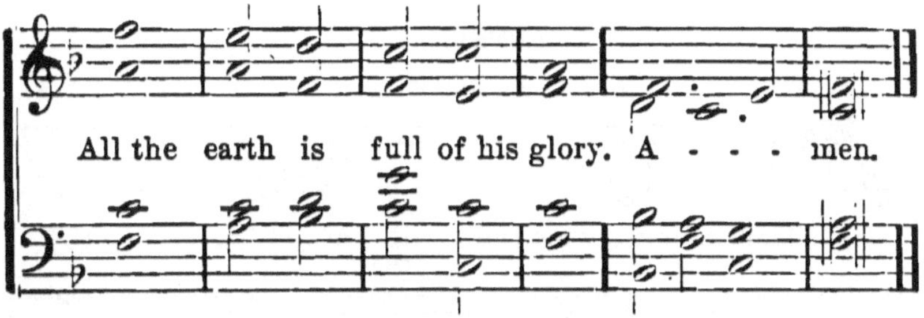

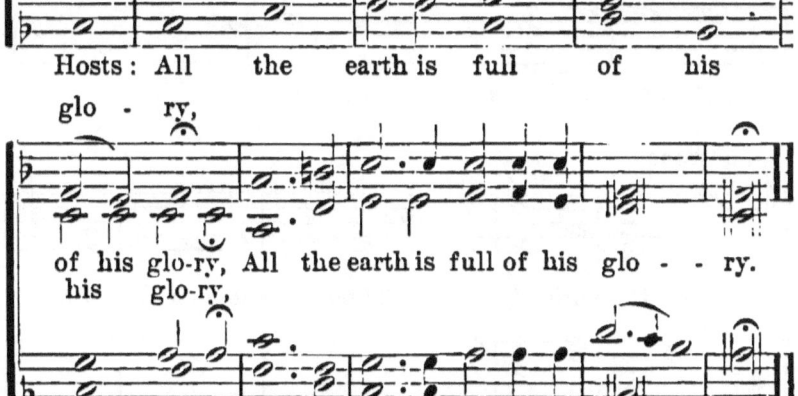

ANTHEM II.
Ps. xvi. 11.

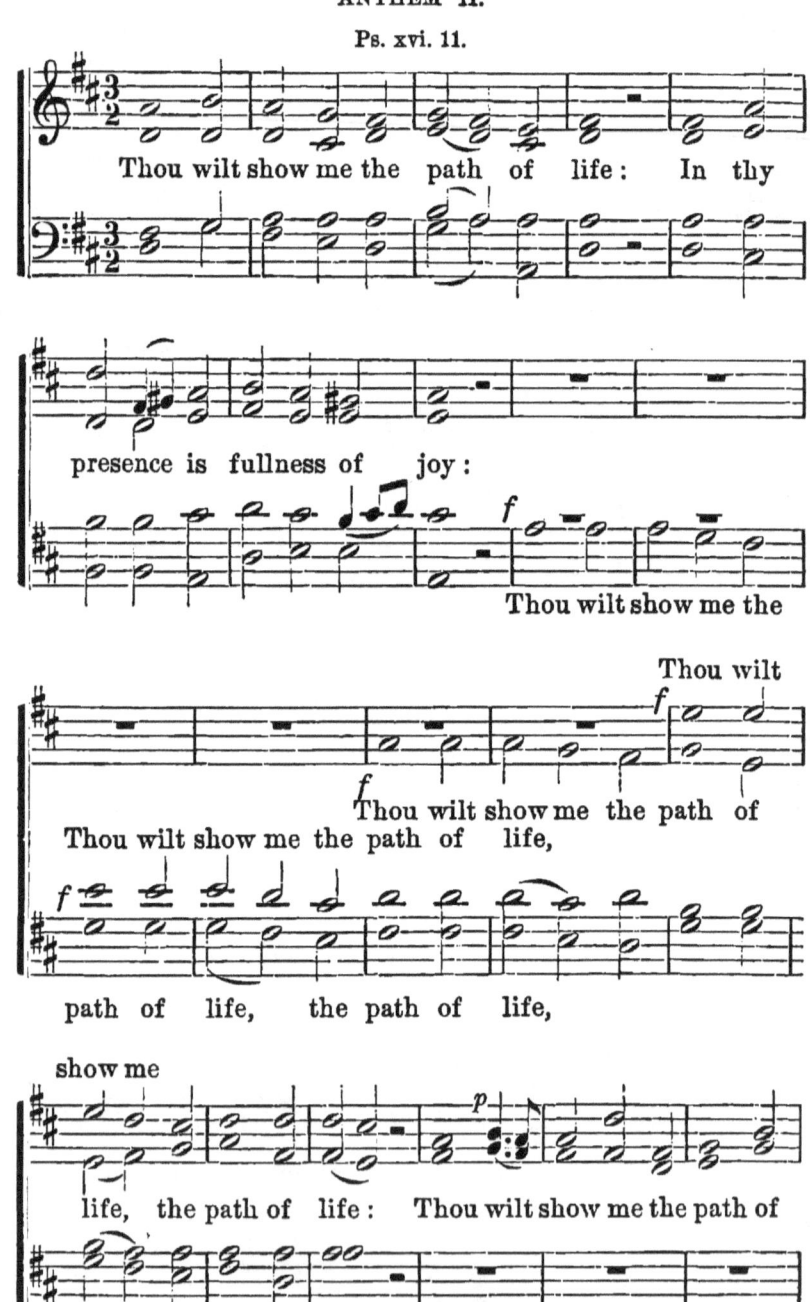

ANTHEM III.

Ps. cxxxiii.

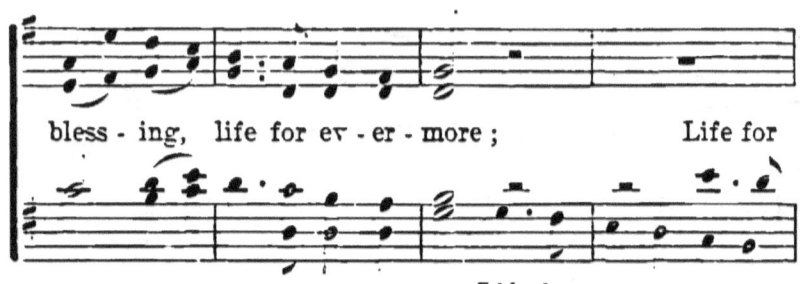

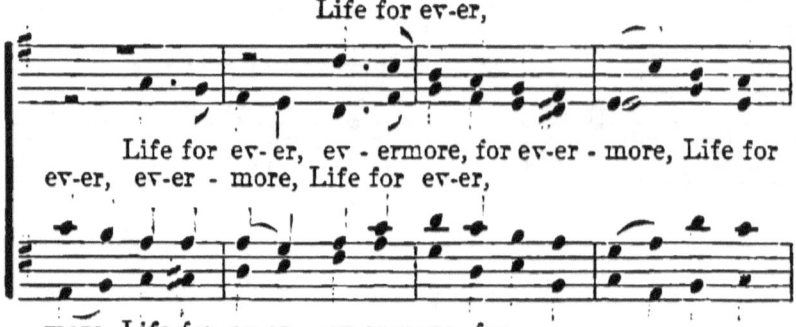

ANTHEM IV.

Ps. xlii. 1.

ANTHEMS. 161

ANTHEM V.
Ps. ix. 9, 10.

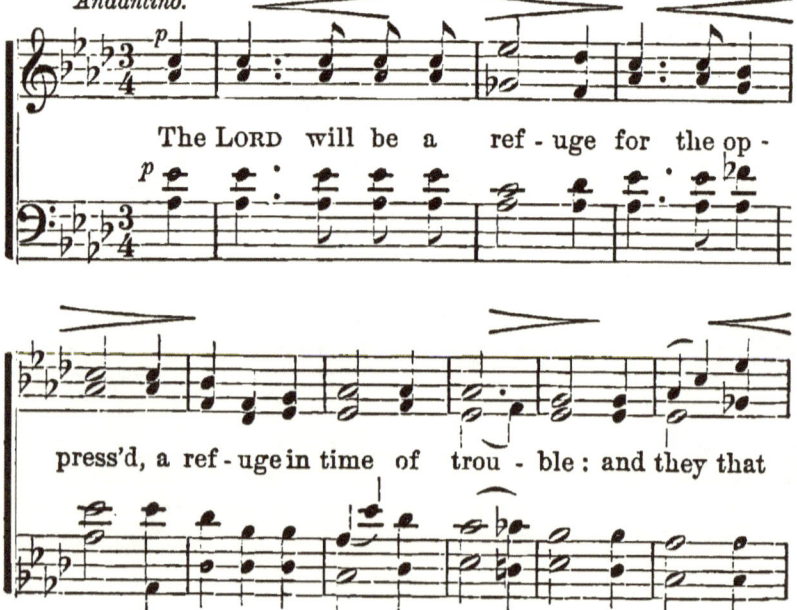

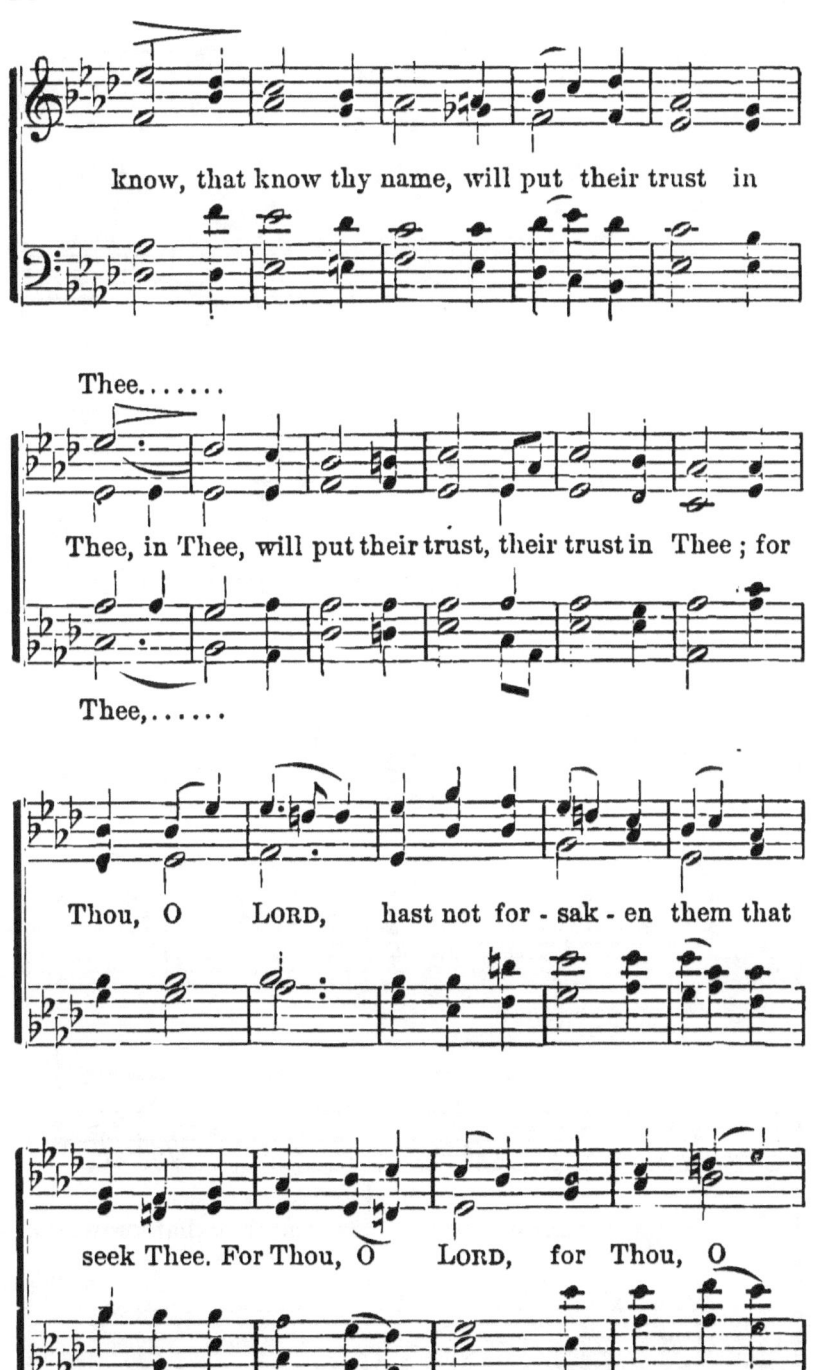

ANTHEM VI.
Isa. liii.

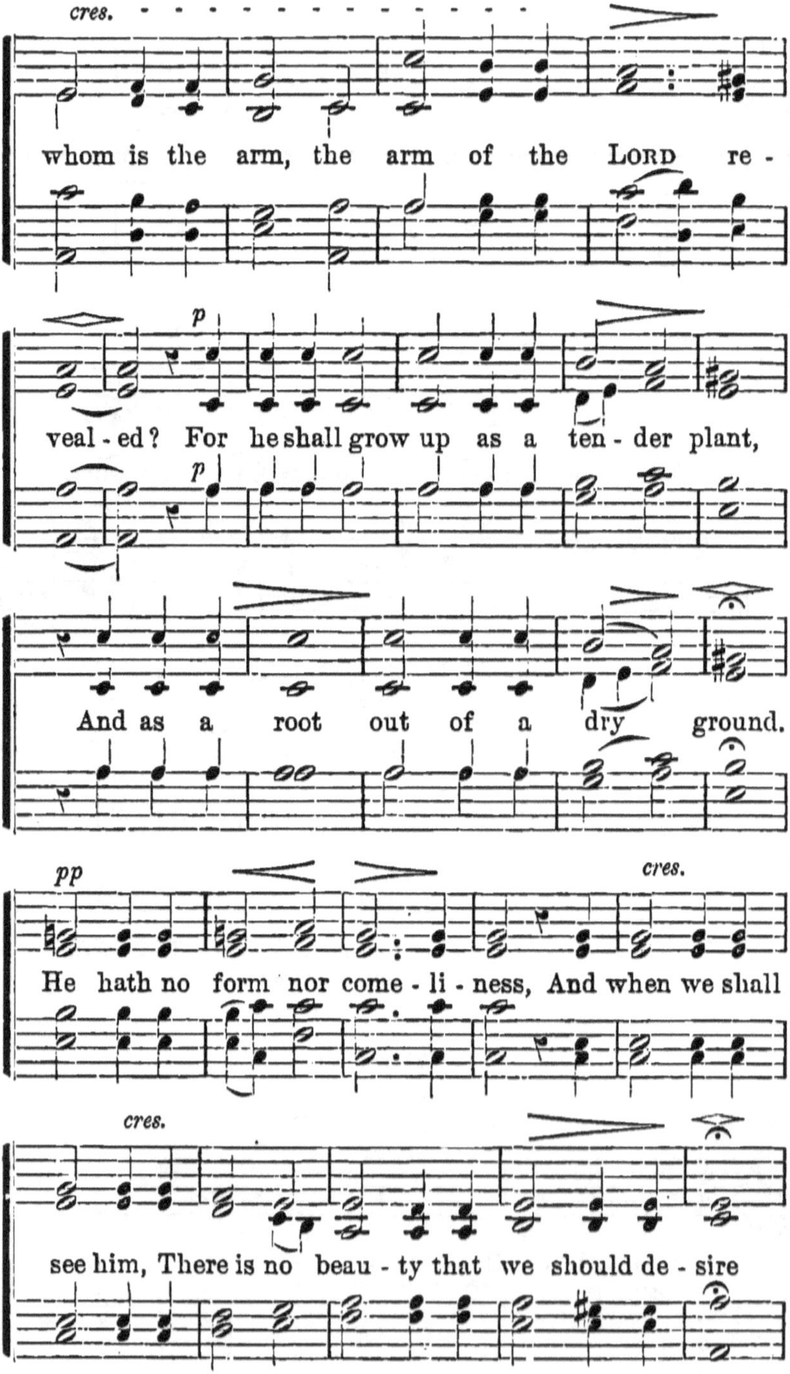
cres.
whom is the arm, the arm of the LORD re -
p
veal - ed? For he shall grow up as a ten - der plant,
And as a root out of a dry ground.
pp
cres.
He hath no form nor come - li - ness, And when we shall
cres.
see him, There is no beau - ty that we should de - sire

ANTHEM VII.

Ps. ciii.

ANTHEM VIII.

Ps. cxliii.

En-ter not in-to judg-ment with thy servant, O LORD, For in thy sight shall no man liv-ing be jus-ti-fied. En-ter not in-to judgment with thy servant, O LORD, For in thy sight shall

ANTHEMS. 175

ANTHEM X.
Isa. xl. 5.

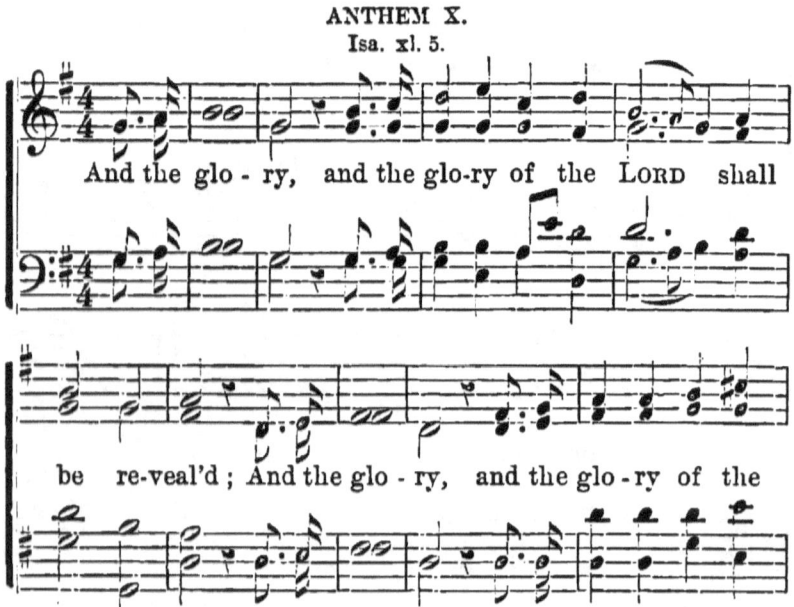

ANTHEMS. 177

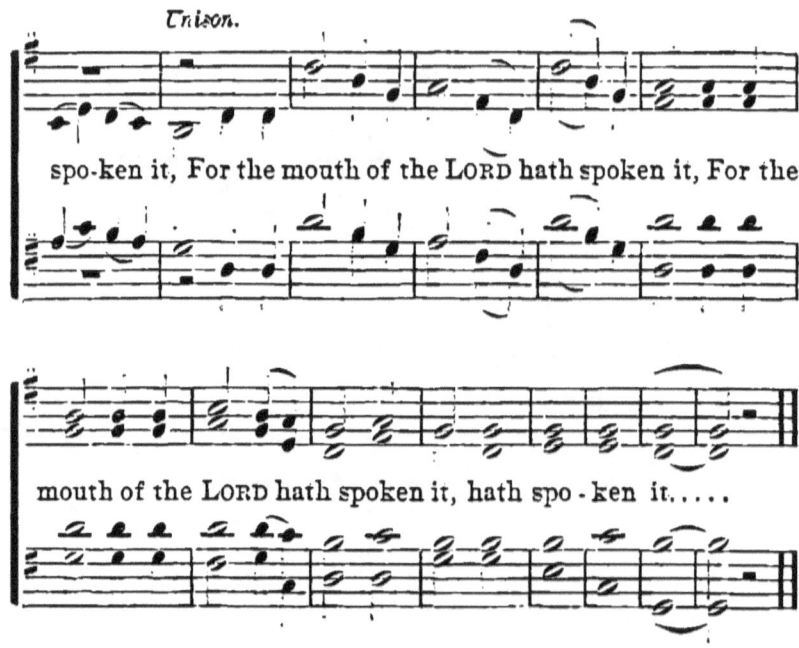

ANTHEM XI.
Is. ix. 6.

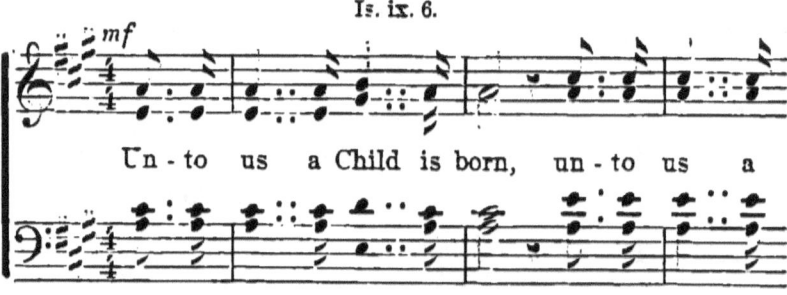

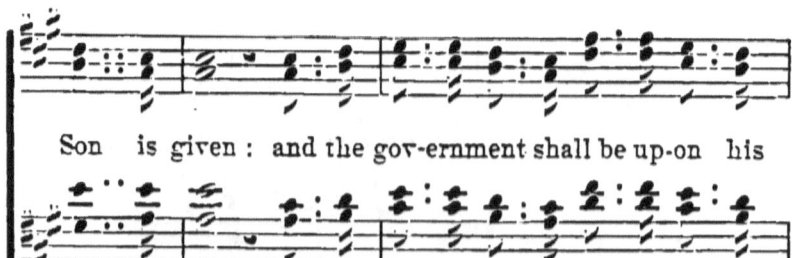

178 ANTHEMS.

ANTHEMS.

ANTHEM XII.

Rev. xii. 10, 12; xv. 3, 4.

ANTHEMS.

ANTHEM XIII.

Luke ii. 14.

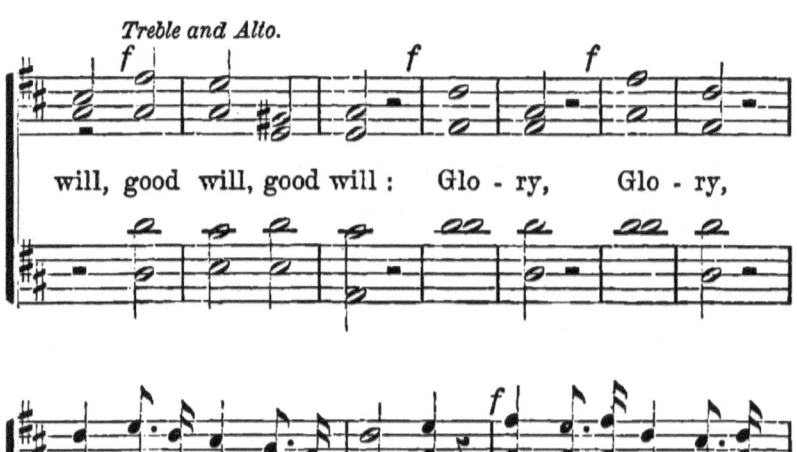
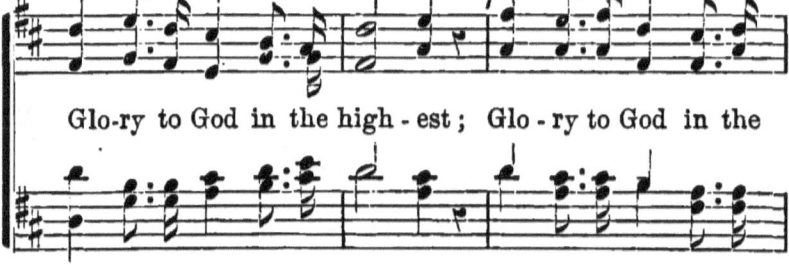

ANTHEMS.

among men good will: and on earth peace, among
men and on earth
men good will: and on earth peace, a-mong
and on earth peace a-mong
men..........
men, among men good will...... good will, good will.
men..........

ANTHEM XIV.
Matt. xxi. 9.

Ho-san - - - na, Ho-san - - - na, Ho-

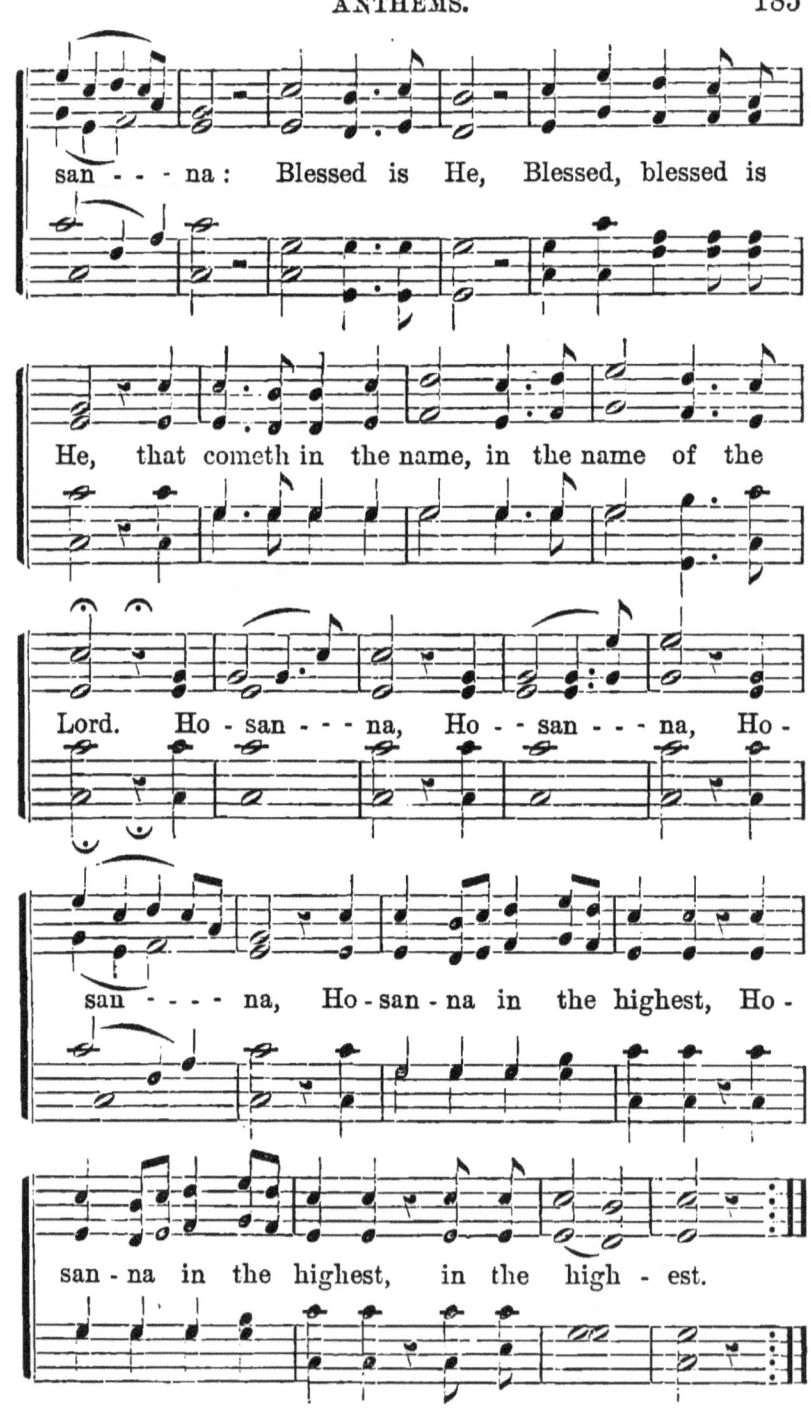

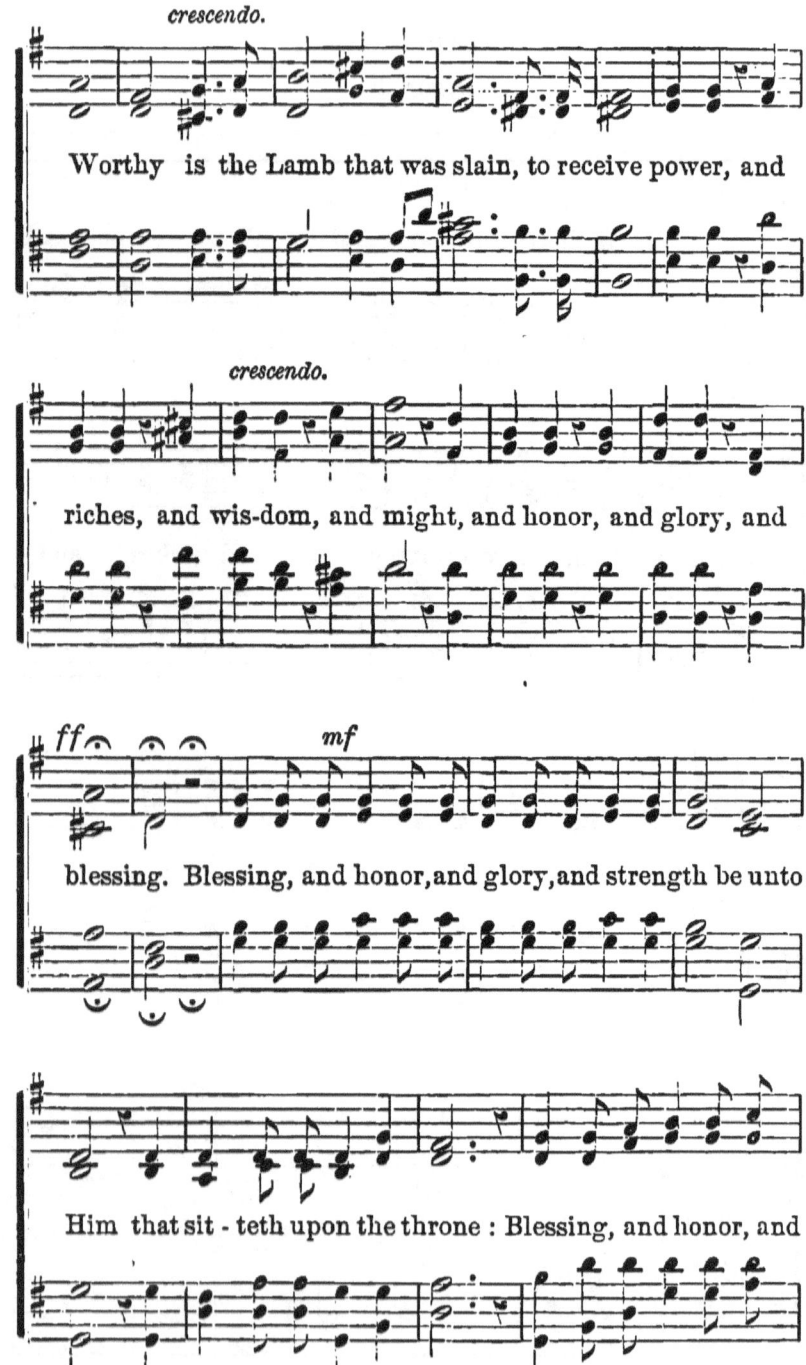

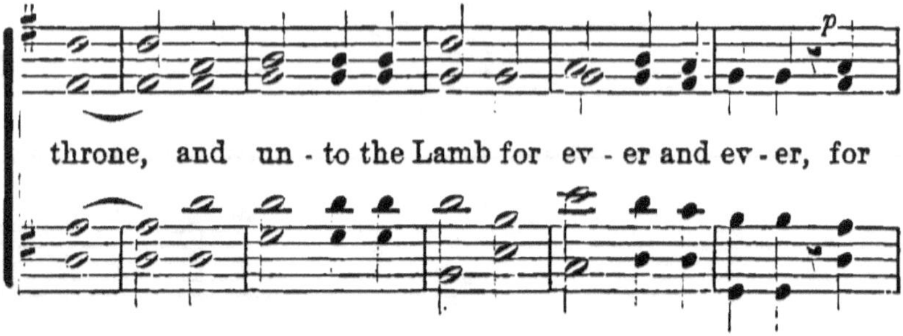

ANTHEMS.

throne, and un - to the Lamb for ev - er and ev - er, for ev - er and ev - er, A - men; for ev - er and ev - er, A - men. A - - - - men.

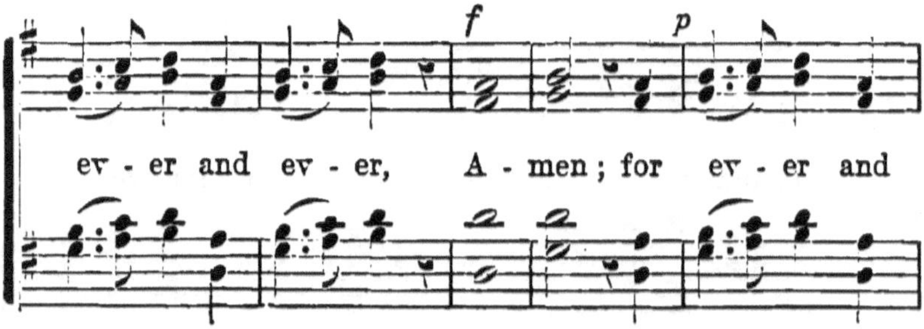

ANTHEM XVI.

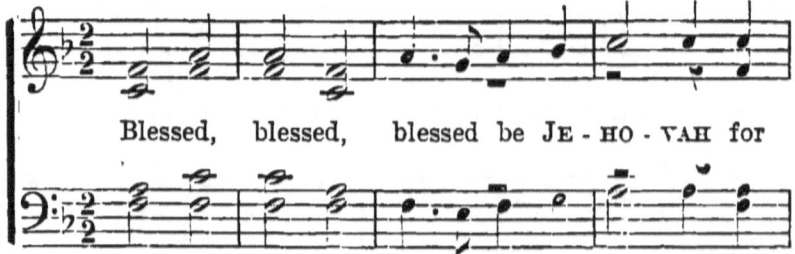

Blessed, blessed, blessed be JE - HO - VAH for

ANTHEMS.

ANTHEM XVII.
Ps. iv. 8:

THE FAITH OF THE NEW CHURCH.

THE FAITH OF THE NEW CHURCH.

THE FAITH OF THE NEW CHURCH.

WE worship the | One | God,
   The Lord, the | Saviour | Jesus | Christ :
In whom is the Father, the Son, and the | Holy | Spirit ;
Whose Hu|manity | is di vine :
Who for our salvation did come | into the | world,
And take our | nature | upon | Him.

He endured temptation even to the passion | of the | cross :
He overcame the hells, and | so de livered | man.
He glorified His hu'mani|ty
By uniting it with the Divinity of | which it | was be|gotten :
So He became the Redeemer | of the | world
Without whom no | mortal | can be | saved :
And they are saved who be lieve in | Him,
And keep the com'mandments | of His | Word :
This is His commandment, that we | love one | another,
As | He has | loved | us.

Unto Him that | loved | us,
And hath washed us from our | sins in | his own | blood:
And hath made us kings and priests unto | God and his | Father,
Be glory and dominion for | ever and | ever. A|men.

TE DOMINUM,

A HYMN OF PRAISE TO THE LORD JESUS CHRIST.

WE praise Thee, O LORD, we magnify thy | holy | Name:
The heavens and earth praise Thee, the sea and | all that | is there in.

2 All thy works praise Thee, and thy | saints | bless Thee:
Thy church doth worship and ac|knowledge Thee alone,

3 The Father eternal, the Word incarnate, the Holy Spirit, the | Comfort er:
In essence and in person One, JE HOVAH, | JESUS, | LORD.

4 To Thee, cherubim and | sera phim:
Angels and blessed spirits lift | up their | voices and | cry:

5 Holy, holy, holy, LORD GOD Al mighty:
Heaven and earth are | full | of thy | glory.

6 Thou didst bow the heavens and come down for our sal-|vation:
Thou didst clothe thyself with our nature and be camest | God with | us.

7 In thy love and pity Thou | didst re|deem us :
And the chastisement of our | peace was up|on | Thee.

8 Thou didst pass through the bitterness of suffering | and temp|tation :
Thou didst humble thyself, even to the | passion | of the | cross.

9 Thou didst burst asunder all the | bonds of | death :
Thou didst rise in divine | majes|ty and | glory.

10 Thou didst ascend on high, Thou didst lead cap|tivity | captive :
The everlasting doors were | opened | to re|ceive thee.

11 High above all the heavens didst Thou | set thy | throne :
Clothed with light inaccessible, girt with om|nipo|tence and | love.

12 Thou art the | King of | glory :
Thou art Je|ho|vah of | hosts.

13 Day unto day will we exalt Thee, O | Lord, our | God :
And worship at thy footstool, for | Thou a|lone art | holy

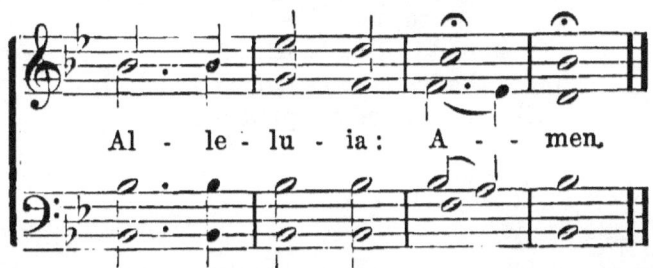

HYMNS AND TUNES.

PRAISE AND ADORATION.

1 JESUS, to thee be endless praise!
  Eternal thanks to thee be given!
Thou didst create all men, to raise
  Their souls to endless bliss in heaven.

2 Hosanna to our only Lord!
  Hosanna to our only King!
Spread the Creator's name abroad,
  Till all mankind his praises sing!

3 Our souls, O Lord, thou didst redeem
  From sin and everlasting woe:
On all thy grace and mercy beam,
  In heaven above, and earth below.

4 Hosanna to our only Lord!
  Hosanna to our only King!
Spread the Redeemer's name abroad,
  Till all mankind his praises sing!

2 PRAISE the Lord! ye heavens adore him!
Praise him, angels, in the height!
Sun and moon rejoice before him,
Praise him, all ye stars of light.
Alleluia! Alleluia!
Earth and heaven, your songs unite.

2 Praise the Lord, for he is glorious!
He hath put our foes to shame;
Over death and hell victorious,
Hosts on high his power proclaim;
Alleluia! Alleluia!
Laud and magnify his name.

3 Praise him for his grace and favor
To our fathers in distress;
Praise him still the same as ever,
Slow to chide, and swift to bless;
Alleluia! Alleluia!
Glorious in his faithfulness.

3. O PRAISE ye the Lord! prepare your glad voice
   His praise in the great assembly to sing;
   In God our Redeemer let Israel rejoice
   And children of Zion be glad in their King.

2 From bondage of hell redeemed by his might,
   Rejoice in his grace, his love and his light;
   For us in his mansion he maketh a place,
   And with his salvation the humble will bless.

3 Then worship the King all glorious above,
   And gratefully sing his power and his love;
   Our Shield and Defender, the Ancient of Days,
   Pavilioned in splendor and girded with praise.

4 FROM all that dwell below the skies,
Let the Creator's praise arise ;
Let the Redeemer's name be sung
Through every land, by every tongue.

2 Eternal are thy mercies, Lord ;
Eternal truth dwells in thy word ;
Thy praise shall sound from shore to shore,
Till suns shall rise and set no more.

5 BE thou, O God, exalted high ;
And as thy glory fills the sky,
So let it be on earth displayed,
Till thou art here, as there, obeyed.

2 Thy praises, Lord, we will resound
To all the listening nations round ;
Thy mercy highest heaven transcends,
Thy truth beyond the clouds extends.

Doxology.

To thee, O Jesus Christ, we raise
Our noblest songs of thanks and praise ;
Be every-where thy name confessed,
God over all forever blest.

PRAISE AND ADORATION.

6 ALL hail the great Immanuel's name!
  Let angels prostrate fall;
  Bring forth the royal diadem,
  And crown him Lord of all.

2 Let countless angels strike the lyre,
  And low before him fall,
  Who tune to love their holy choir,
  And crown him Lord of all.

3 Let every tribe, of every tongue,
  All creatures, great and small,
  Loud swell this universal song,
  And crown him Lord of all.

4 Our heavenly Father, Jesus, Lord,
  Whom King of kings we call;
  We worship thee, Incarnate Word,
  And crown thee Lord of all.   IV.

7 HOLY, holy, holy! Lord God Almighty!
  Early in the morning our song shall rise to thee:
Holy, holy, holy, merciful and mighty;
  Father and Saviour, glory be to thee.

2 Holy, holy, holy! all the saints adore thee,
  Casting down their golden crowns around the glassy sea;
Cherubim and Seraphim falling down before thee,
  Which wert, and art, and evermore shalt be.

PRAISE AND ADORATION.   205

3 Holy, holy, holy! though the darkness hide thee,
    Though the eye of sinful man thy glory may not see,
  Only thou art holy: There is none beside thee
  Perfect in power, in love, and purity.

4 Holy, holy, holy! Lord God Almighty!
    All thy works shall praise thy name, in earth, sky, and
  Holy, holy, holy! merciful and mighty;   [sea:
  Father and Saviour, glory be to thee.

8 JESUS triumphant reigns;
    Let earth adore its Lord;
  Bright cherubs his attendants stand,
    Swift to fulfill his word.

2 In Sion stands his throne;
    His honors are divine;
  His church shall make his wonders known,
    For there his glories shine.

3 His name shall be adored
    Through earth's rejoicing lands:
  Great is his mercy, sure his word,
    His truth forever stands.

4 The God we worship now
    Will guide us till we die;
  Him will we worship, him alone,
    With angel hosts on high.   V.

9 SAVIOUR and Regenerator!
    Thee alone, God we own,
  Father and Creator.

2 Word Incarnate we adore thee!
    Hosts above, God of love,
  Cast their crowns before thee.

3 Father, Son and Holy Spirit,
    One in thee, Lord, we see,
  Who thy grace inherit.

4 May thy Word be our Instructor,
    Night and day, on our way,
  Our divine conductor!

5 Visit us with thy salvation;
    Let thy care still be near,
  Round our habitation.

6 Jesus our divine Protector,
    Guide us still, let thy will
  Be our sole director!

PART II.

BLESSED Lord, what shall we render,
    To thy Name, still the same,
  Gracious, good and tender!

2 Holy, holy, holy Giver
　　Of the food, truly good,
　Nourish us forever!

3 Glory, honor, thanks and blessing
　　Will we give, while we live,
　Never, never ceasing.

4 Thee in glory, great Jehovah,
　　May we see, and to thee
　Raise the Alleluia!

10 GIVE thanks to God; he reigns above:
　　Kind are his thoughts; his name is love:
　His mercy ages past have known,
　And ages long to come shall own.

　2 He feeds and clothes us all the way;
　　He guides our footsteps, lest we stray;
　　He guards us with a powerful hand,
　　And brings us to the heavenly land.

　3 Then let us all with joy record
　　The truth and goodness of the Lord:
　　How great his works; how kind his ways;
　　Let every tongue pronounce his praise.

11 THEE we praise, eternal Lord,
  Thee our only God confessing,
In all earth and heaven adored,
  Father of unending blessing :
All th' angelic powers on high
Loud to thee their praises cry.

2 Holy, holy, holy Lord,
  Earth and heaven declare thy glory :
With thy saints in sweet accord
  Sings the Church the blessed story
Of th' eternal Trinity
Unto man made known in thee.

3 Lord, thy trusting people save,
  Heaven's graces on them shower ;
Light and hope beyond the grave,
  Safety from the evil power ;
Bless their years of earthly strife
With the crown of endless life.

4 Lord and Father, may thy grace
  Rule our hearts where sin abounded ;
All our hope in thee we place,
  Let us never be confounded ;
Dearest God ! we trust in thee
Now and for eternity.

12
O LORD all glorious, Life of life!
 To thee we raise our grateful songs:
Lift up our souls from thoughts of self
 To thee to whom all life belongs.

2 Below all depths thy mercy lies;
 Above all heights thy love ascends:
Thy providence our path surrounds:
 Thy watchful care each step attends.

3 From thee all good desires proceed;
 All holy thoughts we gain from thee;
The good we do is thine alone,
 Thine shall our hearts' thanksgivings be.

4 Reveal thyself to us, O Lord,
 In love, in wisdom, more and more;
That we may find thee ever near,
 And praise and serve thee and adore.   II.

13 PRAISE the Lord who reigns above,
  And rules o'er all below !
Praise the God of truth and love,
  And all his goodness show !
Praise him for his noble deeds !
  Praise him for his matchless power !
Him from whom all good proceeds,
  Let earth and heaven adore !

2 Him in whom we move and live
  Let every creature sing ;
Glory to their Maker give,
  And homage to their King !
Praise the Lord with every breath !
  All his wondrous love record !
He hath conquer'd hell and death ;
  Let all things praise the Lord !

PRAISE AND ADORATION.   211

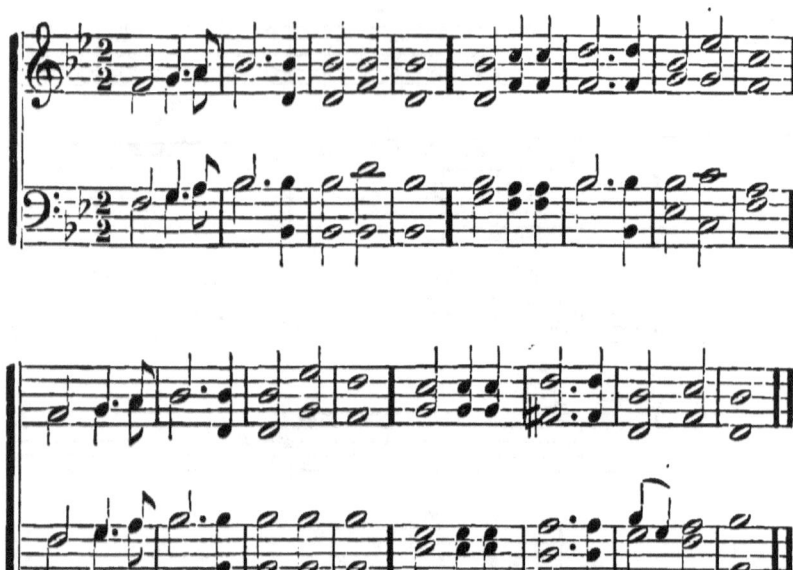

14 JESUS shall reign where'er the sun
   Doth his successive journeys run ;
   His kingdom spread from shore to shore,
   Till moons shall wax and wane no more.

2 To him shall endless prayer be made,
  And endless praises crown his head ;
  His name like sweet perfume shall rise
  With every morning sacrifice.

3 People and realms of every tongue
  Dwell on his love with sweetest song ;
  And infant voices shall proclaim
  Their early blessings on his Name.

4 Let every creature rise and bring
  Peculiar honors to our King ;
  Angels descend with songs again,
  And earth repeat the loud Amen.

II.

15 O BLESS the Lord, my soul;
    Let all within me join,
And aid my tongue to bless his name,
    Whose favors are divine.

2 The Lord forgives thy sins,
    The Lord relieves thy pain,
The Lord doth heal thy sicknesses,
    And give thee strength again.

3 He crowns thy life with love,
    When ransomed from the grave;
He, who redeemed our souls from hell,
    Hath sovereign power to save.

4 O bless the Lord, my soul;
    Let all within me join,
And aid my tongue to bless his name,
    Whose favors are divine.   V.

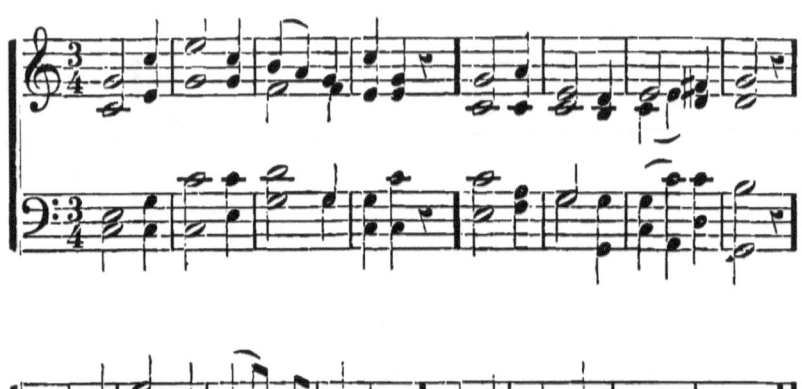

16 PRAISE the Lord! ye heavens, adore him!
   . Praise him, angels in the height;
Sun and moon, rejoice before him,
   Praise him, all ye stars of light.

2 Praise the Lord, for he hath spoken
   Worlds his mighty voice obey;
Changeless wisdom they betoken,
   Love eternal they display.

3 Praise the Lord, for he is glorious,
   Never shall his promise fail;
He will make his truth victorious
   Sin and death shall ne'er prevail.

4 Praise the God of our salvation;
   Hosts on high his power proclaim:
Heaven and earth and all creation
   Praise and magnify his Name.

IX.

17 THY mighty power we sing,
O thou Eternal King,
By heaven adored!
Nations shall bow to thee:
Subject the world shall be
Unto thy Majesty,
Jesus our Lord!

2 Stretch out thy mighty hand!
In this and every land
Evil subdue!
Satan's dominion end,
Ever thy church defend,
O Lord, our God and Friend,
Gracious and true!

3 Rise, O Jerusalem !
   Bring forth the diadem,
      Crown him and sing !
   His sovereign power make known !
   Hail him who rules alone
   On heaven's eternal throne,
      Jesus the King !

18 THOU art the mighty King of kings,
      The Lord of lords most high :
   Israel is safe beneath thy wings ;
      Thy servants shall not die.

2 Through thee we shall the victory gain,
      Though hosts of hell oppose :
   Thou art our God ; and thou wilt reign,
      And conquer all our foes.

3 We trust not in our bow or sword ;
      For weakness is our power :
   In thee we trust, Almighty Lord,
      Through every dangerous hour.

4 To thee we look, thou God of love,
      Thy holy name adore :
   Oh, may we rise to heaven above,
      To love and praise thee more.

IV.

19 SHEPHERD of tender youth,
 Guiding in love and truth
  Through devious ways,
 Christ, our triumphant King!
 We come thy name to sing,
 And here our children bring,
  To join thy praise.

2 Ever be near our side,
 Our Shepherd and our Guide,
  Our staff and song!
 O Jesus Christ our God!
 By thine enduring word
 Lead us where thou hast trod;
  Make our faith strong.

3 So now, and till we die,
   Sound we thy praises high,
   And joyful sing;
   Let all the holy throng
   Who to thy church belong
   Unite and swell the song
   To Thee our King.

20 HOLY, holy, holy Lord,
   Be thy glorious name adored;
   Lord, thy mercies never fail;
   Hail, Eternal Goodness, hail!
   Lord, we know that thou art near;
   Grace impart and holy fear!
   Purer praise we'll joyful bring
   When around thy throne we sing.

 2 There our bosoms filled with love
   Shall the joys of angels prove;
   While through heaven's unmeasured bound,
   Praise to thee shall ever sound.
   Lord, thy mercies never fail;
   Hail, Eternal Goodness, hail!
   Be thy glorious name adored,
   Holy, holy, holy Lord!

21 JESUS, in thee our hopes shall rest,
Fountain of peace, and joy, and love;
Be thy great name on earth confessed,
As by the hosts of heaven above.

2 Thine is all wisdom, thine alone:
Mercy and truth before thee stand;
Justice and judgment form thy throne,
And love divine impels thy hand.

3 No other can thy honors claim,
Or join in thy redeeming care;
No rival bear thy sacred name;
No equal in thy glory share.

4 Worship to thee alone belongs;
Worship to thee alone we give:
Thine be our hearts, and thine our songs,
O Lord, in whom alone we live. I.

22 JESUS, the very thought of thee
   With sweetness fills the breast;
But sweeter far thy face to see,
   And in thy presence rest.

2 No voice can sing, no heart can frame,
   Nor can the memory find
A sweeter sound than Jesus' name,
   The Saviour of mankind.

3 O hope of every contrite heart,
   O joy of all the meek,
To those who fall how kind thou art,
   How good to those who seek!

4 But what to those who find? Ah! this
   Nor tongue nor pen can show;
The love of Jesus, what it is
   None but his loved ones know.

5 Jesus, our only Joy be thou,
   As thou our Prize wilt be;
In thee be all our glory now
   And through eternity.

23 LORD, when thou mak'st thy presence felt,
　　And when the soul hath grasped thee right,
　How fast the dreary shadows melt
　　Beneath thy warm and living light!

2 In thee I find a nobler birth,
　　A glory o'er the world I'll see,
　And paradise returns to earth,
　　And blooms again for us in thee.

3 Thou strong and loving Son of Man,
　　Redeemer from the bonds of sin,
　'Tis thou the living spark dost fan,
　　That sets my breast on fire within.

4 Thou openest heaven once more to men,
　　The soul's true home, thy kingdom, Lord,
　And I can trust and hope again,
　　And feel myself akin to God.

I.

PRAISE AND ADORATION.

24 GOD is love : his mercy brightens
    All the paths in which we rove ;
  Joy he gives and woe he lightens ;
    God is light and God is love.

2 Death and change are busy ever,
    Man decays and ages move ;
  But his mercy waneth never ;
    God is light and God is love.

3 E'en the hour that darkest seemeth
    Will his changeless goodness prove ;
  Through the gloom his brightness streameth ;
    God is light and God is love.

4 He with earthly cares entwineth
    Hope and comfort from above,
  Every where his glory shineth :
    God is light and God is love.

IX.

25 LORD, what offering shall we bring,
　　At thine altars when we bow?
　Hearts, the pure, unsullied spring,
　　Whence the kind affections flow:

2 Willing hands, to lead the blind,
　　Heal the wounded, feed the poor;
　Love, embracing all our kind;
　　Charity, with liberal store.

3 Teach us, O thou heavenly King,
　　Thus to show our grateful mind,
　Thus the accepted offering bring,
　　Love to God and all mankind.　　　　VI.

SUPPLICATION.

26 JESUS, thou mighty God of all,
    Behold thy church assembled here!
On thy great name alone we call,
    In humble love and holy fear.

2 O Light of life, thy truth display,
    And shed around thy beams of love!
O turn our darkness into day,
    And raise our hearts to things above!

3 Here may our fervent praise and prayers
    Like grateful incense, rise on high!
Here may we lose our worldly cares,
    And find thy soothing presence nigh!

4 Here may we learn, with lowly mind,
    The truths that lead to endless peace!
Hear may we feel affections kind,
    And love and charity increase!   I.

27 JESUS, our true and only light!
Illumine those who sit in night;
Let those afar now hear thy voice,
And in thy fold with us rejoice.

2 Seek those, O Lord, who stray from thee,
Let them thy loving guidance see;
Thy peace to contrite hearts be given,
That they be drawn to thee and heaven.

3 Shine on the darkened and the cold,
Recall the wanderers from thy fold;
Unite those now who walk apart,
Confirm the weak and doubting heart.

4 So they, with us, may evermore
Such grace with wondering thanks adore,
And endless praise to thee be given,
By all thy Church in earth and heaven. II.

SUPPLICATION.

28 O LORD, where'er thy people meet,
   There they behold thy mercy-seat;
   Where'er they seek thee, thou art found,
   And where thou art is hallowed ground.

2 Great Shepherd of thy chosen few
  Thy former mercies here renew;
  And still to wayward hearts proclaim
  The sweetness of thy saving Name.

3 Here may we prove the might of prayer
  To strengthen faith and lighten care;
  To teach our faint desires to rise,
  And bring all heaven before our eyes.

4 Lord, we are weak, but thou art near,
  Nor short thine arm, nor deaf thine ear;
  O come with might and mercy down,
  And make our cleansèd hearts thine own.   II.

29 O JESUS, Lord and Saviour,
    The soul's Eternal King,
  Grant now thy grace and favor,
    While we thy praises sing!
Come, Saviour, come, and give thy Spirit course,
O feed us now and evermore, from Love's eternal source!

2 Far, far from thee, our Saviour,
    Our youthful steps might roam,
  By sin and darkness sink in death,
    Nor reach our heavenly home.
Come, Saviour, come, and give thy Spirit course,
O feed us now and evermore, from Love's eternal source!

3 Within thy Church, Lord Jesus,
    O let our souls aspire,
  To see thy Spirit's holy light,
    And feel celestial fire!
Come, Saviour, come, and give thy Spirit course,
O feed us now and evermore, from Love's eternal source!

SUPPLICATION. 227

4 Abide with us, Lord Jesus,
　　Fill us with holy zeal ;
　　Give us to think as angels think,
　　And feel as angels feel.
Come, Saviour, come, and give thy Spirit course,
O feed us now and evermore, from Love's eternal source !

30 GRACIOUS Spirit—Love divine !
　　Let thy light within me shine ;
　　All my guilty fears remove ;
　　Fill me with thy heavenly love.

　2 Life and peace to me impart ;
　　Seal salvation on my heart ;
　　Breathe thyself into my breast,—
　　Earnest of immortal rest.

　3 Let me never from thee stray ;
　　Keep me in the narrow way ;
　　Fill my soul with joy divine ;
　　Keep me, Lord, forever thine.　　　VI.

31 PEACE of God, which knows no measure,
    Heavenly sunlight of the soul,
Peace beyond all earthly treasure,
    Come, and all our hearts control.
Come, almighty to deliver !
    Nought shall make us then afraid ;
We will trust in thee forever,
    Thou on whom our hope is stayed.

SUPPLICATION.

2 O descend, all holy Spirit!
  Let our minds thy wisdom fill;
In our hearts thy throne inherit,
  Dew of heaven, thy peace distil.
Here, within thy earthly dwelling,
  We before thee, lowly bow;
Here thy ancient mercies telling,
  Let us still thy blessing know.   Amen.

32 LOVE divine, all love excelling,
      Joy of heaven, to earth come down,
    Fix in us thy humble dwelling,
      All thy faithful mercies crown.

  2 Jesus, thou art all compassion,
      Pure, unbounded love thou art;
    Visit us with thy salvation,
      Enter every trembling heart.

  3 Breathe, O Lord, thy holy spirit
      Into every troubled breast;
    Let us all thy grace inherit,
      Let us find thy promised rest.

  4 Take away the love of sinning,
      Take our load of guilt away;
    End the work of thy beginning,
      Bring us to eternal day.   IX.

33 LORD of all being! throned afar,
Thy glory flames from sun and star;
Centre and soul of every sphere,
Yet to each loving heart how near!

2 Sun of our life! thy quickening ray
Sheds on our path the glow of day;
Star of our hope! thy softened light
Cheers the long watches of the night.

3 Our midnight is thy smile withdrawn;
Our noontide is thy gracious dawn;
Our rainbow arch thy mercy's sign;
All save the clouds of sin are thine.

4 Lord of all life! below, above,
Whose light is truth, whose warmth is love,
Before thy ever-blazing throne
We ask no lustre of our own.

5 Grant us thy truth to make us free,
And kindling hearts that burn for thee,
Till all thy loving altars claim
One holy light, one heavenly flame. II.

34 IN boundless mercy, gracious Lord appear,
Darkness dispel, the humble mourner cheer;
Vain thoughts remove, melt down the flinty heart,
Draw every soul to choose the better part.

2 Thy presence fills the universal space,
Thy grace appears to all the human race;
Oh! visit us with light and life divine,
Fill every soul,—for every soul is thine.

3 The blessed Jesus is my Lord, my love:
He is my King: from him I would not move.
Hence earthly charms! far, far from me depart,
Nor seek to draw from my dear Lord my heart.

4 That uncreated beauty, which has gained
My raptured heart, has all my glory stained:
His loveliness my soul has prepossessed,
And left no room for any other guest.

35 ETERNAL Source of life and light,
   Supremely good and wise,
To thee we bring our grateful vows ;
   Accept our sacrifice.

2 Our dark and erring minds illume
   With truth's celestial rays :
Inspire our hearts with heavenly love,
   And tune our lips to praise.

3 Conduct us safely, by thy truth,
   Through life's perplexing road ;
And bring us, when our journey's o'er,
   Lord, to thine own abode.

4 For in thy presence e'er abounds
   Fullness of purest joy ;
At thy right hand unceasing flow
   Pleasures without alloy.

IV.

SUPPLICATION.

36 LORD of our life, and God of our salvation,
Star of our night, and hope of every nation,
Hear and receive thy Church's supplication,
    Lord God Almighty.

2 See round thine ark the hungry billows curling,
See how thy foes their banners are unfurling;
Lord, while their darts, envenomed, they are hurling,
    Thou canst preserve us.

3 Lord, thou canst help when earthly armor faileth,
Lord, thou canst save when deadly sin assaileth,
Lord, o'er thy Rock nor death nor hell prevaileth,
    Grant us thy peace, Lord.

4 Grant us thy help till foes are backward driven,
Grant them thy truth, that they may be forgiven,
Grant peace on earth, and, after we have striven,
    Peace in thy heaven.

37 LEAD us, heavenly Father, lead us
    O'er the world's tempestuous sea;
Guide us, guard us, keep us, feed us,
    For we have no help but thee;
Yet possessing every blessing
    If our God our father be.

2 Saviour, shed thy mercy o'er us;
    All our weakness thou dost know;
Thou didst tread the earth before us,
    Thou didst feel its keenest woe:
Lone and dreary, faint and weary,
    Through the desert thou didst go.

SUPPLICATION.

3 Spirit of our God, descending,
　Fill our hearts with heavenly joy;
Love with every feeling blending,
　Pleasures that can never cloy.
Thus provided, pardoned, guided,
　Nothing can our peace destroy.

38 O THAT the Lord would guide my ways
　　　To keep his statutes still!
　　O that my God would grant me grace
　　　To know and do his will!

2 O send thy Spirit down, to write
　　Thy law upon my heart!
　Save me from falsehood and deceit,
　　Thy truth to me impart.

3 Order my footsteps by thy Word,
　　And make my heart sincere;
　Let sin have no dominion, Lord,
　　But keep my conscience clear.

4 Make me to walk in thy commands;
　　'Tis a delightful road;
　Nor let my thoughts, my heart, my hands
　　Offend against my God.　　　　IV.

39 JESUS, Lord of all creation,
　Pure, unbounded love thou art;
Visit us with thy salvation,
　Enter every waiting heart.
Breathe, O breathe thy Holy Spirit
　Into every troubled breast;
Let us all thy grace inherit,
　Let us find the promised rest.

2 Finish, now, thy new creation;
　From our sins O set us free:
May we find thy great salvation
　Come, with healing power, from thee.
Lord, we would on earth adore thee,
　Till in heaven we take our place;
Till we cast our crowns before thee,
　Lost in wonder, love, and praise.　　VIII.

SUPPLICATION.   237

40 O THOU, at whose divine command
      Good seed is sown in every land,
    Thy Holy Spirit now impart,
    And for thy Word prepare each heart.

  2 Not 'mid the thorns of worldly thought,
    Nor soon by passing plunderers caught,
    Nor lacking depth the root to feed,
    May we receive thy Spirit's seed.

  3 But may it, where thy sowers toil,
    Fall in a good and honest soil;
    And spring up from firmest root,
    Through patience, bear abundant fruit.   II.

41
O Thou, to whose all-searching sight
The darkness shineth as the light,
Search, prove my heart; it pants for thee:
O burst these bonds, and set it free.

2 While in this darksome wild I stray,
Be thou my light, be thou my way;
No foes, no violence I fear,
No harm, if thou, O Lord, art near.

3 When rising floods my soul o'erflow,
When sinks my heart in waves of woe,
O Lord, thy timely aid impart,
And raise my head, and cheer my heart.

4 If rough and thorny be the way,
My strength proportion to my day;
Till toil, and grief, and pain shall cease,
Where all is calm, and joy, and peace. II.

PENITENTIAL.

42 JESUS, the weary wanderer's rest,
　　Give me thy easy yoke to bear;
With resignation arm my breast,
　　With humble love and lowly fear.

2 Thankful I take the cup from thee,
　　Mingled according to thy will,
Though bitter to the taste it be,
　　'T is full of heavenly mercy still.

3 Be thou, O Rock of Ages, nigh!
　　So shall each murmuring thought be gone,
And grief, and fear, and care shall fly,
　　As clouds before the mid-day sun.

4 O thou, who bad'st the tempest cease,
　　And lo! the waves obeyed thy will,
Speak to my warring passions, peace!
　　Say to my trembling heart—be still.

I.

43 AS pants the hart for cooling streams,
  When heated in the chase,
So longs my soul, O God, for thee,
  And thy refreshing grace.

2 For thee, my God—the living God,
  My thirsty soul doth pine;
O, when shall I behold thy face,
  Thou Majesty divine!

3 I sigh to think of happier days,
  When thou, O Lord, wast nigh;
When every heart was tuned to praise,
  And none more blest than I.

4 Why restless, why cast down, my soul?
  Hope still, and thou shalt sing
The praise of him who is thy God,
  Thy Saviour, and thy King.

44 O JESUS, Saviour of the lost,
My Rock and Hiding-place,
By storms of sin and sorrow toss'd,
I seek thy sheltering grace.

2 Forgive me guilty, Lord, I cry :
Pursued by foes, I come ;
O save me tempted, or I die ;
A wand'rer, take me home.

3 There safe in thine almighty arms
Let storms come on amain,
No more I fear their dread alarms
Where thou, O Lord, dost reign.

IV.

45 I LOVE the voice Divine that speaks
      The words of life and peace,
    That bids the penitent rejoice,
      And sin and sorrow cease.

 2 No healing balm on earth like this,
      Can cheer the contrite heart;
    No flattering dreams of earthly bliss
      Such pure delight impart.

 3 How merciful and kind thou art
      Thy goodness to reveal;
    Bind up, O Lord, the broken heart,
      The wounded spirit heal.

 4 Let thy bright presence, Lord, restore
      Peace to the anxious breast;
    Conduct me in the path that leads
      To everlasting rest.

IV.

FAITH AND TRUST.

46 GREAT refuge of the weary soul,
On thee, when sorrows rise :
On thee, when waves of trouble roll,
My fainting hope relies.

2 To thee I tell each rising grief,
For thou alone canst heal :
Thy Word can bring a sure relief,
For every pain I feel.

3 O, gracious God, where shall I flee?
Thou art my only trust ;
And still my soul would cleave to thee,
Though prostrate in the dust.

4 Thy mercy seat is open still,
There let my soul retreat :
With humble hope attend thy will,
And wait before thy feet.

IV.

47
1 REST of the weary,
 Joy of the sad,
Hope of the dreary,
 Light of the glad;
Home of the stranger,
 Strength to the end,
Refuge from danger,
 Saviour and Friend!

2 Pillow where lying
 Love rests its head,
Peace of the dying,
 Life of the dead:
Path of the lowly,
 Prize at the end,
Breath of the holy,
 Saviour and Friend!

3 When my feet stumble,
 To thee I'll cry,
Crown of the humble,
 Cross of the high;
When my steps wander,
 Over me bend
Truer and fonder,
 Saviour and Friend.

4 Ever confessing
 Thee, I will raise
Unto thee blessing,
 Glory and praise:
All my endeavor,
 World without end,
Thine to be ever,
Saviour and Friend.

FAITH AND TRUST. 245

48 O Thou from whom all goodness flows,
I lift my soul to thee;
In all my sorrows, conflicts, woes,
Good Lord, remember me.
If trials sore obstruct my way
And ills I cannot flee,
Then let my strength be as my day,
Good Lord, remember me!

2 Whene'er distressed by pain or grief
Thine eye my frame shall see,
Grant patience, rest, and kind relief,
In love remember me.
When on my restless, burdened heart
My sins lie heavily,
Let thy salvation peace impart,
Good Lord, remember me!

3 If on my face, for thy dear Name,
Shame and reproaches be,
All hail reproach, and welcome shame,
If thou remember me!
And when thy love shall call me hence
Thy brighter world to see,
Be thou my haven and defense,
Good Lord, remember me!

49 JESUS, lover of my soul,
    Let me to thy bosom fly,
While the nearer waters roll,
    While the tempest still is high;

2 Hide me, O my Saviour, hide,
    Till the storm of life is past,
Safe into the haven guide,
    O receive my soul at last.

3 Other refuge have I none;
    Hangs my helpless soul on thee:
Leave, O leave me not alone;
    Still support and comfort me:

4 All my trust on thee is stayed;
    All my help from thee I bring;
Cover my defenceless head
    With the shadow of thy wing.   VI.

FAITH AND TRUST.

50 WHERE for safety shall I fly?
Saviour, unto thee I cry.
Dangers everywhere attend,
Let thine arm my soul defend.

2 Round me troops of foes I see,
Help can come from none but thee;
Be my constant strength and stay,
Guard me in the evil day!

3 Thy protecting care I crave,
Power is thine, O Lord, to save;
Matchless wonders thou hast wrought,
Far beyond the reach of thought.

4 Let thy gracious hand impart
Strength and comfort to my heart!
Ever keep me near to thee,
Till I'm called thy face to see.

5 O that home, eternal, blest,
Where the soul shall find its rest;
Lord, till that transporting day,
Onward lead me in thy way.

VI.

51 KEEP me, Saviour, near thy side,
Let thy counsel be my guide;
Never let me from thee rove,
Sweetly draw me by thy love.

2 Earnest thou of heavenly rest,
Comfort of the troubled breast;
Life and joy to me impart,
Take to thee my wandering heart.

3 Thou, blest Shepherd of the sheep,
Wilt thine own in safety keep;
All my doubts and fears control,
Till thy love shall make me whole.

4 Thou, O Lord, in death's dark night,
Be my hope, my strength, my light;
Thou my rock, my anchor fast,
Thou my blessed haven at last.

VI.

52 THOU Lamb of God, thou Prince of Peace,
   For thee my thirsty soul doth pine;
My love, my faith, my hope increase,
   And make me in thy likeness shine.

2 With single eye and humble mind,
   Thy will in all things may I see!
In love be every wish resigned,
   And hallowed every thought to thee!

3 Close by thy side O keep me still,
   Howe'er life's various currents flow;
With steadfast eye to mark thy will,
   And follow thee where'er I go.

4 Thou, Lord, the dreadful fight hast won;
   Alone hast thou the wine-press trod.
Thy hand shall lead me safely on:
   Mighty to save art thou, my God.   I.

53 JESUS! I my cross have taken,
　　All to leave and follow thee;
Naked, poor, despised, forsaken,
　　Thou from hence my all shalt be;
Perish, every fond ambition,
　　All I've sought or hoped or known,
Yet how rich is my condition!
　　God and heaven are still my own!

2 I have called thee, Abba, Father!
　　I have stayed my heart on thee;
Storms may howl, and clouds may gather,
　　All must work for good to me.
Man may trouble and distress me,
　　'T will but drive me to thy breast;
Life with trials hard may press me,
　　Heaven will bring me sweeter rest;

3 Soul, then know thy full salvation,
 Rise o'er sin and fear and care;
Joy to find in every station
 Something still to do or bear.
Soon shall close thy earthly mission,
 Soon shall pass thy pilgrim days,
Hope shall change to glad fruition,
 Faith to sight and prayer to praise.

54 FOREVER blessed be the Lord,
 My Saviour and my shield;
He sends the Spirit of his Word
 To arm me for the field.

2 When sin and hell their force unite,
 He makes my soul his care;
Instructs me in the heavenly fight,
 And guards me through the war.

3 A friend and helper so divine
 My fainting hope shall raise;
He makes the glorious victory mine,
 And his shall be the praise.

IV

55 NEARER, my God, to thee,
    Nearer to thee,
  E'en though it be a cross
    That raiseth me ;
  Still all my song shall be,
  Nearer, my God, to thee,
    Nearer to thee.

2 Though like the wanderer,
    The sun gone down,
  Darkness be over me,
    My rest a stone ;
  Yet in my dreams I'd be
  Nearer, my God, to thee,
    Nearer to thee.

3 There let my way appear
    Steps unto heaven ;
  All that thou sendest me
    In mercy given ;
  Angels to beckon me
  Nearer, my God, to thee,
    Nearer to thee.

              [thoughts
4 Then, with my waking
    Bright with thy praise,
  Out of my stony griefs
    Altars I'll raise ;
  So by my woes to be
  Nearer, my God, to thee,
    Nearer to thee.

5 Or, if on joyful wing,
    Cleaving the sky,
  Sun, moon, and stars forgot,
    Upward I fly,
  Still all my song shall be,
  Nearer, my God, to thee,
    Nearer to thee. *Amen.*

56 O GOD, my heavenly King,
      My Saviour, and my All,
    To thee my every power I bring,
      And at thy footstool fall.

  2 By thee I am supplied
      With every good below :
    Thou art my Shepherd and my Guide,
      In all the way I go.

  3 Fain would I follow thee,
      Nor from thy footsteps stray,
    Whate'er my pains or conflicts be,
      Or snares my foes may lay.

  4 I know that thou art nigh,
      My fortress, shield, and tower :
    On thy rich mercy I'll rely,
      And trust thy mighty power.

57 GOD is my strong salvation,
   What foe have I to fear?
In darkness and temptation
   My light, my help is near.

2 Though hosts encamp around me,
   Firm to the fight I stand;
What terror can confound me
   With God at my right hand?

3 Place on the Lord reliance,
   My soul, with homage wait;
His truth be thine affiance
   When faint and desolate.

4 His might thy heart shall strengthen,
   His love thy joy increase;
Mercy thy days shall lengthen,
   The Lord will give thee peace.

FAITH AND TRUST.

58 COMMIT thou all thy griefs
   And ways into his hands;
To his sure truth and tender care
   Who earth and heaven commands.

2 He every-where has sway,
   And all things serve his might:
His every act pure blessing is,
   His path unsullied light.

3 Still heavy is thine heart?
   Still sink thy spirits down?
Cast off the weight, let fear depart,
   And every care be gone.

4 Leave to his sovereign sway
   To choose and to command;
So shalt thou wondering own his way:
   How wise, how strong his hand!

5 Blest is the man, O God,
   That stays himself on thee!
Who waits for thy salvation, Lord,
   Shall thy salvation see!

59 O fix my heart, my God, my Strength,
And make it strong to bear;
I will be joyful in thy love,
And peaceful in thy care.

2 On thy compassion I rely,
In weakness and distress;
Oh, 'tis a blessed thing for me
To need thy tenderness.

3 Safe in thine all sufficient love,
Almighty to restore,
Oh, let my soul abound in hope,
And praise thee more and more.   IV.

FAITH AND TRUST.

60 THY way, not mine, O Lord,
However dark it be!
Lead me by thine own hand,
Choose out the path for me.

2 Smooth let it be or rough,
It will be still the best;
Winding or straight, it leads
Right onward to thy rest.

3 The kingdom that I seek
Is thine; so let the way
That leads to it be thine;
Else I must surely stray.

4 Take thou my cup, and it
With joy or sorrow fill,
As best to thee may seem;
Choose thou my good and ill;

5 Not mine, not mine the choice,
In things or great or small;
Be thou my guide, my strength,
My wisdom, and my all!

61 HOW gentle God's commands,
   How kind his precepts are;
Come, cast your burdens on the Lord,
   And trust his constant care.

2 His bounty will provide,
   His people safely dwell;
The hand which bears creation up
   Shall guard his children well.

3 Why should this anxious load
   Press down your weary mind?
O seek your heavenly Father's throne
   And peace and comfort find.

4 His goodness stands approved,
   Unchanged from day to day;
I'll drop my burden at his feet,
   And bear a song away.

DIVINE PROVIDENCE.

62 O KING of kings, beneath thy wings
My soul would still repose;
My refuge sure my strength secure,
Against surrounding foes!

2 Thy wondrous ways to grateful praise,
Shall move my heart and tongue;
By hosts above thy deeds of love,
In joyful notes are sung.

3 May I proclaim thy sacred name,
By living, Lord, to thee!
Then shall I rise above the skies,
And thy perfections see.

4 O who can tell what glories dwell,.
Around the eternal throne!
There joys divine, that ne'er decline,
Are by the righteous known.

IV.

63 WHILE thee I seek, protecting Power,
Be my vain wishes stilled,
And may this consecrated hour
With better hopes be filled.

2 Thy love the power of thought bestowed ;
To thee my thoughts would soar ·
Thy mercy o'er my life has flowed,
That mercy I adore.

3 In each event of life, how clear
Thy ruling hand I see !
Each blessing to my soul more dear
Because conferred by thee.

4 In every joy that crowns my days,
In every pain I bear,
My heart shall find delight in praise,
Or seek relief in prayer.

DIVINE PROVIDENCE.

5 When gladness wings my favored hour,
   Thy love my thoughts shall fill;
Resigned, when storms of sorrow lower,
   My soul shall meet thy will.

6 My lifted eye, without a tear,
   The gathering storm shall see;
My steadfast heart shall know no fear,
   That heart shall rest on thee.   IV.

64 FATHER, whate'er of earthly bliss
   Thy sovereign will denies,
Accepted at thy throne of grace
   Let this petition rise:

2 Give me a calm, a thankful heart,
   From every murmur free;
The blessings of thy love impart,
   That I may live in thee.

3 O let the hope that thou art mine
   My path of life attend;
Thy presence through my journey shine,
   And crown my journey's end.   IV.

65 SAVIOUR, Source of every blessing,
  Tune my heart to grateful lays;
Streams of mercy never ceasing
  Call for ceaseless songs of praise.

2 Teach me some melodious measure
   Sung by raptured saints above;
  Fill my soul with sacred pleasure,
   While I sing thy boundless love.

3 Thou didst seek me when a stranger,
   Wandering from the fold of God,
  And, to shield my soul from danger,
   Bore thyself affliction's rod.

4 By thy hand redeemed, defended,
   Safe through life thus far I've come;
  Safe, O Lord, when life is ended,
   Bring me to my heavenly home.   IX.

DIVINE PROVIDENCE. 263

66 O LORD, how boundless is thy love!
    Thy gifts are every evening new;
    And morning mercies from above
    Gently distil like early dew.

2 Thou spread'st the curtains of the night,
    Great Guardian of our sleeping hours;
    Thy sovereign word restores the light,
    And quickens all my drowsy powers.

3 I yield my powers to thy command,
    To thee I consecrate my days;
    Perpetual blessings from thy hand
    Demand perpetual songs of praise.   I.

67 MY spirit on thy care,
   Blest Saviour, I recline:
Thou wilt not leave me to despair,
   For thou art love divine.

2 In thee I place my trust,
   On thee I calmly rest,
I know thee good, I know thee just
   And count thy choice the best.

3 Whate'er events betide,
   Thy will they all perform;
Safe in thy breast my head I hide,
   Nor fear the coming storm.

4 Let good or ill befall,
   It must be good for me;
Secure of having thee in all,
   Of having all in thee.

V.

DIVINE PROVIDENCE.

68 WHOM have we, Lord, in heaven but thee,
    And whom on earth beside?
Where else for succor can we flee,
    Or in whose strength confide?

2 Thou art our portion here below,
    Our promised rest above;
Ne'er may our souls an object know,
    So precious as thy love.

3 Thou, Lord, wilt be our guide through life,
    And help and strength supply;
Sustain us in earth's final strife,
    And welcome us on high.   IV.

69 WHOSO in God alone confideth,
　　Whose hope is fixed in him always,
He 'neath th' Almighty's wing abideth
　　Safe and unmoved in evil days.
Who trusts in God's unchanging love,
Builds on a rock that none can move.

2 O man, cease from thy restless yearning,
　　And wait in cheerful hope, content
To take what his all-wise discerning,
　　His perfect love to thee has sent.
No doubt our inmost wants are known
To him who calleth us his own.

3 He knows when best the joyful hour,
   He sends it as he sees it meet;
   When thou hast proved thy spirit's power,
   And art made free from all deceit,
   Then comes he to thee unaware,
   And makes thee own his loving care.

70 THEY who on the Lord rely
   Safely dwell, though danger's nigh:
   Lo, his sheltering wings are spread
   O'er each faithful servant's head.

2 Vain temptation's wily snare;
  They shall be their Father's care:
  Harmless flies the shaft by day,
  Or in darkness wings its way.

3 When they wake, or when they sleep,
  Angel guards their vigils keep:
  Death and danger may be near;
  Faith and love can never fear.

VI.

71 CAST upon the Lord thy care!
  'Tis enough that he is nigh.
  He will all thy burden bear:
  He will all thy wants supply.

2 He thy soul will safely lead:
  In his tender love confide!
  Call on him in time of need;
  He will be thy Guard and Guide.

3 Lord, I would, I do submit,
  Gladly yield my all to thee:
  What thy wisdom seeth fit,
  Surely must be best for me.

VI.

DIVINE PROVIDENCE.

72 WHILE my Redeemer's near,
My shepherd and my guide,
I bid farewell to every fear;
My wants are all supplied.

2 To ever-fragrant meads,
Where rich abundance grows,
His gracious hand indulgent leads,
And guards my sweet repose.

3 Dear Shepherd, if I stray,
My wandering feet restore,
And guard me with thy watchful eye,
And let me rove no more.   V.

73 GOD moves in a mysterious way
　　His wonders to perform ;
　He plants his footsteps in the sea,
　　And rides upon the storm.

2 Judge not the Lord by feeble sense
　　But trust him for his grace ;
　Behind a frowning providence
　　He hides a smiling face.

3 His purposes will ripen fast,
　　Unfolding every hour :
　The bud may have a bitter taste,
　　But sweet will be the flower.

4 Blind unbelief is sure to err,
　　And scan his work in vain ;
　God is his own interpreter,
　　And he will make it plain.　　　IV.

DIVINE PROVIDENCE.

74 O LORD, our help in ages past,
      Our hope for years to come,
    Our shelter from the stormy blast,
      And our eternal home :

  2 Beneath the shadow of thy throne
      Thy people dwell secure ;
    Sufficient is thine arm alone,
      And our defense is sure.

  3 Before the earth in order stood,
      Or men had learned thy name,
    From everlasting thou art God,
      To endless years the same.

  4 O Lord, our help in ages past,
      Our hope for years to come ;
    Be thou our guard while troubles last,
      And our eternal home !   IV.

75 GOD is the refuge of his saints
When storms of sharp distress invade;
Ere we can offer our complaints,
Behold him present with his aid.

2 There is a stream, whose gentle flow
Supplies the city of our God:
Life, love, and joy still gliding through,
And watering our divine abode.

3 That sacred stream, thy holy Word,
Supports our faith, our fear controls:
Sweet peace thy promises afford,
And give new strength to fainting souls.

4 Zion enjoys her Saviour's love,
Secure against a threatening hour;
Nor can her firm foundation move,
Built on his truth, and armed with power.   II.

THE WORD.

76 FATHER of mercies, in thy Word,
What grace and glory shine!
Forever be thy name adored
For wisdom so divine.

2 The tree of life here fruitful grows,
Adorned with healing leaves:
Sublimer sweets than nature knows
The hungry soul receives.

3 O may these heavenly pages be
My ever dear delight;
And still new beauties may I see,
And still increasing light.

4 Divine Instructor, gracious Lord,
Be thou forever near;
Teach me to love thy holy Word,
And view thy glory there.

IV.

77 WHAT glory gilds the sacred page,
　　Majestic, like the sun :
It gives a light to every age ;
　　It gives, but borrows none.

2 The power that gave it still supplies
　　The gracious light and heat :
Its truths upon the nations rise ;
　　They rise, no more to set.

3 Let everlasting thanks be thine
　　For such a bright display,
As makes a world of darkness shine
　　With beams of heavenly day.

4 My soul rejoices to pursue
　　The steps of him I love,
Till glory break upon my view
　　In brighter worlds above.　　　　IV.

78
 LORD, thy word abideth,
  And our footsteps guideth;
 Who its truth believeth
 Light and joy receiveth.

2 When our foes are near us,
 Then thy Word doth cheer us,
 Word of consolation,
 Message of salvation.

3 When the storms are o'er us,
 And dark clouds before us,
 Then its light directeth
 And our way protecteth.

4 Who can tell the pleasure,
 Who recount the treasure,
 By thy Word imparted
 To the simple-hearted?

5 Word of mercy, giving
 Succor to the living;
 Word of life, supplying
 Comfort to the dying!

6 Oh that we, discerning
 Its most holy learning,
 Lord, may love and fear thee,
 Evermore be near thee!

79 GREAT God, we give thee praise
　　For all thy wond'rous grace,
　Thy kind and condescending ways
　　To our poor fallen race.

2 Thou hast thy love reveal'd
　　Beyond what prophets knew ;
　Thy Holy Book of truth unseal'd,
　　To our astonish'd view.

3 We wander now no more
　　Where darkening errors lead :
　But truth by light divine explore,
　　And wonder while we read.

4 Lord, we adore thy name
　　For light and truth divine !
　From thee the welcome mercies came,
　　And be the glory thine !

80 THE Lord our Saviour is the Way
    To purity and peace;
By doctrine from his Word, he leads
    To everlasting bliss.

2 The Lord our Saviour is the Truth,
    The inward, shining Light,
That reason guides, and gives to faith
    The evidence of sight.

3 The Lord our Saviour is the Life
    Of every soul that lives;
And everlasting life, to those
    Who keep his Word, he gives.

4 Jesus, my Way, my Truth, my Life,
    My God, my All in all;
At thy blest feet, in humble love,
    And lowly fear, I fall.

IV.

81 GLORIOUS things of thee are spoken,
　　Zion, city of our God;
He whose word cannot be broken
　　Formed thee for his own abode;
On the Rock of ages founded,
　　What can shake thy sure repose?
With salvation's walls surrounded,
　　Thou may'st smile at all thy foes.

2 See, the streams of living waters,
  Springing from eternal love,
 Still supply thy sons and daughters,
  And all fear of want remove:
 Who can faint while such a river,
  Ever flows our thirst t'assuage?
 Blessings which, like God, the giver,
  Never fail, from age to age. VIII.

82 TRIUMPHANT ZION, lift thy head
 From dust, and darkness, and the dead;
 Though humbled long, awake at length,
 And gird thee with thy Saviour's strength.

2 Put all thy beauteous garments on,
 And let thine excellence be known;
 Decked in the robes of righteousness,
 Thy glories shall the world confess.

3 No more shall foes unclean invade,
 And fill thy hallowed walls with dread;
 No more shall sin's insulting host
 · Their victory and thy sorrows boast.

4 The Lord on high has heard thy prayer;
 His hand thy ruin shall repair;
 Nor will thy watchful monarch cease
 To guard thee in eternal peace. II.

83 RICH in mercy, Jesus reigns.
Angels own no other King;
Crown him, mortals, in your strains,
While his matchless grace you sing!
Angels wake their lofty lays,
Kindled from celestial fires;
Humbler spirits bid his praise
Sweetly flow from silver lyres.

2 Catch, O catch the pleasing strain!
Gratitude demands the song:
Jesus builds his church again;
Lays her deep foundations strong.

Truth divine her walls supports:
Love has paved her streets of gold:
See her jasper towers and courts!—
Gates of pearl that never fold!

3 Pilgrims, enter and rejoice!
Here your Saviour holds his throne:
'Tis the city of his choice:
'Tis the church he calls his own.
Precious gems, of various hue,
Brightly shine on every side:
Come, the splendid glories view!
Come, and in his courts abide!

84 BUILT by Jehovah's hand,
The holy city see:
Its happy gates wide open stand:
To enter all are free.

2 One bright, eternal day
Shall in the city reign,
Darkness and death are fled away,
Ne'er to return again.

3 O blessed, happy state!
O Lord, we thankful come,
Low at thy footstool humbly wait,
And make thy church our home.

V.

85 SAFE Home, safe Home in port!
Rent cordage, shattered deck,
Torn sails, provisions short,
And only not a wreck :
But O the joy upon the shore,
To tell our voyage perils o'er !

2 The prize, the prize secure !
The warrior nearly fell;
Bare all he could endure,
And bare not always well :
But he may smile at troubles gone
Who sets the victor-garland on !

3 No more the foe can harm :
No more of leagur'd camp,
And cry of night alarm,
And need of ready lamp :
And yet how nearly had he fail'd,—
How nearly had that foe prevailed !

4 The exile is at home!
 O nights and days of tears,
 O longings not to roam,
 O sins, and doubts, and fears;
 What matter now this bitter fray?
 The King has wiped those tears away. *Amen.*

86 CHILDREN of the heavenly King,
 As ye journey, sweetly sing:
 Sing your Saviour's worthy praise,
 Glorious in his works and ways.

2 Ye are traveling home to God,
 In the way the fathers trod;
 They are happy now, and ye
 Soon their happiness shall see.

3 Shout, ye little flock, and blest;
 Soon you'll enter into rest;
 There your seat is now prepared,
 There your kingdom and reward.

4 Lord, submissive make us go,
 Gladly leaving all below;
 Only thou our leader be,
 And we still will follow thee.

VI.

87 JERUSALEM, the golden! O city of the blest!
  O heavenly land of promise! the weary pilgrim's rest;
Safe through the thorny journey; freed from the strife of sin;
Within the walls of jasper; the pearly gates within.

2 What peace beyond all telling; what joy, for them whose feet
   Stand by the crystal river, and walk the golden street!
   With boughs of palms, like victors, arrayed in robes of white,
   With hymns of glad thanksgiving they throng the halls of light.

3 They thirst not, neither hunger, who gain that bright abode,
   With oil of love anointed; as kings and priests to God.
   O dear and blessed vision; the Seer of Patmos tells!
   What glad and hopeful tidings, the prophets voice reveals.

4 Behold the Tabernacle of God is now with men:
   And He will dwell among them and heal their grief and pain,
   And he that overcometh shall be the Father's heir,
   Within the glorious city! and dwell forever there.

88 THOU City of the angels, thou City of the Lord,
   Whose everlasting music is e'er in sweet accord;
   Jerusalem, exulting on that securest shore,
   I hope thee, wish thee, sing thee, and love thee evermore.

2 O fields that know no sorrow! O state that fears no strife!
   O princely bowers, O land of flowers, O realm and home of Life!
   There, through the sacred lilies, and flowers on every side,
   The happy ransomed people go wandering far and wide.

3 O one, O only Mansion! O Paradise of joy!
   Where tears are ever banished and smiles have no alloy;
   With jasper glow thy bulwarks, thy streets with emeralds blaze,
   The sardius and the topaz unite in thee their rays.

4 Thou hast no night, fair heaven; thou hast no time, bright day!
   Dear fountain of refreshment to pilgrims far away!
   Upon the Rock of Ages they raise thy holy tower;
   Thine is the victor's laurel, and thine the golden dower.

5 O sweet and blessed country, the home of God's elect!
   O sweet and blessed country that eager hearts expect!
   In mercy, Saviour, bring us to that dear land of rest,
   Who art our heavenly Father and Saviour ever blest.

89 HIGH in yonder realms of light
    Dwell the raptured saints above—
Far beyond our feeble sight,
    Happy in Immanuel's love.
Pilgrims in this vale of tears,
    Once they knew, like us below,
Gloomy doubts, distressing fears,
    Torturing pain, and heavy woe.

HEAVEN. 287

2 Happy spirits, ye are fled
    Where no grief can entrance find ;
  Lulled to rest the aching head,
    Soothed the anguish of the mind.
  Every tear is wiped away,
    Sighs no more shall heave the breast,
  Night is lost in endless day,
    Sorrow in eternal rest.   VI.

90 O PEACE of all the faithful !
      O calm of all the blest !
    Inviolate, unvaried,
      Divinest, sweetest, best,

2 Yes, peace ! for war is over ;
    Yes, calm ! for storm is past ;
  And goal from finished labor,
    And anchorage at last.

3 O happy, holy portion,
    Refection for the blest !
  True vision of true beauty,
    Sweet cure of all distrest !

4 Strive, man, to win that glory !
    Toil, man, to gain that light !
  Send hope before to grasp it,
    Till hope be lost in sight.

91 THERE is a land of pure delight,
　　Where God the Saviour reigns;
Infinite day excludes the night,
And pleasures banish pains.

2 There everlasting spring abides,
　　And never-withering flowers:
Death, like a narrow sea, divides
This heavenly land from ours.

3 No cloud those blissful regions know,
　　Realms ever bright and fair,
For sin, the source of mortal woe,
Can never enter there.

4 O may the heavenly prospects fire
　　Our hearts with ardent love,
Till wings of faith and strong desire
Bear every thought above.

THE LORD'S DAY.

92 THINE earthly Sabbaths, Lord, we love;
But there's a nobler rest above:
To that our longing souls aspire,
With cheerful hope, and strong desire.

2 No more fatigue, no more distress,
Nor sin, nor death shall reach the place;
No groans shall mingle with the songs,
Which warble from immortal tongues.

3 No rude alarms of raging foes;
No cares to break the long repose;
No midnight shade, no clouded sun;
But sacred, high, eternal noon.

II.

93 THIS is the day of light :
   Let there be light to-day ;
O Day-spring, rise upon our night,
And chase its gloom away.

2 This is the day of rest :
   Our failing strength renew ;
On weary brain and troubled breast
   Shed thou thy freshening dew.

3 This is the day of peace :
   Thy peace our spirits fill ;
Bid thou the blasts of discord cease,
   The waves of strife be still.

4 This is the day of prayer :
   Let earth to heaven draw near ,
Lift up our hearts to seek thee there
   Come down to meet us here.

5 This is the first of days :
   Send forth thy quickening breath,
And wake dead souls to love and praise,
   O Vanquisher of death !

THE LORD'S DAY.

94 WELCOME, sweet day of rest,
   That saw the Lord arise;
   Welcome to this reviving breast,
   And these rejoicing eyes.

2 The King himself comes near
  And feasts his saints to-day;
  Here may we sit, and see him here,
  And love, and praise, and pray.

3 One day of prayer and praise
  His sacred courts within,
  Is sweeter than ten thousand days
  Spent in the ways of sin.

4 My willing soul would stay
  In such a frame as this,
  And serve him in eternal day,
  And everlasting bliss.

V.

95 NEW every morning is thy love,
   Our wakening and uprising prove;
   Through sleep and darkness safely brought,
   Restored to life, and power, and thought.

2 New mercies, each returning day,
  Hover around us while we pray;
  New perils past, new sins forgiven,
  New thoughts of God, new hopes of heaven.

3 If on our daily course our mind
  Be set to hallow all we find,
  New treasures still, of countless price
  God will provide for sacrifice.

4 The trivial round, the common task,
  Will furnish all we need to ask,
  Room to deny ourselves, a road
  To bring us daily nearer God.

5 Only, O Lord, in thy dear love
  Fit us for perfect rest above;
  And help us, this and every day,
  To live more nearly as we pray.

III.

96 NOW that the daylight fills the sky,
    We lift our hearts to God on high :
That he, in all we do or say,
Would keep us free from harm to-day.

2 Would guard our hearts and tongues from strife,
From anger's din would hide our life :
From all ill sights would turn our eyes :
Would close our ears from vanities.

3 Would keep our inmost conscience pure,
Our souls from folly would secure ;
Would bid us check the pride of sense
With due and holy abstinence.

4 So we, when this new day is gone,
And night, in turn, is drawing on,
With conscience by the world unstained,
Shall praise his name for victory gained.   II.

I. *Morning.*

97 SHINE forth, O Sun of boundless love,
The night within our souls remove;
Be thou our Light, be thou our Guide,
O'er every thought and step preside.

2 The light of truth to us display,
That we may know and choose thy way;
Plant holy fear within each heart,
That we may ne'er from God depart.

II. *Noonday.*

1 O GOD of truth, O Lord of might,
Who orderest time and change aright,
And sendest the early morning ray,
And lightest the glow of perfect day.

2 Extinguish thou each sinful fire,
And banish every ill desire;
And while thou keepest the body whole,
Shed forth thy peace upon the soul.

III. *Evening.*

1 O THOU true life of all that live,
Who dost unmoved all motion sway;
Who dost the morn and evening give,
And through its changes guide the day.

2 Thy light upon our evening pour,
  So may our souls no sunset see;
  And death to us an open door,
  To an eternal morning be. L.

98 SAVIOUR, breathe an evening blessing,
    Ere repose our spirits seal;
  Sin and want we come confessing,
    Thou canst save and thou canst heal.

2 Though destruction walk around us,
    Though the arrows past us fly,
  Angel guards from thee surround us,
    We are safe, if thou art nigh.

3 Though the night be dark and dreary,
    Darkness cannot hide from thee;
  Thou art he who, never weary,
    Watchest where thy people be. IX.

99 SUN of my soul! thou Saviour dear,
It is not night if thou be near;
Oh! may no earth-born cloud arise,
To hide thee from thy servant's eyes.

2 When the soft dews of kindly sleep
My wearied eyelids gently steep,
Be my last thought, how sweet to rest
With thy divine protection blest.

3 Abide with me from morn till eve,
For without thee I can not live;
Abide with me when night is nigh,
For without thee I dare not die.

4 If some poor wandering child of thine,
Have spurned, to-day, the voice divine,
Now, Lord, the gracious work begin,
Let him no more lie down in sin.

5 Come near, and bless us when we wake,
Ere through the world our way we take;
Till, in the ocean of thy love,
We lose ourselves in heaven above.

III.

EVENING.

100 SOFTLY now the light of day
Fades upon my sight away;
Free from care, from labor free,
Lord, I would commune with thee.
Thou whose all-pervading eye
Naught escapes, without, within,
Pardon each infirmity,
Open fault and secret sin.

2 Soon the light of this world's day
From my sight shall pass away;
Then from sin, from sorrow free,
Take me, Lord, to dwell with thee.
With the blessed angel throng
In the realms of light above,
Then shall rise my grateful song,
Praising thy redeeming love.

VI.

101 DEAR Saviour, bless us ere we go;
    Thy word into our minds instill;
    And make our lukewarm hearts to glow
    With lowly love and fervent will.

2 The day is gone, its hours have run,
    And thou hast taken count of all,
    The scanty triumphs grace hath won,
    The broken vow, the frequent fall.

3 Grant us, dear Lord, from evil ways
    True absolution and release;
    And bless us, more than in past days,
    With purity and inward peace.

4 Do more than pardon; give us joy,
    Sweet fear, and sober liberty,
    And simple hearts without alloy
    That only long to be like thee.

EVENING.

5 Labor is sweet, for thou hast toiled;
  And care is light, for thou hast cared;
  Ah! never let our works be soiled
  With strife, or by deceit ensnared.

6 For all we love, the poor, the sad,
  The sinful, unto thee we call;
  O let thy mercy make us glad;
  Thou art our Jesus, and our All.   II.

102 GLORY to thee, my God, this night,
    For all the blessings of the light:
    Keep me, O keep me, King of kings,
    Beneath the shadow of thy wings.

2 Forgive, dear Lord, thou holy One,
  The ills that I this day have done;
  That with myself, the world, and thee,
  I, ere I sleep, at peace may be.

3 Lord, let my soul forever share
  The bliss of thy paternal care:
  'T is heaven on earth, 't is heaven above,
  To see thy face, and feel thy love.   III.

103 O BLEST Creator of the light,
　　Who dost the dawn from darkness bring;
And, framing nature's depth and height,
　　Didst with the new-born light begin;

2 Who gently blending eve with morn,
　　And morn with eve, didst call them day;
Thick flows the flood of darkness down:
　　O hear us while to thee we pray.

3 Keep thou our souls from schemes of crime,
　　Nor guilt remorseful let them know;
Nor thinking on the things of time
　　Into eternal darkness go.

4 Teach us to knock at heaven's high door;
　　Teach us the prize of life to win;
Teach us all evil to abhor,
　　And purify ourselves within.

I.

EVENING.

104 BEFORE the ending of the day,
    Creator of the world, we pray
That with thy wonted favor thou
Wouldst be our guard and keeper now.

2 From all ill dreams defend our eyes,
From evil fears and phantasies;
Tread under foot our spirit's foe,
That no temptation we may know.

3 Grant that we ask, Almighty Lord,
Jesus the Christ alone adored,
Blest fulness of the Trinity,
Reigning on high, eternally.

105 JESUS, thou Source of life, and light, and love,
Thou King of kings, and Lord of lords above,
Eternal, self-existent, and divine,
In thee ineffable perfections shine :
On thy unchanging love our souls depend,
Almighty Father and Eternal Friend !

2 From thee, great Spring of uncreated might,
The vast resplendent orbs of glowing light,
And all created beings take their rise,
That walk the earth, or dwell above the skies.
Profusely wide unnumber'd blessings flow;
Heaven they enrich, and gladden earth below.

3 In thy wide grasp, and comprehensive eye,
Worlds upon worlds, and suns unnumber'd, lie;
Systems enclosed in thy perception roll,
Whose all-informing mind directs the whole:
Led by thy hand, their certain ways they know,
Placed in that sight from whence they cannot go.

4 Around thy throne the flaming seraphs stand,
And touch the golden lyre with trembling hand,
Transported with the ardors of thy praise,
The holy, holy, holy anthem raise.
To them, responsive, let creation sing
The omnipresent and almighty King! Amen.

106 HAIL! gladdening Light, of that pure glory poured
Which is the Love eternal, heavenly, blest,
Holiest of holies, Jesus Christ our Lord!
Now are we come to the sun's hour of rest.
All times are ordered by thy word alone,
Therefore the day and night thy glories own.

2 The lights of evening now around us shine;
We hymn the blest Humanity Divine.
Worthiest art thou at all times to be sung,
By grateful hearts, with undefiled tongue.
Thou art the Lord: giver of life, alone,
Therefore shall all the worlds thy glories own. Amen.

107 THROUGH thee as we together came,
In singleness of heart,
And met, Lord Jesus, in thy name,
So in thy name we part.

2 Nearer to thee our spirits lead,
And still thy love bestow,
Till thou hast made us free indeed,
Through trial, here below.

3 When to the right or left we stray,
Leave us not comfortless,
But guide our feet into the way
Of everlasting peace.

IV.

108 SUPPLIANT, lo! thy children bend,
      Father, for thy blessing now;
    Thou canst teach us, guide, defend;
      We are weak, almighty thou!

 2 With the peace thy Word imparts
     Be the taught and teacher blessed;
   In our lives and in our hearts,
     Father, be thy laws impressed.

 3 Pour into each longing mind
     Light and knowledge from above,
   Charity for all mankind,
     Trusting faith, enduring love.　　VI.

109 LORD, before thy throne we bend ;
Lord, to thee our prayers ascend ;
Servants to our Master true,
We would yield thee homage due ;
Unto thee our thanks we give
In whose life alone we live ;
Children, to our God we fly :
Gracious Father, hear our cry !

2 From the heavens, thy dwelling place,
Grant thy saving strength and grace;
In temptation's dangerous hour
Leave us not beneath its pow'r;
Keep us safe from vain alarms
In thine everlasting arms;
God, our Saviour, still be nigh,
Lord of life and victory!

3 Whilst our earthly path we tread,
May thy love our footsteps lead!
When our journey here is past,
May we rest with thee at last!
Let these earthly Sabbaths prove,
Foretastes of our joys above;
While their steps thy pilgrims bend
To the rest which knows no end!

110 ERE another day shall close,
Ere again we seek repose,
Lord! our song ascends to thee;
At thy feet we bow the knee.
For the mercies of the day,
For this rest upon our way,
Thanks to thee alone be given,
Lord of earth, and King of heaven!

111 O BLEST Redeemer, from thy radiant throne,
Where tongues angelic sing thy triumphs won,
Look down on those who bear thy sacred name,
And with thy glorious deeds their hearts inflame!

2 Restore their ways! renew them, by thy grace,
Thy laws to follow, and thy steps to trace;
Thy bright example to thy doctrine join,
And by their conduct prove their faith divine!

2 O be thy Providence their constant friend !
Thro' life still guard them, and in death attend !
With everlasting arms their cause embrace,
And crown the paths of piety with peace !

And O ! when call'd before their Judge divine,
May they in Zion's wedding-garments shine ;
With thee sit down, and find their great reward,
In full conjunction with their God and Lord !

112 SAVIOUR, again to thy dear name we raise
With one accord our parting hymn of praise ;
We stand to bless thee ere our worship cease,
Then, lowly kneeling, wait thy word of peace.

2 Grant us thy peace upon our homeward way ;
With thee began, with thee shall end the day ;
Guard thou the lips from sin, the hearts from shame,
That in this house have called upon thy Name.

3 Grant us thy peace, Lord, thro' the coming night,
Turn thou for us its darkness into light ;
From harm and danger keep thy children free,
For dark and light are both alike to thee.

4 Grant us thy peace throughout our earthly life,
Our balm in sorrow, and our stay in strife ;
Then, when thy voice shall bid our conflict cease,
Call us, O Lord, to thine eternal peace. *Amen.*

113
A BIDE with me! Fast falls the eventide;
The darkness deepens; Lord! with me abide
When other helpers fail and comforts flee,
Help of the helpless! oh abide with me.

2 Swift to its close ebbs out life's little day;
Earth's joys grow dim; its glories pass away;
Change and decay in all around I see;
O thou who changest not! abide with me!

3 I need thy presence every passing hour;
What but thy grace can foil the tempter's power?
Who like thyself my guide and stay can be?
Through cloud and sunshine, oh abide with me!

4 Hold thou thy Word before my closing eyes,
  Shine through the gloom and point me to the skies;
  Heaven's morning breaks and earth's vain shadows flee;
  In life, in death, O Lord! abide with me.

114 LORD, dismiss us with thy blessing;
  Fill our hearts with joy and peace;
  Let us each, thy love possessing,
    Triumph in redeeming grace:
      O refresh us,
      O refresh us,
    Traveling through this wilderness.

2 Thanks we give, and adoration,
    For thy Gospel's joyful sound;
  May the fruits of thy salvation
    In our hearts and lives abound:
      May thy presence,
      May thy presence,
    With us evermore be found.

BAPTISM.

115 GUIDE me, O thou great Jehovah,
    Pilgrim through this barren land;
  I am weak, but thou art mighty;
    Hold me with thy powerful hand:
  Bread of heaven, Bread of heaven,
  Feed me now and evermore.

2 Open, Lord, the crystal fountain
    Whence the living waters flow;
  Let the fiery, cloudy pillar
    Guide me all my journey through:
  Strong Deliverer, Strong Deliverer,
  Be thou still my Strength and Shield.

BAPTISM. 313

3 When I tread the verge of Jordan,
    Bid my anxious fears subside ;
  Bear me through the swelling current,
    Land me safe on Canaan's side :
  Songs of praises, Songs of praises
  I will ever give to thee,   VII.

116 SAVIOUR, who thy flock art feeding
      With the shepherd's kindest care,
    All the feeble gently leading,
      While the lambs thy bosom share.

  2 Now, these little ones receiving,
      Fold them in thy gracious arm ;
    There we know, thy Word believing,
      Only there secure from harm !

  3 Never, from thy pasture roving,
      Let them be the lion's prey ;
    Let thy tenderness, so loving,
      Keep them all life's dangerous way.

  4 Then, within thy fold eternal,
      Let them find a resting-place ;
    Feed in pastures ever vernal,
      Drink the rivers of thy grace !   IX.

THE HOLY SUPPER.

117 AT thy table, Lord of life,
    May our souls find peace and rest,
On our Saviour may we lean,
    Safe repose upon thy breast.

2 Thou dost call us to this feast,
    Thou hast said, "Remember me:"
May we come with trustful hearts,
    Hearts devoted, Lord, to thee.

3 May thy grace our souls awake;
    Make them glow with holy love;
While we take the bread and cup,
    Set our hearts on things above.   VI.

THE HOLY SUPPER.

118 O GOD, unseen yet ever near,
     Thy presence may we feel;
  And, thus inspired with holy fear,
     Before thine altar kneel.

2 Here may thy faithful people know
     The blessings of thy love,
  The streams that through the desert flow,
     The manna from above.

3 We come, obedient to thy word,
     To feast on heavenly food;
  Our meat, the body of the Lord,
     Our drink, his precious blood.

4 Thus may we all thy words obey,
     For we, O God, are thine;
  And go rejoicing on our way,
     Renewed with strength divine.

119 O LORD! and is thy table spread,
And doth thy cup with love o'erflow?
Thither be all thy children led,
And let them all its sweetness know.

2 Hail, sacred feast which Jesus makes,
Rich banquet of his flesh and blood!
Thrice happy he who here partakes
That sacred stream, that heavenly food.

3 Oh, let thy table honored be,
And furnished well with joyful guests;
And may each soul salvation see
That here its sacred pledges tastes.

4 Nor let thy spreading gospel rest
Till through the world thy truth has run;
Till with this bread all men be blest
Who see the light, or feel the sun.

I.

THE HOLY SUPPER.

120 BREAD of the world, in mercy broken,
   Wine of the soul, in mercy shed,
 By whom the words of life were spoken,
   And by whose voice thy flock is led;

2 Look on the heart by sorrow broken,
   Look on the tears by sinners shed;
 And be thy feast to us the token
   That by thy love our souls are fed. *Amen.*

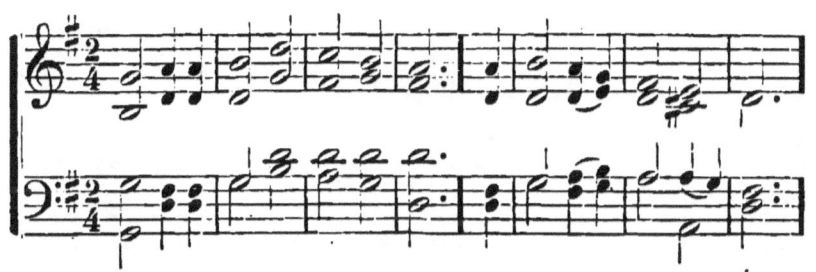

121 SHEPHERD of souls, refresh and bless
　　Thy chosen pilgrim flock :
　With manna in the wilderness,
　　With water from the rock.

2 We would not live by bread alone,
　　But by thy word of grace ;
　Thus in thy strength would travel on
　　To our abiding place.

3 Be known to us in breaking bread,
　　But do not then depart :
　Saviour, abide with us and spread
　　Thy table in our heart.

4 Lord, sup with us in love divine ;
　　Thy body and thy blood,
　That living bread, that heavenly wine,
　　Be our immortal food.

ORDINATION.

122 O GUARDIAN of the church divine,
The sevenfold gifts of grace are thine;
And kindled by thy hidden fires,
The soul to highest aims aspires.

2 Thy priests with wisdom, Lord, endue,
Their hearts with love and zeal renew;
Turn all their weakness into might,
O thou the source of life and light.

3 Spirit of truth, on us bestow
The faith in all its power to know;
That with the saints of ages gone,
And those to come, we may be one.

4 Protect thy church from every foe,
And peace, the fruit of love, bestow;
Convert the world, make all confess
The glories of thy righteousness.   II.

DEDICATION.

123 LORD JESUS, God of heaven,
By men on earth adored,
This temple now to thee is given :
Accept the offering, Lord.

2 Here may thy glory rest ;
Here may thy truth be known ;
Be thou by every heart confess'd
As Lord and God alone.

3 Here, Lord, thyself reveal,
Thy love divine impart ;
The doctrines of thy kingdom seal
On every humble heart.

4 May peace, within these walls,
A constant guest be found ;
With plenty and prosperity,
These palaces be crowned.

V

ANNIVERSARIES. 321

124 LONG as I live, I'll bless thy name,
My King, my God of love:
My work and joy shall be the same
In brighter worlds above.

2 Great is the Lord, his power unknown;
O let his praise be great:
I'll sing the honors of thy throne,
Thy works of grace repeat.

3 Thy love shall dwell upon my tongue;
And while my lips rejoice,
The men who hear my sacred song
Shall join their cheerful voice.

4 Fathers to sons shall tell thy name,
And children learn thy ways;
Ages to come thy truth proclaim,
And nations sound thy praise.

IV.

125 LO! for us the wilds are glad,
     All in cheerful green arrayed ;
     Opening sweets they all disclose,
     Bud and blossom as the rose.

  2 Hark ! the wastes have found a voice ;
     Lonely deserts now rejoice,
     Gladsome alleluias sing
     To the great Almighty King.

  3 Lo ! abundantly they bloom :
     Lebanon is hither come.
     Carmel's stores the heavens dispense—
     Sharon's fertile excellence.

  4 May these barren wastes of ours
     Bloom, and put forth fruits and flowers ;
     Flowers of wisdom, fruits of love,
     Gifts imparted from above.   VI.

ANNIVERSARIES.

126 LET children hear the mighty deeds
        Which God performed of old;
    Which in our younger years we saw,
        And which our fathers told.

2 He bids us make his glories known,
    His works of power and grace;
  And we'll convey his wonders down
    Through every rising race.

3 Our lips shall tell them to our sons,
    And they again to theirs,
  That generations yet unborn
    May teach them to their heirs.

4 Thus shall they learn, in God alone
    Their hope securely stands,
  That they may ne'er forget his works,
    But practice his commands.

IV.

324 HYMNS AND TUNES.

127 Now thank we all our God,
    With heart, and hands, and voices,
Who wondrous things hath done,
    In whom his world rejoices;
Who from our mother's arms
    Hath blessed us on our way
With countless gifts of love,
    And still is ours to-day.

2 O may this bounteous God
    Through all our life be near us,
With ever joyful hearts
    And blessed peace to cheer us;
And keep us in his grace,
    And guide us when perplexed,
And free us from all ills
    In this world and the next.

3 All praise and thanks to God,
    The Father, now be given,
The Saviour, King, and Lord
    Of all in earth and heaven,
The one eternal God,
    Whom earth and heaven adore;
For thus it was, is now,
    And shall be evermore.

326 HYMNS AND TUNES.

128 Come, ye thankful people, come,
Raise the song of Harvest-Home!
All is safely gathered in
Ere the winter-storms begin;
God, our Maker, doth provide
For our wants to be supplied;
Come to God's own temple, come,
Raise the song of Harvest-Home!

2 What is earth but God's own field,
Fruit unto his praise to yield?
Wheat and tares therein are sown,
Unto joy or sorrow grown;
Ripening with a wondrous power,
Till the final Harvest-Hour:
Grant, O Lord of Life, that we
Holy grain and pure may be.

3 For we know that thou wilt come,
And wilt take thy people home;
From thy field wilt purge away
All that doth offend, that day;
And thine angels charge at last
In the fire the tares to cast,
But the fruitful ears to store
In thy garner evermore.

4 Come, then, Lord of mercy, come,
Bid us sing thy Harvest-Home!
Let thy saints be gathered in,
Free from sorrow, free from sin;
All, upon the golden floor,
Praising thee for evermore:
Come, with thousand angels, come,
Bid us sing thy Harvest-Home!

NATIONAL HYMN.

129 GREAT God! thou dost all nations rule,
And their affairs control;
Thy power extends o'er all the earth,
Thy love from pole to pole.

2 Our native land in mercy view!
From heaven, O Lord, look down!
Thy kingdom in each heart erect!
Maintain thy rightful crown!

3 On people and on ruler let
Thy blessing, Lord, be shed;
To God and country true, may we
In wisdom's paths be led.

4 As thee their God our fathers owned,
So thou art still our King:
Thou only canst our peace maintain,
Or our deliverance bring.

5 To thee the glory we ascribe,
From whom salvation came;
In God, our shield, we will rejoice,
And ever bless thy Name.

INCARNATION AND REDEMPTION.　　329

130　HARK the glad sound! the Saviour comes,
　　　　The Saviour promised long:
　　　Let every heart prepare a throne,
　　　　And every voice a song.

2 He comes, the prisoners to release,
　　In Satan's bondage held;
　The gates of brass before him burst,
　　The iron fetters yield.

3 He comes, the broken hearts to bind,
　　The bleeding souls to cure,
　And with the treasure of his grace
　　To bless the humble poor.

4 Our glad hosannas, Prince of Peace,
　　Thine Advent shall proclaim;
　And heaven's eternal arches ring
　　With thy beloved Name.

330 HYMNS AND TUNES.

Advent.

131 SLEEPERS, wake, a voice is calling,
It is the watchman's voice upon thy walls,
O City of Jerusalem !
Lo ! he cries the hour of midnight,
The voice is gone out into all the world,—
Where are ye Servants of the Lord !
For lo ! the Bridegroom comes ;
Arise and take your lamps ! Alleluia !
Awake, his kingdom is at hand ;
Go forth, go forth to meet your Lord !

Easter.

132 UP, ye Christians, join in singing,
And praises to our Saviour bringing,
For risen is the Conqueror.
Lo ! his march is now undoubted,
And all the powers of death are routed ;
Lo ! open lies the sepulcher.
O fair and glorious beam !
O joy in fullest stream ! Alleluia !
With hero-might he wins the fight,
And scatters all the hosts of night.

Ascension.

133 JESUS, Lord, our Captain glorious !
O'er sin, and death, and hell victorious,
Wisdom and might to thee belong.
We confess, proclaim, adore thee,
We bow the knee, we fall before thee ;
Thy love henceforth shall be our song.
The cross meanwhile we bear,
The crown ere long to wear ; Alleluia !
Thy reign extend, world without end,
Let praise from all to thee ascend.

134 THE Advent of our King
     Our praise must now employ;
　Come let us hymns of welcome sing
     In strains of holy joy.

2 The Everlasting Lord
    Incarnate deigns to be;
  The Mighty girdeth on his sword
    To set his servants free.

3 Daughter of Zion, rise
    To meet thy lowly King;
  Nor let thy faithless heart despise
    The peace he comes to bring.

4 Before the dawning day
    Let sin's dark deeds be gone;
  The old man all be put away,
    The new man all put on.　　V.

135 DOWN from the worlds of radiant light
Behold the Saviour come,
To ransom souls from endless night
And bring the wand'rers home.

2 He calls us to his dear embrace
From misery and despair,
Bids us receive his wondrous grace,
And seek salvation there.

3 We come, Emmanuel, at thy call,
Believe thy glad'ning Word,
Renounce our sins, ourselves, our all,
And glory in our Lord.

4 Salvation to Messiah's name
With grateful hearts we sing,
And join our voices to proclaim
Our Saviour and our King.

5 Immortal praise to God belongs
For such unfathomed love;
Join, all below, in rapturous songs,
And shout, ye hosts above.

136 ALONE to God on high be praise
    And thankful adoration,
That we may now, and all our days,
    Rejoice in his salvation.
Let high in heaven his praises sound,
Peace and good-will on earth abound,
    All feud and strife be ended.

2 Ye Christian people, all rejoice,
    Each soul with joy upspringing;
Pour forth one song with heart and voice,
    With love and gladness singing.
Give thanks to God, the Lord above,
Thanks for his miracle of love;
    In love hath he redeemed us.

3 Lord Jesus Christ, alone to thee
    Be praise and glory given;
Who reignest, God, eternally,
    In all the earth and heaven.
The Prince of Peace, the incarnate Word,
The wonderful, the mighty Lord,
    The Father everlasting.

137
ANGELS, from the realms of glory,
    Wing your flight o'er all the earth;
Ye who sang creation's story,
    Now proclaim Messiah's birth:
        Come and worship,
        Worship Christ, the new-born King.

2 Shepherds in the field abiding,
    Watching o'er your flocks by night;
God with man is now residing,
    Yonder shines the infant light:
        Come and worship, etc.

3 Sages, leave your contemplations;
    Brighter visions beam afar:
Seek the great Desire of nations,
    Ye have seen his natal star:
        Come and worship, etc.

4 Watchers at the altar bending,
    Waiting long in hope and fear,
Suddenly the Lord, descending,
    In his temple doth appear:
        Come and worship, etc.

CHRISTMAS.

138 HARK! what mean those holy voices,
    Sweetly sounding through the skies?
Lo! the angelic host rejoices,
    Heavenly alleluias rise.
Listen to the wond'rous story,
    Which they chant in hymns and joy :—
Glory in the highest, glory,
    Glory be to God on high!

2 Peace on earth, good-will from heaven,
    Thus they sing with harps of gold;
Christ is born, the Son is given,
    Of the prophets long foretold.
Haste, ye mortals, to adore him,
    Heaven and earth his praises bring;
Men and angels fall before him,
    Hail your Saviour, Lord, and King.   VIII.

139 HARK! the herald angels sing
 Glory to the new-born King;
Peace on earth, and mercy mild,
God and sinners reconciled!
Joyful, all ye nations, rise,
Join the triumph of the skies;
With th' angelic host proclaim,
Christ is born in Bethlehem!
 Hark! the herald angels sing
 Glory to the new-born King.

2 Hail! the heaven-born Prince of peace!
Hail! the Sun of Righteousness!
Light and life to all he brings,
Risen with healing in his wings.
Mild he lays his glory by,
Born that man no more may die:
Born to raise the sons of earth,
Born to give them second birth.
    Hark! the herald angels, etc.

140   HARK! the skies with music sound,
        Heav'nly glory beams around;
      Christ is born! the angels sing,
      Glory to the new-born King.

2 Peace is come, good will appears,
Sinners, wipe away your tears;
Christ for you in flesh to-day
Humbly in the manger lay.

3 Shepherds tending flocks by night,
Heard the song and saw the light;
Took their reeds, and softest strains
Echo'd through the happy plains.

4 Mortals, hail the glorious King!
Richest incense cheerful bring;
Praise and love Emmanuel's name,
And his boundless grace proclaim.   VI.

141 COME, Redeemer, blessed Jesus,
　　　Born to set thy people free!
　　From our sins and fears release us,
　　　Let us find our rest in thee.

2 Israel's strength and consolation,
　　Hope of all the earth thou art;
　Dear desire of every nation,
　　Joy of every humble heart.

3 Born thy people to deliver,
　　Born a child, and yet a king;
　Born to reign supreme forever,
　　Now thy gracious kingdom bring.

4 By thine own eternal spirit
　　Rule in all our hearts alone;
　So may we a place inherit
　　With the blest before thy throne.　　IX.

INCARNATION.

142 LET every heart exulting beat
With joy at Jesus' name of bliss;
With every pure delight replete
And passing sweet its music is.

2 Jesus the comfortless consoles,
Jesus each sinful fever quells,
Jesus the power of hell controls,
Jesus each deadly foe repels.

3 O speak his glorious name abroad!
Jesus let every tongue confess,
Let every heart and voice accord
The healer of our souls to bless.

4 All might, all glory be to thee,
Refulgent with this name divine;
All honor, worship, majesty,
Jesus, for evermore be thine.

143 BRIGHTEST and best of the sons of the morning,
Dawn on our darkness, and lend us thine aid ;
Star of the East, the horizon adorning,
Guide where the infant Redeemer is laid.

2 Cold, on his cradle, the dew-drops are shining ;
Low lies his bed with the beasts of the stall ;
Angels adore him, in slumber reclining,—
Maker, and Monarch, and Saviour, of all.

3 Say, shall we yield him, in costly devotion,
Odors of Edom and off'rings divine?
Gems of the mountain, and pearls of the ocean,
Myrrh from the forest, and gold from the mine?

4 Vainly we offer each ample oblation ;
Vainly with gifts would his favor secure ;
Richer by far is the heart's adoration ;
Dearer to God are the prayers of the poor.

INCARNATION. 343

144 BETHLEHEM in land of Judah,
Who shall all thy glory tell?
Out of thee the Lord from heaven
Came to rule his Israel.

2 Fairer than the sun at morning
Was the star that told his birth,
To the world its God announcing
Seen in fleshly form on earth.

3 Eastern sages at his cradle
Make oblations rich and rare;
See them give, in deep devotion,
Gold, and frankincense, and myrrh.

4 Sacred gifts of mystic meaning;
Incense doth their faith disclose,
Gold their hearts' best love proclaimeth,
Myrrh obedience foreshows.

5 Jesus, whom the Gentiles worshiped
At thy glad Epiphany,
Unto thee, our only Father,
God, and Saviour, glory be.

For the Sunday before Easter.

145 ALL glory, laud, and honor,
    To thee, Redeemer, King!
To whom the lips of children
    Made sweet Hosannas ring.
        All glory, etc.

2 Thou art the King of Israel,
    Thou David's royal Son,
Who in the Lord's name comest,
    The King and Blessed One.
        All glory, etc.

3 The company of angels
    Are praising thee on high,
And mortal men, and all things
    Created make reply.
        All glory, etc.

4 The throngs who came to meet thee
    With palms before thee went;
Our praise and prayer and anthems
    Before thee we present.
        All glory, etc.

5 To thee, before thy Passion,
    They sang their hymns of praise;
To thee, now high exalted,
    Our melody we raise.
        All glory, etc.

6 Thou didst accept their praises,
    Accept the prayers we bring,
Who in all good delightest,
    Thou good and gracious King.
        All glory, etc.

146 ANGELS, roll the rock away;
Death, yield up thy mighty prey:
See! he rises from the tomb,
Bright with heaven's immortal bloom.
'T is the Saviour! Angels, raise
Your triumphant songs of praise;
Let the world's remotest bound
Hear the joy-inspiring sound.

2 O ye people, lift your eyes,
High in glory see him rise;
Hosts of angels on the road
Hail and sing th' incarnate God.
Praise him, all ye heavenly choirs,
Praise, and sweep your golden lyres;
All on earth, in humble strain,
Sing the mighty Saviour's reign!

3 Where, O death, is now thy sting?
Over thee the Lord is King;
Where, O grave, thy victory?
Christ no more in thee doth lie.
Heaven unfolds her portals wide,
Glorious Hero, through them ride;
King of Glory, mount thy throne,
Heaven and earth are all thine own.

4 Jesus Christ, our risen Lord,
  Ever be thy name adored;
  God and Man! alone in thee
  Dwells the blessed Trinity:
  Glory, honor, power, and might,
  Be to thee, O Prince of Light,
  Lord of all the heavenly host,
  Father, Son, and Holy Ghost.

Al-le-lu-ia.

147 THE strife is o'er, the battle done;
     The triumph of the Lord is won;
     O let the song of praise be sung. Alleluia!

  2 The powers of death have done their worst,
    And Jesus hath his foes dispersed;
    Let shouts of praise and joy outburst. Alleluia!

  3 On this third morn he rose again
    In glorious majesty to reign;
    O let us swell the joyful strain. Alleluia!

  4 He closed the yawning gates of hell;
    The bars from heaven's high portals fell;
    Let songs of joy his triumphs tell. Alleluia!

148 JESUS lives! No longer now
  Can thy terrors, Death, appall us;
 Jesus lives! by this we know
  Thou, O Grave, canst not enthrall us.
            Alleluia!

2 Jesus lives! henceforth is death
   But the gate of Life immortal;
  This shall calm our trembling breath
   When we pass its gloomy portal.
            Alleluia!

3 Jesus lives! for us he died;
   Then, alone to Jesus living,
  Pure in heart may we abide,
   Glory to our Saviour giving.
            Alleluia!

4 Jesus lives! our hearts know well
   Naught from us his love shall sever;
  Life, nor death, nor powers of hell,
   Tear us from his keeping ever.
            Alleluia!

ASCENSION. 349

5 Jesus lives! to him the throne
  Over all the world is given:
  May we go where he is gone,
  Rest and reign with him in heaven.
                    Alleluia!

149 THOU art gone up on high,
      To realms beyond the skies,
    And round thy throne unceasingly
      Sweet songs of praise arise.

  2 Thou art gone up on high,
      But thou didst first come down
    Through earth's most bitter misery
      To pass unto thy crown.

  3 But we are lingering here
      With sin and care oppressed;
    Lord, send thy promised Comforter,
      And lead us to our rest.

  4 Here, girt with griefs and fears,
      Our onward course must be;
    But only let this path of tears
      Lead us at last to thee.   V.

150 COME, thou holy Spirit, come;
And from thine eternal home
Shed the ray of light divine;
Come, thou Father of the poor,
Come, thou source of all our store,
Come, within our bosoms shine!

2 Thou of Comforters the best,
Thou the soul's most welcome Guest,
Sweet Refreshment here below!
In our labor rest most sweet,
Grateful shadow from the heat,
Solace in the midst of woe!

3 O most blessed Light Divine,
   Shine within these hearts of thine,
     And our inmost being fill;
   If thou take thy grace away,
   Nothing pure in man will stay—
     All our good is turned to ill.

4 Heal our wounds; our strength renew;
   On our dryness pour thy dew;
     Wash the stains of guilt away;
   Bend the stubborn heart and will,
   Melt the frozen, warm the chill,
     Guide the steps that go astray.

5 On the faithful, who adore
   And confess thee, evermore
     In thy sevenfold gifts descend ·
   Give them virtue's sure reward,
   Give them thy salvation, Lord,
     Give them joys that never end.

151 BLESSED city, heavenly Salem,
　　Vision dear of peace and love,
Who of living stones art builded
　In the height of heaven above,
And, with angel hosts encircled,
　As a bride to earth dost move.

2 From celestial realms descending,
　　Bridal glory round thee shed,
Meet for him whose love espoused thee,
　To thy Lord shalt thou be led;
All thy streets and all thy bulwarks
　Of pure gold are fashioned.

The Doxology.
Glory to thy Royal Bridegroom,
　Salem, sing rejoicingly;
He, thy Lord, thy Light, thy Temple,
　Dwelleth evermore with thee;
His be blessing and thanksgiving,
　Now and to eternity.

THE HOLY CITY. 353

152 JERUSALEM, arise,
　　The heavenly glory view;
　The light is come, lift up thine eyes,
　　All things are now made new.

2 Now ended is the reign
　　Of error's gloomy night:
　The Sun of heaven appears again,
　　And beams celestial light.

3 Now living waters flow
　　To cheer the humble soul;
　From sea to sea the rivers go,
　　And bless where'er they roll.

4 Jesus shall rule alone,
　　The world shall hear his Word;
　By one blest name shall he be known,
　　The universal Lord.　　V.

THE SECOND COMING.

153 Now blessing, honor, glory, praise,
     By angel hosts are sung ;
   The church below the voice doth raise
     To join the heavenly throng.

  2 Adored be he who comes to bless
      The nations with his love,
    To show his truth and righteousness,
      And every cloud remove.

  3 Blessed be he who comes to reign
      In Zion's happy land !
    Jerusalem is built again,
      And shall forever stand.

  4 No more his kingdom shall decay,
      No more the temple fall ;
    Here Jesus reigns with endless sway,
      The king and Lord of all.   IV.

DOXOLOGIES.

Referred to in the Roman Numerals at the end of the Hymns.

I. L. M.

GLORY eternal be to thee,
   O God, the Father, Spirit, Son,
Blest Fulness of the Trinity,
   Revealed in Jesus Christ alone.

II. L. M.

GLORY and praises ever be,
O Jesus Christ, our Lord, to thee,
Whom all the heavenly hosts adore,
God over all for evermore.

III. L. M.

GRANT that we ask, Almighty Lord,
Jesus, the Christ, alone adored,
Blest Fulness of the Trinity,
Reigning on high eternally.

IV. C. M.

ALL glory be to thee, O Lord,
   The Father, Spirit, Son,
Alone be thou our God adored
   While endless ages run.

V. S. M.

To thee, O Lord, alone
   Whom heaven and earth adore,
Be glory as it was, is now,
   And shall be evermore.

VI. 7s.

Glory, praise, and blessing be,
   Lord, our Saviour, unto thee ;
Thee let heaven and earth adore,
   God o'er all for evermore.

VII. 8s & 7s. 6 lines.

Lord, to thee in whom is dwelling
   All the Godhead bodily,
Hymn and chant and glad thanksgiving,
   And unending praises be,—
Honor, glory, and dominion,
   And eternal victory.

VIII. 8s & 7s. 8 lines.

Lord, to thee in whom is dwelling,
   All the Godhead bodily,
Father, Son, and Holy Spirit,
   One in perfect unity,
Hymn and chant and glad thanksgiving,
   And unending praises be,—
Honor, glory, and dominion,
   And eternal victory.

IX. 8s & 7s. 4 lines.

Lord, to thee, in whom is dwelling
   All the Holy Trinity,
Blessing, honor, and thanksgiving,
   And eternal glory be.

X. L. M.

Praise God, from whom all blessings flow,
Praise Him, all creatures here below,
Praise Him above, ye heavenly host,
Praise Father, Son, and Holy Ghost.

INDEX OF THE SELECTIONS.

FIRST LINES.	SELECTION
Alleluia: For the Lord God omnipotent reigneth....	80
Although the fig tree shall not blossom.	87
And in that day thou shalt say, O Lord, I will praise Thee.	128
And in the same country were shepherds abiding in the field.	74
And in this mountain shall the Lord of Hosts make to all people..	10
And it shall come to pass in the last days....	9
And they shall build houses and inhabit.	138
And they shall build the old wastes.	145
Arise, O Lord, into thy rest	163
Arise, shine, for thy light is come.	136
As the hart panteth for the brooks of water.	7
Behold, how good and how pleasant it is	3
Behold, my servant shall deal prudently.	162
Behold, the tabernacle of God is with men.	119
Blessed are the perfect in the way	49
Blessed be the Lord God of Israel.	76
Blessed is every one that feareth the Lord.	135
Blessed is the man that walketh not in the counsel of the ungodly	20
Blessed is the man whom Thou dost chasten, O Lord.	43
Blessed is the nation whose God is the Lord.	124
Bless the Lord, O my soul; and all that is within me, bless his holy name.	70
Bless the Lord, O my soul. O Lord my God, Thou art very great.	157
Bow down thine ear, O Lord, hear me.	30
But now thus saith the Lord, that created thee, O Jacob.	131
Come, and let us go up to the mountain of the Lord.	21
Come, and let us return to the Lord.	11
Come, ye children, hearken unto me.	24
Comfort ye, comfort ye my people, saith your God.	4
Create in me a clean heart, O God.	64
Deal bountifully with thy servant.	50
For Thou, O Lord, art my refuge.	89
For thy Maker is thine husband	133
For Zion's sake will I not hold my peace	126
Give ear, O ye heavens, and I will speak.	144
Give ear to my prayer, O God.	32
Give ear to my words, O Lord...	1
Give the king thy judgments, O God.	141
God be merciful unto us, and bless us.	14
God is not a man, that He should lie.	140
God is our refuge and strength	98
Good and upright is the Lord.	123
Have mercy upon me, O God.	48
Hearken unto me, ye that know righteousness.	139
Hear me when I call, O God of my righteousness.	47
Hear my cry, O God; attend to my prayer.	36
Hear my prayer, O Lord: Give ear to my supplications	29
Hear, O Lord; I cry with my voice.	34
Hear ye this, O house of Jacob.	121
He sendeth forth springs into brooks.	147

INDEX OF THE SELECTIONS.

FIRST LINES.	SELECTION
He that dwelleth in the secret place of the Most High	93
He that is clean of hands, and pure in heart	159
He was oppressed, and he was afflicted	162
Ho, every one that thirsteth, come ye to the waters	26
Holy, holy, holy, Lord God Almighty	78
How beautiful upon the mountains	118
How goodly are thy tents, O Jacob	143
How great is thy goodness	81
How lovely are thy tabernacles, O Lord of Hosts	12
How manifold are thy works, O Lord	155
I cried by reason of mine affliction unto the Lord	45
I cried with all my heart; Hear me, O Lord	60
If thou take away from the midst of thee the yoke	125
If thou turn away thy foot from the Sabbath	125
I have done judgment and justice	58
I love the Lord, because He hath heard my voice	90
In God will I praise his word	99
In Thee, O Lord, do I put my trust	33
It is good to give thanks to the Lord	2
I was glad when they said unto me	8
I will bless the Lord at all times	23
I will extol Thee, my God, O King	83
I will heal their backsliding	122
I will hear what God the Lord will speak	86
I will lift up mine eyes to the mountains	71
I will mention the loving-kindness of the Lord	161
I will praise Thee, O Lord, with all my heart	103
I will sing of the mercies of the Lord for ever	92
Judge me, O God, and plead my cause	16
Judge me, O Lord; for I have walked in mine integrity	44
Let them exalt Him in the congregation of the people	108
Let thy mercies come also unto me, O Lord	62
Lift up your heads, O ye gates	159
Look down from heaven, and behold	65
Look upon Zion, the city of our solemnities	160
Lord, now lettest Thou thy servant depart in peace	77
Make a joyful noise unto God, all the earth	95
Make a joyful noise unto the Lord, all the earth	5
Many, O Lord my God, are thy wonderful works	105
My days are like a shadow that declineth	38
My heart rejoiceth in the Lord	85
My soul cleaveth unto the dust	51
My soul doth magnify the Lord	75
O come, let us sing to the Lord	25
O give thanks unto the Lord; call upon his name	97
O give thanks unto the Lord; for He is good	22
O give thanks unto the Lord; for He is good	100
O give thanks unto the Lord, for He is good	104
O God, my heart is fixed	6
O God, Thou art my God; early will I seek Thee	17
O how I love thy law	56
Oh that Thou wouldst rend the heavens, that Thou wouldst come down	113
O Lord, God of Hosts, hear my prayer	13
O Lord, how are they increased that trouble me	102
O Lord, rebuke me not in thine anger	42
O Lord, Thou hast searched me and known me	40
O Lord, who shall abide in thy tabernacle	31
O sing unto the Lord a new song; sing unto the Lord all the earth	91
O sing unto the Lord a new song, for He hath done wondrous works	109
O thou afflicted, tossed with tempest, and not comforted	134
Out of the depths have I cried unto Thee, O Lord	41
O Zion, that bringest good tidings	111

INDEX OF THE SELECTIONS.

FIRST LINES.	SELECTION
Praise the Lord, O Jerusalem	150
Praise waiteth for Thee, O God, in Zion	152
Praise ye the Lord: For it is good to sing praises to our God	154
Praise ye the Lord: Happy is he that hath the God of Jacob for his help	156
Praise ye the Lord. O give thanks to the Lord, for He is good	106
Praise ye the Lord. Praise God in his sanctuary	110
Praise ye the Lord. Praise ye the Lord from the heavens	101
Princes have persecuted me without a cause	61
Rejoice greatly, O daughter of Zion	112
Righteous art Thou, O Lord; and upright are thy judgments	63
Seek ye the Lord, while He may be found	27
Sing, O barren, thou that didst not bear	127
Surely he hath borne our griefs	162
Teach me, O Lord, the way of thy statutes	53
Teach me thy way, O Lord; I will walk in thy truth	28
The bread of God is He that cometh down from heaven	120
The days of our years are three-score years and ten	87
The earth is the Lord's, and the fulness thereof	159
The heavens are thine, the earth is also thine	96
The kingdoms of this world are become our Lord's and his Christ's	79
The law of the Lord is perfect, converting the soul	68
The Lord hath prepared his throne in the heavens	73
The Lord hear thee in the day of trouble	107
The Lord is gracious, and full of compassion	15
The Lord is merciful and gracious	72
The Lord is my light and my salvation	19
The Lord is my Shepherd; I shall not want	69
The Lord is the portion of mine inheritance and of my cup	88
The Lord reigneth; He is clothed with majesty	153
The Lord upholdeth all that fall	82
Then shall the eyes of the blind be opened	130
The people that walked in darkness	114
There shall come forth a Rod out of the stem of Jesse	116
The Spirit of the Lord Jehovih is upon me	115
The steps of a good man are ordered by the Lord	67
The wilderness and the barren place shall be glad for them	129
The wolf shall dwell with the lamb	117
They that go down to the sea in ships	104
Thou art my portion, O Lord	54
Thou dost visit the earth, and water it	146
Thou hast been favorable, O Lord, to thy land	84
Thy hands have made me and fashioned me	55
Thy mercy, O Lord, is in the heavens	18
Thy testimonies are wonderful	59
Thy way, O God, is in the sanctuary	151
Thy word is a lamp to my feet	57
To whom then will ye liken Me	149
Trust in the Lord, and do good	66
Unto Thee, O Lord, do I lift up my soul	35
Violence shall no more be heard in thy land	137
We have thought of thy kindness, O God	158
What shall I render to the Lord	94
Wherewith shall a young man cleanse his way	52
Wherewith shall I come before the Lord	46
Who hath believed our report	162
Who hath measured the waters in the hollow of his hand	148
Who is a God like to Thee, that pardoneth iniquity	39
Who is this that cometh from Edom with dyed garments from Bozrah	161
Yea, all kings shall bow down to him	142
Yet now hear, O Jacob, my servant	132

AUTHORS OF THE CHANTS.

CHANT.
- i. Giovanni Animuccia, 1558.
- ii. Geo. J. Webb.
- iii.
- iv. Geo. J. Webb.
- v. Henry Purcell, 1658.
- vi. Geo. J. Webb.
- vii. Dr. Gauntlett.
- viii. Arr. fr. Gregorian 5th Tone.
- ix. Arranged from Gregorian.
- x. Geo. J. Webb.
- xi. Vincent Novello.
- xii. Richard Farrant, 1564.
- xiii. Arranged from Gregorian.
- xiv. Henry Purcell, 1658.
- xv. J. Battishill, 1738.
- xvi.
- xvii. Rev. J. P. Stuart.
- xviii. Gregorian 5th Tone, 1st End.
- xix. Dr. Greene, 1696.
- xx. Dr. Worgan.
- xxi. Charles King, 1704.
- xxii. E. G. Monk.
- xxiii. Arranged from Gregorian.
- xxiv. Gregorian 2d Tone,
- xxv. Geo. J. Webb.
- xxvi. George F. Root.
- xxvii.
- xxviii.
- xxix. Dr. Gauntlett.
- xxx. D. P. Hayes.
- xxxi. George F. Root.
- xxxii. Dr. Croft.
- xxxiii. Rev. Mr. Fitzherbert.
- xxxiv. Geo. J. Webb.
- xxxv. Rev. G. Heathcote.
- xxxvi. Arranged from Gregorian.
- xxxvii. Arr. fr. an old Roman Chant.
- xxxviii. Arr. fr. an old Roman Chant.
- xxxix. Geo. J. Webb.
- xl.
- xli. Richard Clark, 1786.
- xlii. Geo. J. Webb.
- xliii. Gregor. " Peregrine " Tone.
- xliv.
- xlv. Dr. Blow.
- xlvi. Mr. Pratt.
- xlvii. " Tonus Regius."
- xlviii. Gregorian 7th Tone, 4th End.
- xlix, l. Geo. J. Webb
- li. Arr fr. Gregorian 1st Tone.
- lii—liv. Geo. J. Webb.
- lv. Rev. T. B. Hayward.
- lvi. Lord Mornington.
- lvii. Arr.fr.Orlando de Lasso,1520.
- lviii. Geo. J. Webb.
- lix. Arr. fr. Gregorian 7th Tone.
- lx. Geo. J. Webb.

CHANT.
- lxi. Dr. Croft.
- lxii. Arranged from Gregorian.
- lxiii. Geo. J. Webb.
- lxiv. Arranged from Gregorian.
- lxv. Rev. T. B. Hayward.
- lxvi. Hine.
- lxvii. Rev. W. Jones, 1786.
- lxviii. Geo. J. Webb.
- lxix. Rev. T. B. Hayward.
- lxx.
- lxxi. Geo. J. Webb.
- lxxii.
- lxxiii. Dr. Boyce, 1710.
- lxxiv. Gregorian 1st Tone, 1st End.
- lxxv.
- lxxvi. Dr. Woodward.
- lxxvii.
- lxxviii. Geo. J. Webb.
- lxxix. Dr. Croft, 1700.
- lxxx. Gregorian 3d Tone, 1st End.
- lxxxi. James Kent, 1700.
- lxxxii. Geo. J. Webb.
- lxxxiii. Gregorian 5th Tone, 2d End.
- lxxxiv. Dr. Dupuis, 1733.
- lxxxv, lxxxvi. Geo. J. Webb.
- lxxxvii. Rev. G. Heathcote.
- lxxxviii. Arranged from Palestrina.
- lxxxix. Geo. J. Webb.
- xc. Gregor. 7th Tone, 1st End.
- xci, xcii. Geo. J. Webb.
- xciii. Richard Langdon, 1750.
- xciv. Dr. Chard.
- xcv. Rev. Mr. Henley.
- xcvi. Dr. Randall.
- xcvii. Geo. J. Webb.
- xcviii. Arranged from Gregorian.
- xcix. Dr. Philip Hayes, 1739.
- c. Rev. Dr. Aldrich.
- ci. Gregorian 5th Tone, 2d End.
- cii, ciii. Geo. J. Webb.
- civ. Vincent Novello.
- cv. Dr. G. K. Jackson.
- cvi. Arranged from Gregorian.
- cvii. Gregorian 6th Tone.
- cviii. Arranged from Gregorian.
- cix. Geo. J. Webb.
- cx. Gregorian 1st Tone, 1st End.
- cxi. Geo. J. Webb.
- cxii. Dr. Jackson.
- cxiii. Arranged from Palestrina.
- cxiv. Thomas Tallis, 1558.
- cxv, cxvi. Geo. J. Webb.
- cxvii.
- cxviii. Geo. J. Webb.
- cxix.
- cxx—cxxxi. Geo. J. Webb.
- cxxxii. Gregorian 8th Tone,1st End.

INDEX OF ANTHEMS.

CHANT.
- cxxxiii. Arranged from Gregorian.
- cxxxiv. Gregorian 8th Tone, 2d End.
- cxxxv. Dr. Dupuis.
- cxxxvi, cxxxvii. Geo. J. Webb.
- cxxxviii. Kent.
- cxxxix. 1st Tone, 1st Ending, harmonized by Bernabei, with melody in the Tenor.
- cxl—cxlii. Geo. J. Webb.
- cxliii. Arranged from Gregorian.
- cxliv. Geo. J. Webb.

CHANT.
- cxlv. John Robinson.
- cxlvi.
- cxlvii. William Russell, 1777.
- cxlviii. Dr. G. K. Jackson.
- cxlix.
- cl—cliii. Geo. J. Webb.
- cliv.
- clv.
- clvi. Dr. Dupuis.
- clvii. Richard Farrant.
- clviii. Geo. J. Webb.

INDEX OF ANTHEMS.

CHANT ANTHEMS.

NO.   PAGE
1. Blessed is the man that walketh not in the counsel of the ungodly.... *Geo. J. Webb.* 129
2. Thou dost visit the earth, and water it................. *Geo. J. Webb.* 132
3. Blessed be the Lord, because He hath heard the voice of my supplications............ *Geo. J. Webb.* 135
4. Violence shall no more be heard in thy land............ *Geo. J. Webb.* 138
5. Thy hands have made me and fashioned me..... *Geo. J. Webb.* 141
6. As the hart panteth for the brooks of water............ *Geo. J. Webb.* 144
7. Thou hast been favorable, O Lord, to thy land.......... *Geo. J. Webb.* 147
8. Behold, I come quickly, and my reward is with me...... *Geo. J. Webb.* 150
9. Praise ye the Lord. Praise God in his sanctuary........ *Geo. J. Webb.* 151

ANTHEMS.

1. Holy, Holy, Holy, Jehovah of Hosts........................*Allegri.* 154
2. Thou wilt show me the path of life........................*Anon.* 155
3. Behold, how good and how pleasant it is............... *Geo. J. Webb.* 157
4. Like as the hart desireth the water brooks......... ..*Vincent Novello.* 159
5. The Lord will be a refuge for the oppress'd......... *Geo. J. Webb.* 161
6. Who hath believed our report?............*Arr. from Josquin de Prés.* 164
7. Bless the Lord, O my soul..... ....*Geo. J. Webb.* 169
8. Enter not into judgment with thy servant............. *T. Attwood.* 172
9. When the Lord shall build up Zion................... *Vincent Novello.* 174
10. And the glory of the Lord shall be reveal'd............ *Geo. J. Webb.* 175
11. Unto us a Child is born........... .... *Geo. J. Webb.* 177
12. Now is come the salvation, and the strength, and the kingdom of our God....... ....*Kent.* 180
13. Glory to God in the highest....... ...... *Geo. J. Webb.* 182
14. Hosanna! Blessed is He that cometh in the name of the Lord......... *Geo. J. Webb.* 184
15. Worthy is the Lamb that was slain.................. *Geo. J. Webb.* 186
16. Blessed be Jehovah for evermore...........................*Anon.* 189
18. I will lay me down in peace and sleep....................*Neukomm.* 191

    The Faith of the New Church... ....*Geo. J. Webb.* 192
    The Faith of the New Church, Simple Arrangement of.*Rev. F. Sewall.* 196

    Te Dominum..*Rev. F. Sewall.* 197

INDEX OF THE HYMNS.

FIRST LINES	AUTHORS.	HYMN
Abide with me! Fast falls the eventide	Lyte.	113
All glory, laud, and honor	Theodulph of Orleans.	145
All hail the great Immanuel's name	Perronet, alt.	6
Alone to God on high be praise	after Decius.	136
Angels, from the realms of glory	Montgomery.	137
Angels, roll the rock away	T. Scott.	146
As pants the hart for cooling streams	Tate & Brady.	43
At thy table, Lord of life	Anon.	117
Before the ending of the day	Ancient Hymn.	104
Bethlehem in land of Judah	Hymns An. & Mod., alt.	144
Be thou, O God, exalted high	Tate & Brady.	5
Blessed city, heavenly Salem	Urbs beata.	151
Blessed Lord, what shall we render	Engl. Conf.	9
Bread of the world, in mercy broken	Heber.	120
Brightest and best of the sons of the morning	Heber.	143
Built by Jehovah's hand	Engl. Conf.	84
Cast upon the Lord thy care	Engl. Conf.	71
Children of the heavenly King	Cennick.	86
Come, Redeemer, blessed Jesus	Epis. Coll., alt.	141
Come, thou holy Spirit, come	Robert II of France.	150
Come, ye thankful people, come	Henry Alford.	128
Commit thou all thy griefs	Gerhardt.	58
Dear Saviour, bless us ere we go	Hymns An. & Mod.	101
Down from the worlds of radiant light	J. Proud.	135
Ere another day shall close	Anon.	110
Eternal Source of life and light	Cappe's Sel.	35
Father of mercies, in thy Word	Mrs. Steele.	76
Father, whate'er of earthly bliss	Mrs. Steele.	64
Forever blessed be the Lord	Watts.	54
From all that dwell below the skies	Watts.	4
Give thanks to God; he reigns above	Watts.	10
Glorious things of thee are spoken	Newton.	81
Glory to thee, my God, this night	Ken., alt.	102
God is love: his mercy brightens	Engl. Conf.	24
God is my strong salvation	Montgomery.	57
God is the refuge of his saints	Watts.	75
God moves in a mysterious way	Cowper.	73
Gracious Spirit—Love divine	Stocker.	30
Great God! thou dost all nations rule	Engl. Conf.	129
Great God, we give thee praise	Engl. Conf.	79
Great refuge of the weary soul	Engl. Conf.	46
Guide me, O thou great Jehovah	W. Williams.	115
Hail! gladdening Light, of that pure glory poured	Keble.	106
Hark the glad sound! the Saviour comes	Doddridge.	130
Hark! the herald angels sing	C. Wesley.	139

INDEX OF THE HYMNS.

FIRST LINES.	AUTHORS.	HYMN
Hark! the skies with music sound	Anon.	140
Hark! what mean those holy voices	Cawood.	138
High in yonder realms of light	Raffles.	83
Holy, holy, holy Lord	Engl. Conf.	20
Holy, holy, holy! Lord God Almighty	Heber, alt.	7
How gentle God's commands	Doddridge.	61
I love the voice divine that speaks		45
In boundless mercy, gracious Lord, appear	Attrib. to Swedenborg.	34
Jerusalem, arise	Engl. Conf.	152
Jerusalem, the golden! O city of the blest	H. Howard.	87
Jesus! I my cross have taken	H. F. Lyte.	53
Jesus, in thee our hopes shall rest	Engl. Conf.	21
Jesus lives! No longer now	Hymns An. & Mod.	143
Jesus, Lord of all creation	Engl. Conf.	39
Jesus, Lord, our Captain glorious	Ch. Psalter & Hymn Bk.	133
Jesus, lover of my soul	C. Wesley.	49
Jesus, our true and only light	C. Winkworth.	27
Jesus shall reign where'er the sun	Watts.	14
Jesus, the very thought of thee	Bernard of Cluny.	22
Jesus, the weary wanderer's rest	C. Wesley.	42
Jesus, thou mighty God of all	Engl. Conf.	26
Jesus, thou Source of life, and light, and love	Engl. Conf.	105
Jesus, to thee be endless praise	Engl. Conf.	1
Jesus triumphant reigns	Anon.	8
Keep me, Saviour, near thy side	Cento F. S.	51
Lead us, heavenly Father, lead us	Edmeston.	37
Let children hear the mighty deeds	Watts.	126
Let every heart exulting beat	Hymns An. & Mod.	142
Long as I live, I'll bless thy name	Watts.	124
Lo! for us the wilds are glad	Engl. Conf.	125
Lord, before thy throne we bend		19
Lord, dismiss us with thy blessing	Burder.	114
Lord Jesus, God of heaven	Engl. Conf.	123
Lord of all being! throned afar	O. W. Holmes	33
Lord of our life, and God of our salvation		36
Lord, thy word abideth	Hymns An. & Mod.	78
Lord, what offering shall we bring	J. Taylor.	25
Lord, when thou mak'st thy presence felt	Noralis.	23
Love divine, all love excelling	C. Wesley.	32
My spirit on thy care	Lyte.	67
Nearer, my God, to thee	Sarah F. Adams.	55
New every morning is thy love	Keble.	95
Now blessing, honor, glory, praise	J. Proud.	153
Now thank we all our God	Martin Rinckart.	27
Now that the daylight fills the sky	7th Century.	96
O bless the Lord, my soul	Watts.	15
O blest Creator of the light	Ancient Hymn.	103
O blest Redeemer, from thy radiant throne	Engl. Conf.	111
O fix my heart, my God, my strength	Engl. Conf.	59
O God, my heavenly King	Engl. Conf.	56
O God of truth, O Lord of might	7th Century.	97
O God, unseen yet ever near	Keble.	118
O guardian of the church divine	Hymns An. & Mod.	122
O Jesus, Lord and Saviour	Dr. J. Bayley.	29
O Jesus, Saviour of the lost	Bickersteth.	44
O King of kings, beneath thy wings	Engl. Conf.	62

FIRST LINES.	AUTHORS.	HYMN
O Lord all glorious, Life of life,	Engl. Conf.	12
O Lord! and is thy table spread	Doddridge.	119
O Lord, how boundless is thy love	Watts.	66
O Lord, our help in ages past	Watts.	74
O Lord, where'er thy people meet	Cowper.	28
O peace of all the faithful	Bernard of Cluny.	50
O praise ye the Lord! prepare your glad voice	Anon.	3
O that the Lord would guide my ways	Watts.	38
O thou, at whose divine command	Alford.	40
O thou from whom all goodness flows	Thos. Haweis.	48
O thou, to whose all-searching sight	C. Wesley.	41
O thou true life of all that live	7th Century.	97
Peace of God which knows no measure	Anon.	31
Praise the Lord who reigns above	Engl. Conf.	13
Praise the Lord! ye heavens, adore him	Hymns An. & Mod.	2
Praise the Lord! ye heavens, adore him	Bishop Mant.	16
Rest of the weary	J. S. B. Monsell.	47
Rich in mercy, Jesus reigns	Engl. Conf.	83
Safe home, safe home in port	Neale.	85
Saviour, again to thy dear name we raise	Ellerton.	112
Saviour and Regenerator	Engl. Conf.	9
Saviour, breathe an evening blessing	Edmeston.	98
Saviour, Source of every blessing	Robinson.	65
Saviour, who thy flock art feeding	Anon.	116
Shepherd of souls, refresh and bless	Moravian.	121
Shepherd of tender youth	Alexandrinus.	19
Shine forth, O Sun of boundless love	7th Century.	97
Sleepers, wake, a voice is calling	Nicolai.	131
Softly now the light of day	Episcopal Coll.	100
Sun of my soul! thou Saviour dear	Keble.	99
Suppliant, lo! thy children bend	Gray.	108
The advent of our King	Anon.	134
Thee we praise, eternal Lord	after Ambrosius.	11
The Lord our Saviour is the Way	Engl. Conf.	80
There is a land of pure delight	Watts, alt.	91
The strife is o'er, the battle done	Hymns An. & Mod.	147
They who on the Lord rely	Spirit of the Psalms.	70
Thine earthly sabbaths, Lord, we love	Doddridge.	92
This is the day of light	Ellerton.	93
Thou art gone up on high	Anon.	149
Thou art the mighty King of kings	Engl. Conf.	18
Thou city of the angels, thou city of the Lord	Bernard of Cluny.	88
Thou Lamb of God, thou Prince of peace	C. Wesley.	52
Through thee, as we together came	Anon.	107
Thy mighty power we sing	Engl. Conf.	17
Thy way, not mine, O Lord	Bonar.	60
Triumphant Zion, lift thy head	Doddridge.	82
Up, ye Christians, join in singing	German.	132
Welcome, sweet day of rest	Watts.	94
What glory gilds the sacred page	Cowper.	77
Where for safety shall I fly	Engl. Conf.	50
While my Redeemer's near	Steele.	72
While thee I seek, protecting Power	H. M. Williams.	63
Whom have we, Lord, in heaven but thee	Anon.	68
Whoso on God alone confideth	Neumarck.	69

INDEX OF TUNES AND COMPOSERS.

	COMPOSERS.	HY.
Accrington (5)	F. S.	9
Agape	W. F. Sherwin.	19
Agnus Dei.	Mozart.	39
All Saints	W. Knapp.	82
Amsterdam	Dr. Nares.	13
Arlington	Dr. Arne.	80, 118
Autumn	Scotch.	138
Badea	German.	123
Bath (5)	F. S.	36
Bavaria	German.	53
Bemerton (1)	Greatorex.	62
Bethany (1)	Dr. L. Mason.	55
Blumenthal	Blumenthal.	109, 110
Bristol	Dr. Hodges.	77
Bristol	Old English.	135
Carol	Old Melody.	140
Chesterfield	Dr. Haweis.	76
Christmas	Handel.	91
Constance (5)	F. S.	60
Coronation	O. Holden.	6
Dallas	Cherubini.	51
Dane	Beethoven.	65
Dennis (1)	Nägeli.	61
Detroit	E. P. Hastings.	94
Dornance (8)	I. B. Woodbury.	32
Dover	English.	56
Duke Street	J. Hatton.	21
Dundee	Scotch.	74
Dykes	J. B. Dykes.	7
Elijah	Mendelssohn.	49
Eltham	Dr. L. Mason.	20
Eucharist (5)	F. S.	119
Eventide	W. H. Monk.	113
Ewing	A. Ewing.	87, 88
Federal Street (1)	H. K. Oliver.	83, 101
Firmament (7)	G. F. Root.	12
Gilbert's (3)	W. B. Gilbert.	137
Gloria in Excelsis	Decius.	136
Gould	T. P. Warren.	143
Greenville	Rousseau.	114
Hamburg (1)	Gregorian.	26, 42
Harvest Home	E. Elvey.	128
Haydn	Haydn.	63
Hayne (4)	Meinecke.	92
Hermann	H. Strachauer.	81
Holley (1)	Geo. Hews.	30
Horton (1)	Schneider.	25
Italian Hymn	Giardini.	17
Jerusalem	Chauvenet's Coll.	152
Keble (5)	F. S.	99

	COMPOSERS.	HY.
Lanesboro'	English.	35
Larue	German.	66
Lebanon	English.	125
Leipsic	Old German.	52
Litany	Spanish.	100
London New	Scotch.	73
Lucis Creator (5)	F. S.	103
Lutzen	German.	129
Lyons	Haydn.	3
Magdalene	after Spohr.	43
Manoah (1)	Greatorex.	45
Martyrdom	Wilson.	46
Mear	Old English.	153
Mecklenburg	German.	116
Mehul	Mehul.	14
Mendelssohn	Mendelssohn.	139
Mercy (6)	Gottschalk.	71
Messiah (2)	Kingsley.	83
Missionary Chant	Zeuner.	10, 122
Morning Star (4)	Meinecke.	41
Mozart	Mozart.	23
Naomi (1)	Dr. L. Mason.	64
Nun danket alle	Crüger.	127
Old Hundred	Unknown.	4, 5
Olmutz (1)	Dr. L. Mason.	67
Oporto (1)	Wm. Mason.	24
Otto	English.	89
Palestine		44
Parting Hymn	E. J. Hopkins.	111, 112
Pentecost (5)	F. S.	150
Pilgrim (5)	F. S.	29
Pleyel's Hymn	Pleyel.	86
Praise (5)	F. S.	1
Quebec	H. Baker.	96
Rachel (5)	F. S.	149
Rathbun	J. Conkey.	16
Ravenshaw	German.	78
Rector potens (5)	F. S.	97
Regent Square	H. Smart.	2
Resurgam (5)	F. S.	58
Rotterdam	I. Gould.	142
Safe Home	Hymns of Eastern Ch.	85
Sanglier	German.	48
Schumann	Schumann.	95
Seymour	Von Weber.	108
Sherborne	Mendelssohn.	50
Sicilian Hymn		98
Silver Street	Smith.	8
Skara	F. S.	34
Spohr	Spohr.	54
St. Agnes	J. B. Dykes.	38

COMPOSERS.	HY.
St. Albinus.........*Dr. Gauntlett.*	148
St. Alphege.......*Dr. Gauntlett.*	90
St. Andrew............*Cherubini.*	63
St. Ann's.............*Dr. Croft.*	124
St. Bernard (7)........*G. F. Root.*	22
St. Cecilia (5).............*F. S.*	47
St. George.........*Dr. Gauntlett.*	15
St. Hilda..............*Barnby.*	31
St. James (5) *Harmonized by F. S.*	70
St. John.........*Old Melody.*	115
St. Luke........*H. C. Gilmore.*	120
St. Martins............*Tansur.*	126
St. Michael........*Day's Psalter.*	134
St. Nicolai................*German.*	146
St. Polycarp....................	27
St. Theodulph.........*German.*	145
St. Thomas........*A. Williams.*	79, 84
Stuttgart ....*German.*	144
Suabia................*Lutheran.*	93
Swabia................*German.*	57

COMPOSERS.	HY.
Tallis ... ...*Tallis.*	102
Te Deum ....*German.*	11
Te lucis........*6th Century.*	104
Thorney Abbey..................	59
Tottenham..........*T. Greatorex.*	18
Trinity... ... .*Pierracini.*	28
Trust...........*Mendelssohn.*	141
Valdimir (5)..............*F. S.*	151
Verona...........*J. H. Deane.*	37
Vincenzo (5) ....*F. S.*	72
Victory.........*Palestrina.*	147
Vienna..............*Havergal.*	117
Wachet auf..... *German.* 131, 132,	133
Ward (1)...............*Scotch.*	75
Wer nur den lieben....*Neumarck.*	69
Whiteland..............*German.*	40
Wordsworth...........105,	106
Worship (4) ....*Meinecke.*	107
York..............*Old English.*	130

NUMERICAL INDEX OF TUNES AND COMPOSERS.

HY.	TUNE.	COMPOSER.
1.	Praise (5)...............	*F. S.*
2.	Regent Square........	*H. Smart.*
3.	Lyons................	*Haydn.*
4.	Old Hundred..........	*Unknown.*
5.	Old Hundred..........	*Unknown.*
6.	Coronation	*O. Holden.*
7.	Dykes...............	*J. B. Dykes.*
8.	Silver Street	*Smith.*
9.	Accrington (5)	*F. S.*
10.	Missionary Chant.......	*Zeuner.*
11.	Te Deum..............	*German.*
12.	Firmament (7)....	*G. F. Root.*
13.	Amsterdam...........	*Dr. Nares.*
14.	Mehul...............	*Mehul.*
15.	St. George........	*Dr. Gauntlett.*
16.	Rathbun.............	*J. Conkey.*
17.	Italian Hymn.........	*Giardini.*
18.	Tottenham........	*T. Greatorex.*
19.	Agape............	*W. F. Sherwin.*
20.	Eltham...... ...	*Dr. L. Mason.*
21.	Duke Street	*J. Hatton.*
22.	St. Bernard (7).......	*G. F. Root.*
23.	Mozart..............	*Mozart.*
24.	Oporto (1)	*Wm. Mason.*
25.	Horton (1)...........	*Schneider.*
26.	Hamburg (1)	*Gregorian.*
27.	St. Polycarp	
28.	Trinity.	*Pierracini.*
29.	Pilgrim (5)............	*F. S.*
30.	Holley (1)............	*Geo. Hews.*
31.	St. Hilda............	*Barnby.*
32.	Dornance (8)....	*I. B. Woodbury.*
33.	Federal Street (1)..	*H. K. Oliver.*
34.	Skara (5).............	*F. S.*
35.	Lanesboro'.........	*English.*
36.	Bath (5)	*F. S.*
37.	Verona	*J. H. Deane.*
38.	St. Agnes........	*J. B. Dykes.*
39.	Agnus Dei........	*Mozart.*
40.	Whiteland	*German.*
41.	Morning Star (4)	*Meinecke.*
42.	Hamburg (1) ..	*Gregorian.*
43.	Magdalene...	*after Spohr.*
44.	Palestine	
45.	Manoah (1)..........	*Greatorex.*
46.	Martyrdom...........	*Wilson.*
47.	St. Cecilia (5).............	*F. S.*
48.	Sanglier...........	*German.*
49.	Elijah... ...	*Mendelssohn.*
50.	Sherborne.......	*Mendelssohn.*
51.	Dallas	*Cherubini.*
52.	Leipsic.........	*Old German.*
53.	Bavaria.........	*German.*
54.	Spohr...........	*Spohr.*
55.	Bethany (1).	*Dr. L. Mason.*
56.	Dover.............	*English.*
57.	Swabia.............	*German.*
58.	Resurgam (5)........	*F. S.*

NUMERICAL INDEX OF TUNES AND COMPOSERS. 367

HY.	TUNE.	COMPOSER.
59.	Thorney Abbey	....
60.	Constance (5)	F. S.
61.	Dennis (1)	Nägeli.
62.	Bemerton (1)	Greatorex.
63.	St. Andrew	Cherubini.
64.	Naomi (1)	Dr. L. Mason.
65.	Dane	Beethoven.
66.	Larne	German.
67.	Olmutz (1)	Dr. L. Mason.
68.	Haydn	Haydn.
69.	Wer nur den lieben	Neumarck.
70.	St. James (5)	Harmonized by F. S.
71.	Mercy (6)	Gottschalk.
72.	Vincenzo (5)	F. S.
73.	London New	Scotch.
74.	Dundee	Scotch.
75.	Ward (1)	Scotch.
76.	Chesterfield	Dr. Haweis.
77.	Bristol.	Dr. Hodges.
78.	Ravenshaw	German.
79.	St. Thomas	A. Williams.
80.	Arlington	Dr. Arne.
81.	Hermann	H. Strachauer.
82.	All Saints	W. Knapp
83.	Messiah (2)	Geo. Kingsley.
84.	St. Thomas	A. Williams.
85.	Safe Home	
	Hymns of the Eastern Church.	
86.	Pleyel's Hymn	Pleyel.
87.	Ewing	A. Ewing.
88.	Ewing	A. Ewing.
89.	Otto	English.
90.	St. Alphege	Dr. Gauntlett.
91.	Christmas	Handel.
92.	Hayne (4)	Meinecke.
93.	Suabia	Lutheran.
94.	Detroit	E. P. Hastings.
95.	Schumann	Schumann.
96.	Quebec	H. Baker.
97.	Rector potens (5)	F. S.
98.	Sicilian Hymn	
99.	Keble (5)	F. S.
100.	Litany	Spanish.
101.	Federal Street (1)	H. K. Oliver.
102.	Tallis.	Tallis.
103.	Lucis Creator (5)	F. S.
104.	Te lucis	6th Century.
105.	Wordsworth	

HY.	TUNE.	COMPOSER.
106.	Wordsworth	
107.	Worship (2)	Meinecke.
108.	Seymour	Von Weber.
109.	Blumenthal	Blumenthal.
110.	Blumenthal	Blumenthal.
111.	Parting Hymn	E. J. Hopkins.
112.	Parting Hymn	E..J. Hopkins.
113.	Eventide	W. H. Monk.
114.	Greenville	Rousseau.
115.	St. John	Old Melody.
116.	Mecklenburg	German.
117.	Vienna	Havergal.
118.	Arlington	Dr. Arne.
119.	Eucharist (5)	F. S.
120.	St. Luke	H. C. Gilmore.
121.	Dedham	Gardner.
122.	Missionary Chant	Zeuner.
123.	Badea	German.
124.	St. Ann's	Dr. Croft.
125.	Lebanon	English.
126.	St. Martin's	Tansur.
127.	Nun danket alle	Crüger.
128.	Harvest Home	E. Elvey.
129.	Lutzen	German.
130.	York	Old English.
131.	Wachet auf	German.
132.	Wachet auf	German.
133.	Wachet auf	German.
134.	St. Michael	Day's Psalter.
135.	Bristol	Old English.
136.	Gloria in Excelsis	Decius.
137.	Gilbert's (3)	W. B. Gilbert.
138.	Autumn	Scotch.
139.	Mendelssohn	Mendelssohn.
140.	Carol	Old Melody.
141.	Trust	Mendelssohn.
142.	Rotterdam	I. Gould.
143.	Gould	T. P. Warren.
144.	Stuttgart	German.
145.	St. Theodulph	German.
146.	St. Nicolai	German.
147.	Victory	Palestrina.
148.	St. Albinus	Dr. Gauntlett.
149.	Rachel (5)	F. S.
150.	Pentecost (5)	F. S.
151.	Valdimir (5)	F. S.
152.	Jerusalem	Chaurenet's Coll.
153.	Mear	Old English.

COPYRIGHTS.

(1) Tunes owned by Messrs. OLIVER DITSON & Co., whose permission to use them in this book has been courteously granted to the compilers.
(2) By permission of the author, Mr. GEORGE KINGSLEY.
(3) From *Goodrich & Gilbert's Musical Hymnal*, by courtesy of Messrs. E. P. DUTTON & Co.
(4) From *The Meinecke Collection*, by permission.
(5) By permission of the author, Rev. FRANK SEWALL.
(6) By permission of Messrs. WM. HALL & SON.
(7) By permission of Messrs. JOHN CHURCH & Co.
(8) By permission of Messrs. F. J. HUNTINGTON & Co.

A TABLE

OF

LESSONS FOR FESTIVAL SERVICES:

At Morning and Evening Worship.

DAYS.	PSALMS.	OLD TESTAMENT.	NEW TESTAMENT.
Advent Sunday, the 4th before Christmas	*M.* 37, 40, 42.	Gen. 3 : 1-15..	Luke 1 : 1-39.
The Promise of Redemption...	*Ev.* 105, 106.....	Is. 1.........	Luke 3 : 1-6.
Christmas Day..............	*M.* 2, 19, 45, 85..	Is. 7 : 10-16...	Luke 2 : 1-20.
The Incarnation.............	*Ev.* 110, 111, 132.	Is. 9 : 1-8....	John 1 : 1-14.
The 40 days before Easter.... Commemorating the Lord's Fasting and Temptation.	*M.* 6, 32, 38.	Is. 58.	Matt. 4 : 1-11.
Lessons for the First Day...	*Ev.* 102, 130, 143.	Joel 2........	Rev. 3.
The Sunday before Easter, called Palm Sunday .... *The Lord's Entry into Jerusalem*	*M.* 31, 32, 33. ... *Ev.* 119: 121-176.	Dan. 9. .... Zech. 9 : 9–17.	John 12. Matt. 21.
Thursday before Easter.......	*M.* 107.	Is. 63.........	John 13.
Institution of the Holy Supper.	*Ev.* 136, 137, 138.	Jer. 31.	John 17.
Good Friday.................	*M.* 22, 40, 54. ...	Gen. 22 : 1–19.	Luke 23 : 1-49.
The Passion of the Lord......	*Ev.* 69, 70, 88....	Is. 52 : 13–53..	John 18 : 1-19.
Easter Eve....................	*M.* 18, 23.	Ex. 13.........	Luke 23 : 50-56.
The Burial...................	*Ev.* 13, 14, 16, 17.	Is. 38 : 10-20..	Matt. 27 : 57-66.
Easter Day...................	*M.* 30, 97, 99. ...	Ex. 12	Matt. 28.
The Resurrection of the Lord..	*Ev.* 113, 114, 115, [113.	Is. 25.........	John 20 : 1-18.
The Sunday after Easter.......	*M.* 103, 104.	Ex. 14........	Luke 24 : 13-35.
Teaching of the Risen Lord...	*Ev.* 72, 73.......	Is. 26.........	John 20 : 19-31.
Ascension Day, the fortieth after Easter..............	*M.* 8, 21, 24.	Ex. 15...	Luke 24 : 36-53.
The Glorification of the Lord.	*Ev.* 47, 108.	Ex. 19........	Mark 16 : 14-20.
Pentecost	*M.* 48, 68........	Ex. 34.	John 14: 15-31.
The Giving of the Holy Spirit.	*Ev.* 104, 144, 146.	Joel 2 : 21–32.	Rev. 1.
The Holy City.... .... *The Lord's Presence with His Church...*	*M.* 27, 76, 87. .... *Ev.* 122 to 147 ..	Is. 54......... Zach. 2........	Matt. 28 : 18-20. Rev. 21.
Thanksgiving Day, or *The Feast of Ingathering*........	*M.* 103, 104, 107..	Deut. 8.......	Luke 12 : 15-40.

www.ingramcontent.com/pod-product-compliance
Lightning Source LLC
Chambersburg PA
CBHW022102300426
44117CB00007B/554